War Between Brothers

THE AMERICAN STORY

WAR BETWEEN BROTHERS

by the Editors of Time-Life Books, Alexandria, Virginia

Contents

A Nation Divided

During the early afternoon of April 14, 1861, on a tiny island fortress in Charleston harbor, a battered Stars and Stripes was being lowered through the smoke-filled air. For two days the stronghold had withstood bombardment from the guns that ringed the harbor. Miraculously, none of the defenders had been killed; a horse had been the only fatality. But now, its barracks in ruins, its outer wall cratered, Fort Sumter—symbol of Federal power in secessionist South Carolina—was surrendering to the newly founded Confederate States of America.

In charge of the fort's defense and its garrison of 68 soldiers was Major Robert Anderson, grandson of the man who had defended another of the harbor's fortresses against the British during the fighting of the Revolutionary War. Indeed, to the cheering crowds that had gathered in Charleston that afternoon, a second American revolution was now under way.

As Anderson struck his shot-torn flag, his artillerymen fired off the first round of a planned 100-gun salute. The Federal gunners were about halfway through their salute when tragedy struck. A soldier rammed another cartridge down the muzzle of his cannon, apparently before sparks from the previous round were thoroughly swabbed out. One of the sparks ignited the cartridge prematurely, and the explosion that resulted ripped his right arm from his body, killing him instantly. The wind carried smoldering bits of cloth to a nearby pile of cartridges, and a second explosion mortally wounded another gunner and injured four more. Anderson cut short the salute. Two hours later, with drummers beating "Yankee Doodle," the men of Sumter marched out of the battered fort, Anderson himself carrying its Stars and Stripes. When he died, he thought, he would be buried in the flag.

After waiting respectfully for the last of the Northern troops to leave, Confederate general Pierre Gustave Toutant Beauregard put ashore at Fort Sumter. The man who had directed the bombardment was an engineer officer, but while a cadet at the West Point military academy he had shown such promise as an artilleryman that his instructor had insisted that Beauregard stay on as his assistant for another year. The instructor had been Major Robert Anderson.

Now, after Anderson and his garrison had boarded ships for home, Beauregard gave orders for two flags to be raised over the ramparts of Sumter. The flags climbed their staffs and snapped open in the sea breeze, and a roar of approval rose from thousands of jubilant Southerners on the mainland and on small boats circling the island fortress. One flag carried the palmetto-and-crescent emblem of South Carolina. The other was a newer flag, with three broad bars—two red, one white—and in the top left corner, seven stars, 27 fewer than on the United States flag it replaced. For this was the Stars and Bars of the Confederacy *(opposite),* and its seven stars represented the Southern states that had already seceded from the Union: South Carolina, Mississippi, Florida, Alabama, Georgia, Louisiana, and Texas.

Within two months of the fall of Sumter, these original seven would be joined by four others: Virginia, Arkansas, Tennessee, and North Carolina. And in a gesture of defiance the Confederates transferred their capital from Montgomery, Alabama, to Richmond, Virginia, just 100 miles from the seat of the Federal government.

The capture of Fort Sumter had been an almost painless victory. "Thank God! Thank God!" the governor of South Carolina had proclaimed from the balcony of the Charleston Hotel. "The day has come; the war is open, and we will conquer or perish. We have defeated their 20 million, and we have humbled the proud flag of the Stars and Stripes that never before was lowered to any nation on earth." Future victories would not be won so easily, however. For if Sumter caused rejoicing in the South, its effect in the North was to trigger an outburst of war fever. The country was headed down the road to civil war.

The Old Dominion would be the first target of the army that President Abraham Lincoln was building in Washington. Under pressure from the public and the press, the U.S. government now prepared to launch its armies toward the rival capital.

But even though the best-known battles of the Civil War would take place in the eastern theater—particularly in the hills and valleys of Virginia, Maryland, and Pennsylvania—it would also be fought out over the vast territory that stretched from the Appalachians to the banks of the Mississippi River and beyond, to Texas and New Mexico. In 10,000 engagements, which ranged from minor skirmishes to huge clashes like those at Antietam and Gettysburg, Federal would fight Confederate, Rebel would fight Yank. The American Story was about to enter its bloodiest chapter.

A great pantheon of American heroes would take the stage during the coming years: Stonewall Jackson, Robert E. Lee, Jeb Stuart, U. S. Grant, William Tecumseh Sherman, Frederick Douglass. Other names would enter the national consciousness: a church called Shiloh, a crossroads known as Chancellorsville, a village named Appomattox Court House.

In the middle of July 1861, Union troops crossed the Potomac River and began to march into northern Virginia—and "On to Richmond!" Another little-known place was about to achieve sudden fame. For the armies of North and South were set to meet at a small Virginia stream called Bull Run.

**A Nation Divided
July 1861**

UNITED STATES

SLAVE STATES IN THE UNITED STATES

TERRITORIES

CONFEDERATE STATES

"Shot and shell went screaming over Sumter as if an army
of devils were swooping around it."

MEMBER OF THE UNION GARRISON

CHAPTER *1*

THE COUNTRY AT WAR

"Oh, that I had the genius of Napoleon....If I could only get the enemy to attack me...I should stake my reputation on the handsomest victory that could be hoped for."

CONFEDERATE GENERAL P. G. T. BEAUREGARD, JULY 8, 1861

The morning of July 21, 1861, an army of 35,000 men was marching south to make good on the Union's rallying cry—"On to Richmond!" At Bull Run in Virginia, 90 miles north of the Confederate capital and 25 miles west of Washington, General Pierre Gustave Toutant Beauregard was waiting for the enemy, confident that he would stop them. Flowing in a roughly west to east direction, Bull Run provided an excellent defensive position for the troops he had deployed along an eight-mile stretch of the south bank. The deployment conformed to the instructions that Confederate president Jefferson Davis and his military adviser, General Robert E. Lee, had given him: Outnumbered by about 10,000 men, the army at Bull Run was to halt the Yankee invasion; Beauregard was not to take his Confederates on the offensive.

But after surveying Bull Run and the rolling hills nearby, Beauregard had devised a bold plan of his own. The germ of the plan lay in the stream itself, or rather in its banks: Along most of their length they were too high and steep to get an army across without turning the troops into sitting ducks. There were only a few fords and one bridge where the Yankees could cross, and Beauregard concluded, more on a hunch than on any solid evidence, that the Yankees were heading toward one particular ford.

That ford occupied the center point of Beauregard's defensive line along Bull Run. Upstream he placed a small force to guard the left of his defensive line. What he had in mind for the remainder of his troops ran counter to his instructions: Seizing the initiative, he would cross Bull Run downstream, on the Rebel right, and outflank the Union army. The enemy would be trapped between the defensive line and the flanking force, and the way to Washington would be open. Beauregard would march on the Union capital. The war would be over at a stroke, and he would have secured victory for the Confederacy, and his beloved Southland could follow its own destiny.

Such audacity was in character for the small, dapper Louisiana Creole, whose plantation background, excessive courtesy, and French-accented English gave him an air of the exotic. Mindful of his appearance, he maintained the color of his hair with European dyes. He had a dramatic streak, too. When Louisiana seceded from the Union, he resigned his commission in the U.S. Army and offered his services to his state. But when command of Louisiana's forces went to another officer, an irate Beauregard enlisted as a private in a local regiment of fellow Creole aristocrats. Five days later he was made brigadier general in the Confederate army. Given charge of the Southern forces at

Soldiers like these members of the 1st Virginia Infantry were ready to fight for their homeland when the Southern states broke from the Union. Expecting an early victory, volunteers on both sides of the conflict rushed eagerly into service lest the war end before they had a chance to see any action. Few were prepared for the harsh realities of a conflict that would drag on for four years.

Charleston, South Carolina, he forced the surrender of Fort Sumter in the first engagement of the war. Beauregard became the hero of the Confederacy, and when Jefferson Davis needed a general to defend Richmond, the 43-year-old Beauregard was the obvious choice. He left the capital for northern Virginia on May 31 and, after setting up his field headquarters there, began devising his plan for a victory that would far outshine the glory of Sumter.

Around 9:00 a.m. Beauregard received a report that was at odds with his hunch about the direction in which the Yankee army was going: The enemy had crossed Bull Run upstream, beyond the left end of his defensive line, and engaged the

Fearing that his troops had insufficient training to take on the Rebels in Virginia, General Irvin McDowell *(fifth from right, above)* pleaded with President Abraham Lincoln for more time. But Lincoln could wait no longer. "You are green, it is true," the president told him, "but they are green also; you are all green alike." A self-assured P. G. T. Beauregard *(inset)* showed none of McDowell's hesitation. After his easy victory at Fort Sumter, the Confederate general eagerly anticipated the first major battle of the war.

small Confederate force that was stationed there. The first battle of the war had barely begun, and what was happening had the makings of disaster for the South. If the Yankees swept behind the Rebel forces strung out along the south bank of Bull Run, they would seize the vital railroad located at Manassas Junction, just two miles from the stream, and the road to Richmond would be open. Setting aside his offensive strategy for the moment, Beauregard dispatched reinforcements upstream to meet the threat to the left of his line.

The commander of the Federal army that had stolen a march on him was well known to Beauregard. General Irvin McDowell had attended the West Point military academy with Beauregard,

Finding that the Confederates were barring his path across Bull Run, McDowell had veered upstream to sweep around their left flank and was beginning to drive behind the lines of defense that had been drawn up along the stream. Bearing new silk regimental flags as they advanced, the Yankees felt certain of victory. Only a small force of Rebels stood in their way here, and although fighting doggedly, the Southerners were being pushed before the advancing Federals. "I felt that I was in the presence of death," remembered one Georgian. "My first thought was, 'This is unfair; somebody is to blame for getting us all killed. I didn't come out here to fight this way; I wish the earth would crack open and let me drop in.' "

In contrast to the soldier's foreboding, a celebra-

"We were expecting a big fight. It came; it is over; the enemy is gone. I cannot give you an idea of the terrors of this battle."

SOUTH CAROLINA PRIVATE WHO FOUGHT AT BULL RUN

graduating at the bottom of a class in which the Louisianan had distinguished himself by graduating second. But now, 23 years after their time together at the academy, it appeared that McDowell was about to turn the tables on his former classmate.

McDowell's army was made up of men from all over the North: frontiersmen from Michigan, Bowery toughs and Irish firemen from New York, blue bloods from Boston, farm boys from Ohio. As varied as their places of origin were their uniforms. Some wore gaudy outfits that imitated the dress of the French Zouave regiments of North Africa: baggy red pants, short blue coats, with scarlet sashes at their waists and tasseled fezzes for hats. Recalling a different martial tradition, one captain of a New York regiment called the Highlanders set out in a full-dress kilt, and some of his men wore tartan trousers. Many in this "blue army" even marched in gray. They would discover, to their confusion and their cost, that their opponents had Zouaves of their own and regiments dressed in blue.

tory mood prevailed among the clusters of civilians dotting the hills north of Bull Run. They had traveled the 25 miles from Washington with the Federal army to see the action, bringing along picnic hampers and bottles of champagne for toasting a Union victory. For like most Northerners they were convinced that there could be only one result: Given the North's superiority in manpower and matériel, they expected the battle to be an easy win in what must surely be a short war.

By noon it seemed that such expectations were well founded. General McDowell, wearing full uniform and dress white gloves, watched as the Confederates retreated and his men gave pursuit. He stood up in his stirrups and waved his hat in the air as he rode up and down his lines shouting, "Victory! Victory! The day is ours."

McDowell's troops were as confident as their leader. "We felt like veritable heroes," one soldier remembered. For some of the men it seemed the battle would be over too soon. "Give us a chance at them, General," a young soldier yelled at McDowell, "before they all run away." One of the man's companions was less sure the fighting was finished: "Shut up your damned head," he told him. "You'll get chances enough, maybe, before the day is over." Driving the Rebels before them, the Federals marched on toward a rise named Henry House Hill.

Among the troops rushing to meet the Federals at Henry House Hill was a 3,000-man brigade of Virginians led by General Thomas Jonathan Jackson. The 37-year-old Jackson had a reputation for being somewhat peculiar. A robust-looking six footer with piercing blue eyes and an oddly high-pitched voice, he sucked on lemons to relieve a stomach disorder and would not touch pepper because it made his legs ache. When he laughed, he threw his head back, his mouth would open, and barely a sound would come out. Even by army standards, he was a stickler for discipline. His harshness as a prewar instructor at the Virginia Military Institute had earned him death threats from at least one cadet; others had challenged him to duels. But as a commander, Jackson was second to none, leading by example, harnessing fighting spirit and discipline, and winning the respect of his men. As another gen-

eral put it, "Praying and fighting appeared to be his idea of the whole duty of man."

Jackson's brigade was still on the march when fighting broke out on Henry House Hill. Hearing the sound of gunfire, John Henry, who lived with his family in a two-story frame house on the hill, ran outside. His 85-year-old mother, Judith Henry, a bedridden widow, remained inside with her daughter Ellen, who took shelter in the fireplace chimney. Lucy Griffith, their servant, hid under Judith Henry's bed. When Jackson neared the top of the hill, he saw Rebel troops retreating toward him, pursued by Yankees whose numbers seemed to grow by the minute. Quickly assessing the situation—and the defensive possibilities of the high ground—Jackson ordered his men to lie down on the southeast side of the hill, below the crest and out of the view of the advancing Yankees.

In the thick of the fighting on Henry House Hill was Confederate general Barnard Bee, a gallant veteran soldier. Bee's troops were falling back before the Federals when the general spotted Jackson's men taking up their defensive position. Bee immediately galloped over to them, furious that the newly arrived infantry had not engaged the enemy, and demanded to know who was in charge. He was directed to Jackson, who was wearing his old United States Army cap pulled down over his sunburned, bearded face. "General," cried Bee, almost hysterical, "they are beating us back." Jackson appeared unworried: "Sir, we'll give them the bayonet."

Bee seemed to take Jackson's words as an order, even though the two men were equal in rank. He saluted and rode back to his own troops, who by this time had been hit so hard that he was barely able to recognize them. All of his field officers had been killed or captured, and there was no one in command. Bee desperately barked out orders, trying to rouse his men to attack. He shouted something else too. The noise of the battle made it hard to hear, but to soldiers nearby it sounded as though he was saying, "There is Jackson standing like a stone wall! Rally behind the Virginians!"

Afterward there were two interpretations of what Bee might have meant. Some thought he was praising Jackson and his men for not flinching under fire. Others thought that Bee intended no compliment at all. Seeing Jackson's soldiers lying down and not yet engaged in the battle while his own troops were taking so much punishment, Bee was, in this view, angrily comparing Jackson to an immovably fixed stone wall. Bee toppled from his horse with a mortal wound soon after, so no one had a chance to ask him what he had meant. Whatever his answer would have been, he had given Jackson his enduring nickname, Stonewall.

Back at the middle of the Confederate line, P. G. T. Beauregard had become increasingly nervous. He could hear the sounds of battle upstream but was reluctant to commit more troops there. To do so would mean abandoning his plan for going on the offensive altogether. When another general, Joseph Johnston, urged him to order additional reinforcements to the fighting upstream, Beauregard seemed paralyzed. Finally, around noon,

A Vermonter who served at Bull Run re-created the scene below in which Union troops advance up the slope of Henry House Hill toward Rebels concealed in the woods on the right. This hill, where the Henry family had its home *(top left)*, saw the fiercest combat in the daylong battle.

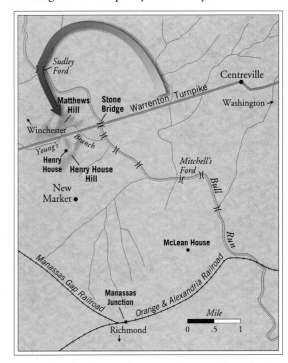

In a bold opening move, Union troops *(blue arrow)* marched around the left of the Confederate line at Bull Run.

Carried into battle on July 21 by a private from South Carolina, this Bible stopped a bullet and saved him from serious injury or death. Not so fortunate were the dead Confederate soldiers below; they were among the first casualties of the day.

Johnston decided to take action himself: "The battle is there," he said with a gesture in the direction of the Confederate left flank. "I am going!" Johnston strode over to his horse, mounted, and galloped off.

Johnston's action seemed to galvanize Beauregard and snap him out of his indecision. Grasping the fact that he had to fight the battle as it was rather than as he had intended, he ordered all available troops upstream. Then he put spurs to his horse and rode off after Johnston.

When Johnston and Beauregard arrived on Henry House Hill shortly after noon, they found Jackson's troops still in their place, lying "as flat as flounders," as one soldier put it. Although some firing continued, a lull had fallen over the fighting. Convinced that the Rebels were in full retreat, McDowell had ordered his soldiers to halt and reorganize before they continued the advance. The break gave the Confederate commanders the time they needed to strengthen their position on the hill, and they immediately set about forming a line of defense around Jackson's men. Johnston would ride to the rear and direct other reinforcements to this part of the field. Beauregard would lead at the front.

With his eyes flashing and face flushed with excitement, the Louisianan rode back and forth along the Confederate line, jabbing his sword in the direction of the enemy and urging his men to stand fast. He called out to a group of New Orleans artillerymen who had just arrived on the battlefield, "Hold this position and the day is ours. Three cheers for Louisiana!" Just then, a shell exploded beneath his horse, disemboweling it. Aware that the gunners' eyes were on him, the general calmly called for a nearby horse, remounted, and rode off to another part of the line, the cheers of his men ringing in his ears. Coming upon a Georgia regiment, he took off his bright red artilleryman's cap and shouted, "I salute the Eighth Georgia with my hat off! History shall never forget you!" And when the standard of a South Carolina unit fell, he cried, "Hand it to me, let me bear the Palmetto Flag." The heat was now sweltering, the humidity oppressive, but the Confederate position was indeed stabilizing. The lull in the battle was about to lift.

From his position on Henry House Hill, Thomas Jackson watched as a dozen horse-drawn Yankee field guns began to move up the slope in his direction. Jackson guessed that the Federals were planning a close-range bombardment to weaken the Confederates in preparation for a renewed infantry assault. A single word—"Attention!"— was passed down the line of Virginians. Jackson knew that artillery batteries were never advanced without the support of foot soldiers, and he waited to see just how the Yankees planned to back up the guns, which were becoming more and more exposed to Confederate fire as they moved up the slope.

While Jackson was studying the enemy's movements, at least one Union officer was having serious doubts about what he was doing. Captain Charles Griffin had been promised that his gunners would be supported by a regiment of New York "Fire" Zouaves, whose men were more notable for their blood-red firemen's shirts than for their military experience. Griffin doubted they would hold their ground once the Rebels started shooting. Ordered to move his cannon forward by Major William Barry, his commanding officer, Griffin had replied: "I will go. But mark my words, they will not support us."

Union officer George Custer with Rebel prisoner and former West Point cadet James B. Washington.

THE BONDS OF WEST POINT

In the course of being shaped into officers, the young men at the United States Military Academy at West Point formed strong bonds of friendship. But the war would transform comrades into enemies. Shortly before the conflict began, Southerner Braxton Bragg voiced the feelings of many West Pointers in a letter to classmate William Tecumseh Sherman, who had just declared his Union loyalty. "You are acting on a conviction of duty . . . ," Bragg wrote. "A similar duty on my part may throw us into an apparent hostile attitude, but it is too terrible to contemplate."

The war's first shots pitted West Pointer against West Pointer, as Confederate general P. G. T. Beauregard ordered his men to fire on Fort Sumter and its commander, Major Robert Anderson—once Beauregard's academy artillery instructor. Much grimmer confrontations would follow. In 55 of the 60 major battles to come, academy graduates would lead the Yankee and the Rebel forces.

But some bonds survived. During one encounter, Thomas "Tam" Rosser rode out in full view of George Custer's soldiers to reconnoiter, taunting Yankee sharpshooters by showing his cape's red lining. Custer ordered his men not to fire and the next day dispatched a note to the classmate turned enemy. "Tam, do not expose yourself so," Custer admonished. "Yesterday I could have killed you."

When the Federal guns came within 100 yards of the Confederate line, they drew fire. It seemed to some of the gunners that the shooting came from around the Henry house, and they turned their cannon to face in that direction. A shot smashed into Judith Henry's bedroom. She was thrown to the floor and received wounds in the neck and the side. A piece of flying debris tore off one of her feet. While she was comforting her daughter, whose eardrums were terribly damaged by the reverberating explosions, Judith Henry bled to death. Outside, her son John lay facedown on the ground, crying, "They've killed my mother! They've killed my mother!"

Meanwhile, the Fire Zouaves were trotting up the west slope of Henry House Hill, most of them having shed their blue army jackets because of the heat. Above them there was not so much as a glimpse of the enemy, not a shot from the top of the hill. As they neared the top, the Zouaves passed through the Federal batteries and into a small cornfield that belonged to the Henry family. In his quarter of Henry House Hill, Jackson was moving among his men, reassuring them. "All's well, all's well," he repeated. "When their heads are seen above the hill, let the whole line rise." The Federals closed to within 50 yards of the Virginians. They got no closer. A volley of bullets crashed through the corn, turning the air blue and sulfurous with smoke. Jackson's men sent volley after volley into the Zouaves, whose scarlet shirts made them easy targets.

The survivors scrambled back down the hill toward the rest of the Union army. But before they could regain their own lines, a detachment of Confederate horsemen fell upon them.

Slashing with their swords and firing at close range, they cut through the retreating soldiers. One cavalryman tried to jump over a Zouave, but his horse's hoofs caught the man square in the chest and sent him flying. As the soldier struggled to his feet, the rider stuck the end of his short-barreled carbine rifle in the man's stomach and pulled the trigger. "I could not help feeling a little sorry for the fellow as he lifted his handsome face to mine," the Confederate wrote later, "for the carbine blew a hole as big as my arm clear through him."

Captain Griffin witnessed the rout of the Zouaves. As he was casting about with mounting fear for a way to protect his isolated and vulnerable guns, he saw a line of blue-coated men emerge from a grove of trees several hundred yards away. They looked like Federals, but Griffin doubted that they actually were. The day had been a dusty one, and all uniforms had acquired a coat of grime and were starting to look alike. He ordered two guns to turn and fire on them. Just before they did so, however, Ma-

Jackson's brigade, quickly moved forward and seized the now-silent batteries.

Major Barry made it safely down the hill, but he was certain that Griffin had been killed in the fiasco and blamed himself for the captain's death. He was watering his horse at a creek behind the Federal lines and reflecting on how he had dismissed the captain's fears when another man stopped at the stream to let his horse drink. It was Griffin, and when he saw Barry he asked caustically, "Major, do you think the Zouaves will support us?"

"I was mistaken."

"Do you think that was our support?"

"I was mistaken."

"Yes," Griffin growled. "You were mistaken all around!" With that, he rode off.

Astride his new mount up on Henry House Hill, P. G. T. Beauregard scented victory. For two hours the fighting had swirled around Griffin's cannon, which changed hands in a series of attacks

> *"Should troops be passing about the neighborhood you and mother need not fear them, as your entire helplessness, I should think would make you safe."*
>
> LETTER FROM JUDITH HENRY'S SON HUGH TO HIS SISTER ELLEN, TWO MONTHS BEFORE BULL RUN

jor Barry stopped them. "Captain, don't fire there," he shouted, convinced that these were more troops sent to defend the artillery pieces. Griffin shouted back, "They are Confederates, as certain as the world, they are Confederates!"

"No, I know they are your battery support."

By this time the oncoming line of men was 50 yards from Griffin. Certain that they were the enemy, the artilleryman wheeled his cannon in their direction once more, and Barry overruled him again. Captain Griffin had had it right. The infantrymen leveled their muskets and unleashed a volley in their direction, and the next moment the ground was littered with dead and wounded Yankees and artillery horses. The surviving gunners fled back down the hill. The blue-coated Rebels, who were members of

and counterattacks. But discipline had ebbed away from the exhausted Union troops. Piecemeal, one regiment at a time, they had been sent against the reinforced Rebel line. But then, about 3:00 p.m., came news that plunged the Confederate general into despair: A large dust cloud was approaching from the southwest, indicating considerable numbers of men on the march. Beauregard's first thought was that it was another Union force sent to help McDowell. If that was so, the Confederate commander would have little option but to withdraw.

Beauregard watched as the column came into sight about a mile distant. Through his field glasses, the general could see the flag at the head of the column. However, the cloth hung limp against the staff in the still air, so he couldn't tell whether the approaching force was hostile or friendly. Increasingly anxious, he prepared a message ordering a retreat, then wavered. "Let us wait a few minutes to confirm our suspicions," he told a courier, "before finally resolving to yield the field."

A sudden breeze sprang up and settled the matter, filling and lifting the limp flag. To Beauregard's relief, he saw that it belonged to one of his own units, and it was arriving on the field at Henry House Hill at precisely the right moment. The sight of the reinforcements broke the spirit of the Yankees. "We scared the enemy worse than we hurt him," observed one of the new arrivals. But the effect was the same. The Federals began to fall back.

Seeing his chance, Beauregard ordered an advance along the entire Confederate line. Jackson responded immediately. Ordering his men forward, he instructed them to fire a volley, charge, then rely on the bayonet. "And when you charge," Jackson added, "yell like furies!"

The yell that rose from their throats that hot afternoon—a shrill, high-pitched cry that was part triumphant shout, part foxhound's yelp—would be heard on a thousand fields of battle over the next four years. The effect of the Rebel yell on the Union soldiers was terrifying. "There is nothing like it this side of the infernal region," remembered one Yankee. "The peculiar corkscrew sensation that it sends down your backbone under these circumstances can never be told. You have to feel it." Exhilarated, Beauregard watched from his horse as the Federals began to pour back over Bull Run.

The main road back to Washington told the story of the Northern defeat. Strewn along it were 28 cannon too cumbersome to move in the retreat. And scattered among the abandoned rifles and knapsacks littering the road were parasols, shawls, and ladies' slippers left behind by the fleeing civilians who had come to watch the battle. Most of them had gotten away safely, fleeing as fast as their buggies would carry them.

Among the Northerners who didn't manage to escape was Alfred Ely, a congressman from New

"Little Rose" leans against her mother, Rose O'Neal Greenhow, in this 1862 photograph taken in Washington's Old Capitol building, where the socialite turned spy was confined. In June 1862, after pledging not to return to the North during the war, Greenhow was transported to Virginia and released.

THE SOCIALITE SPY

During the summer of 1861, Washington socialite Rose O'Neal Greenhow became a spy for the Confederacy. Military news, whispered in the 44-year-old widow's ear by well-placed dinner companions, quickly found its way south. On July 10, 1861, Greenhow courier Betty Duvall, disguised as a farm girl, traveled into Virginia to meet with Confederate general P. G. T. Beauregard. In the coils of her dark hair was a tiny black silk pouch. The coded message inside and a subsequent Greenhow note confirmed what the general had heard from other sources: The Union army would advance toward Manassas in six days. Beauregard made preparations for a Rebel victory at Bull Run.

Greenhow continued to provide intelligence but was soon under suspicion. On August 23, Allan Pinkerton, chief of the Union army's Secret Service, arrested her at home and lay in wait for other Rebel agents. The widow's eight-year-old daughter, Rose, slipped outside, climbed a tree, and shouted, "Mother's been arrested!" Despite Little Rose's warning, several agents came and were arrested.

After her release from prison in 1862, Greenhow traveled to England seeking support for the South. In 1864 she was on her way home when her ship ran aground in North Carolina's Cape Fear River. She insisted that a small boat be launched for her so she could escape. It capsized in rough water, and the famous spy was drowned.

York. Keen to see how a unit from his own state was faring, he had edged a little too close to the action. An officer from South Carolina discovered him hiding near a bridge over the stream. Raising his pistol to Ely's head, the enraged Rebel screamed, "God damn your white-livered soul! I'll blow your brains out on the spot." Only the quick intervention of some other Confederates saved Ely from certain death. Taken prisoner, he spent five months in a Southern jail before being released.

Before darkness began to fall over Virginia, a tall, gaunt figure dressed in black steered his horse through the rear of the Rebel lines. Torn by suspense, Confederate president Jefferson Davis had been unable to stay in Richmond to await the outcome of the battle. A West Point graduate who at one time had hoped to command the Southern armies, Davis had come to Bull Run in order to see what was happening for himself.

He passed through what he considered alarmingly high numbers of stragglers going in the opposite direction before he came upon General Joe Johnston, who assured him that the battle had been won. The two men made their way to Beauregard's quarters, where Davis sat down to draft a dispatch announcing the outcome of the battle to the war department in the Confederate capital. "Night has closed upon a hard-fought field," he began. "Our forces have won a glorious victory."

The man who considered himself most responsible for that victory was still out on the field somewhere. For P. G. T. Beauregard it had been a glorious day. When an aide told him that Davis had arrived and wanted to see him, the general retorted, "I cannot wait upon the President himself till I have first seen and attended to the wants of my wounded." It was 10:00 p.m. before Beauregard felt he could return to his quarters. There he provided Davis with more details about the battle and noticed with irritation that the president's signature was the only one at the bottom of the dispatch to Richmond. Davis had not handed it to his generals to add their signa-

A LAST LETTER HOME

A week before he was killed at Bull Run, Union major Sullivan Ballou wrote his wife:

The indications are very strong that we shall move in a few days.... Lest I should not be able to write again, I feel impelled to write a few lines that may fall under your eye when I shall be no more....

The memories of the blissful moments I have spent with you come creeping over me, and I feel most gratified to God and to you that I have enjoyed them so long. And hard it is for me to ... burn to ashes the hopes of future years, when, God willing, we might still have lived and loved together, and seen our sons grown up to honorable manhood, around us. I have, I know, but few and small claims upon Divine Providence, but something whispers to me— perhaps it is the wafted prayer of my little Edgar, that I shall return to my loved ones unharmed. If I do not my dear Sarah, never forget how much I love you, and when my last breath escapes me on the battle field, it will whisper your name....

But, O Sarah! if the dead can come back to this earth and flit unseen around those they loved, I shall always be near you; in the gladdest days and in the darkest nights, advised to your happiest scenes and gloomiest hours, *always, always,* and if there be a soft breeze upon your cheek, it shall be my breath, as the cool air fans your throbbing temple, it shall be my spirit passing by.

tures, implying, Beauregard thought, that Davis was claiming the credit for the victory himself.

Beauregard need not have worried. The Confederacy had proved to be victorious in the first major engagement of the war, and a grateful public was generous with its praise.

From the outset of the great struggle between the states, most Southerners knew the odds against them: They had less industry than the North, a smaller population, and fewer resources, but they were not daunted by these disadvantages. Whatever they thought of slavery—and few poor Rebels would have owned slaves—they were able to view the conflict with a clarity that often was not shared by their Yankee counterparts. To the average Virginian, Tennessean, or Texan, the issue was a simple one: His land had been invaded, he had been called to arms to defend his home and his state, and, like all good citizens, he had responded. Besides, one Rebel fighter was worth at least two Yankees—and, it seemed, Beauregard had just proved that at Bull Run.

Hailed in the press, inundated with adoring letters, and celebrated in song, Beauregard was, as he had been after the victory at Fort Sumter, the hero of the hour. Never had so many American babies been christened Pierre. Women sent him gifts and wrote him poems, and he was feted everywhere that he went. Enjoying the adulation, Beauregard was eager for more action. As he saw it, there would now be little fighting in Virginia before winter arrived, and he asked for a transfer. Beauregard had also taken to criticizing Richmond's prosecution of the war, and President Davis was happy to meet his general's request. In the winter of 1862, Beauregard was transferred to the western theater, across the Appalachian Mountains.

The general was right about the course of the war in Virginia. For the time being the North, appalled at the 2,896 Federal soldiers killed, wounded, or missing at Bull Run, posed little threat to the Confederate capital. Northern citizens now understood that this would not be a one-battle war. But they determined, too, that it was a war that had to be won. Lincoln would turn from Irvin McDowell to other generals to lead the Union army "on to Richmond." It would take time to organize, train, and equip the army well. In the meantime, the fighting would move to the West, where the two sides would clash along the banks of the Tennessee River, at a place known ever after as Shiloh.

Beyond the Appalachians, rivers were the key to transportation—and to military victory. If the Federals were to win control of the Mississippi, Ohio, Cumberland, and Tennessee Rivers, they would gain access to the heart of the Southland. To keep these valuable highways in their own hands, the Confederates had built two strongholds just below the Tennessee-Kentucky line, Fort Henry on the Tennessee River and Fort Donelson on the Cumberland. In February 1862, an obscure Union brigadier general named Ulysses S. Grant led a combined naval and infantry advance on the forts. On February 6 Fort Henry buckled under a pounding

from Grant's guns, and Fort Donelson surrendered 10 days later. The double victory was an important one for the North, and General Grant, a quiet, modest sort of man, suddenly found himself in the limelight. The note he sent demanding the submission of Fort Donelson electrified the public: "No terms except an immediate and unconditional surrender can be accepted." U. S. Grant was quickly dubbed Unconditional Surrender Grant.

The Rebel commander in this part of the country was Albert Sidney Johnston, the highest-ranking field officer in the Confederate army. In the face of the advancing Yankees, he withdrew his forces, leaving his home state of Kentucky and much of Tennessee open to the Federals. General Johnston headed for Corinth, Mississippi, to guard its vital railroad junction connecting the western and eastern parts of the Confederacy. With him traveled P. G. T. Beauregard, recently arrived from Virginia.

Grant, meantime, had pushed south along the Tennessee. He stationed most of his troops on the

Marked by ordinary plank headboards sunk into a swampy part of the battlefield, these Yankee graves bear silent testimony to the Union defeat at Bull Run. But the Federals would be back to fight dozens more battles in Virginia, and to carry the war to the other parts of the Confederacy, like Mississippi and Tennessee in the West.

western bank of the river at a tiny port called Pittsburg Landing, just 22 miles from Corinth, and put General William Tecumseh Sherman—Cump for short—in command there. A smaller force was posted at Crump's Landing, four miles northeast of Pittsburg Landing. Grant established his headquarters at Savannah, Tennessee, on the east bank of the river three miles north of Crump's Landing. There he awaited reinforcements from General Don Carlos Buell, who was marching from Nashville to join him. The Confederates' only hope was to strike the enemy before Grant and Buell could combine their forces. In the first week of April 1862 the Rebel army moved from Corinth toward the Tennessee.

The evening of April 5 General Beauregard found himself with nowhere to sleep. The next day would bring battle with the Yankees. But in the preparations for the assault, he had forgotten to give orders for his tent to be pitched.

There was ample reason for the general's distraction. Only a few hundred yards away from the Confederate lines the outlying elements of the Union army were camped on the plateau that rolled westward from the bluffs reared up along the river near Pittsburg Landing. The two largest armies yet assembled in the war would sleep within earshot of each other that night.

The plan had been for Beauregard's entire force to fall on the unsuspecting enemy at dawn and drive them back to the river—and out of Tennessee. But Beauregard knew that the Confederate advantage lay in surprise, and he was afraid that all surprise had been lost. Despite orders to observe strict silence, shouts, gunshots, and bugles continued to echo in the clear, cold night. "Now they will be entrenched to the eyes," the despairing Beauregard said of the Federals. He recommended to Albert Sidney Johnston that the attack be called off and the army marched back to Corinth.

Johnston took a different view from that of his excitable junior. A favorite of Jefferson Davis, who had declared him worth a force of 10,000 men,

Union artillerymen drill with siege rifles at one of the 68 forts built to shield Washington from attack. Considered a marvel of military engineering at the time, the forts were connected by miles of trenches for infantry troops.

FEAR, FESTIVITY IN THE CAPITALS
WASHINGTON AND RICHMOND AT WAR

When the men of the 7th New York marched into Washington on April 25, 1861, the city turned out to give them a hero's welcome. Since the outbreak of war, the Confederacy had been clamoring for "the capture of Washington City, at all and every human hazard," and the threatening words were reinforced by the Confederate campfires that could be seen glowing at night across the Potomac. One of the first orders of business was to begin construction of a ring of 68 forts to defend the capital.

The city of 63,000 was unprepared for its new role as the nerve center of a Union at war. Barely 60 years old, Washington was a work in progress. The Capitol was still uncompleted, and Lincoln demanded that construction continue as "a sign we intend the Union to go on." There was no lodging for the thousands of soldiers flowing through the city toward battle zones, and newly arrived regiments took up makeshift quarters in the Capitol and the handful of other government buildings that could accommodate them. During the first winter of the war, Washington had to provide for the 200,000-man Army of the Potomac camped around the city.

For Washington's elite, war signaled a heady infusion of socially prominent officers and their wives. The old guard and the newcomers enjoyed a round of festive receptions, balls, and dinners. The Lincolns were the official leaders of Washington society, and an invitation to the White House was much coveted. But the reality of the long struggle that lay ahead dawned on Washington's residents in July 1861, when the South dealt the Union a humiliating blow at the First Battle of Bull Run. Soon the city

In the war's early days a civilian militia, mustered below on the South Lawn, defended the White House. The president's wife, Mary Todd Lincoln *(right)*, stood at the apex of Washington society.

The base of the Capitol's dome stands out against the sky in this view down Pennsylvania Avenue. Like many other Washington streets in this period, the avenue was unpaved.

English novelist William Makepeace Thackeray praised prewar Richmond *(below)* as a "comfortable, friendly, cheery little town—the most picturesque I have seen in America."

The mistress of the Confederate president's Richmond residence was Varina Howell Davis *(left)*.

Residents of Richmond celebrated the Confederate victory at the First Battle of Bull Run with a 100-gun salute at the Virginia State House. Within a year, fighting would take place within earshot of the city.

began to take on the appearance of a sprawling hospital for the wounded and sick soldiers who came to receive treatment.

Two days after Lincoln greeted the New York volunteers from the steps of the White House, the Virginia Secession Convention invited Jefferson Davis, the Confederacy's newly elected president, to make Richmond, Virginia, his capital. Like Washington, this city of 38,000 inhabitants was unprepared for the transformation to come. Only 100-odd miles from Washington, Richmond was the target of the North's early military strategy. Lincoln and his generals were urged by politicians and the press to take the Rebel city. Headlines proclaimed, "Forward to Richmond! The Rebel Congress Must Not Be Allowed to Meet."

The reasons for capturing Richmond were more than symbolic. Two major railroad lines radiated out from the Confederate stronghold throughout the South, facilitating the transportation of war matériel as well as communications. Richmond also boasted the Tredegar Iron Works, one of the country's largest and most productive.

The hub of the new Confederacy soon swelled with politicians, soldiers, adventurers, speculators, and hundreds of the other hangers-on who materialize in wartime. This influx of humanity so crowded Richmond that Mary Chesnut, a keen observer of the city during the war and a prominent figure in local society, claimed the city was filled "to suffocation—hardly standing room left." The arrival of Jefferson Davis, his young wife Varina Howell Davis, and his cabinet members added a new luster to Richmond's social scene. Born into a prominent Mississippi family, Mrs. Davis set the tone for genteel socializing. In contrast to Bull Run's sobering message to the Union, Southerners greeted their victory with dancing in the streets and cries of "On to Washington."

Johnston gave promise of being one of the South's most brilliant military leaders. More than six feet tall, broad shouldered, and handsome, he was a commanding, dignified presence. "We shall attack at daylight tomorrow," he told Beauregard calmly but firmly. When the Louisianan was out of earshot, he confided his determination to one of his staff officers: "I would fight them if they were a million."

Beauregard was still convinced that going ahead as planned was a mistake. The last straw was the sound of a beating drum. Angrily he sent an officer to halt the drumming. In minutes the man returned with a startling reminder of how close the two armies lay: The drum Beauregard could hear was beating in the enemy camp. Full of fears for what the morning would bring, the hero of Fort Sumter and Bull Run found himself an ambulance wagon to serve as a shelter for the night and tried to catch a few hours of sleep.

Early on the morning of April 6, General William Sherman received yet another report of enemy activity along his front lines. For several days now accounts of skirmishes with the Rebels had been coming in from his pickets, the troops who were assigned to forward positions to guard against a surprise attack. Although Sherman was skeptical about the veracity of these reports, he decided to go out and investigate for himself.

Sherman felt there was little cause for anxiety, because the plateau on which his 35,000-man army had been camped for the last month offered considerable security. A patchwork of woods, farmland, and orchards roughly three miles square, the plateau was protected on one side by high bluffs overlooking the Tennessee River and on its flanks by flooded creeks running through deep ravines. In the unlikely event of an attack, the Rebels would have no choice but to come through the three-mile gap between the creeks. And if names meant anything, he had chosen a good place to locate his tent headquarters. It was near Shiloh Church, a one-room Methodist meeting house. *Shiloh* was a Hebrew word meaning "place of peace."

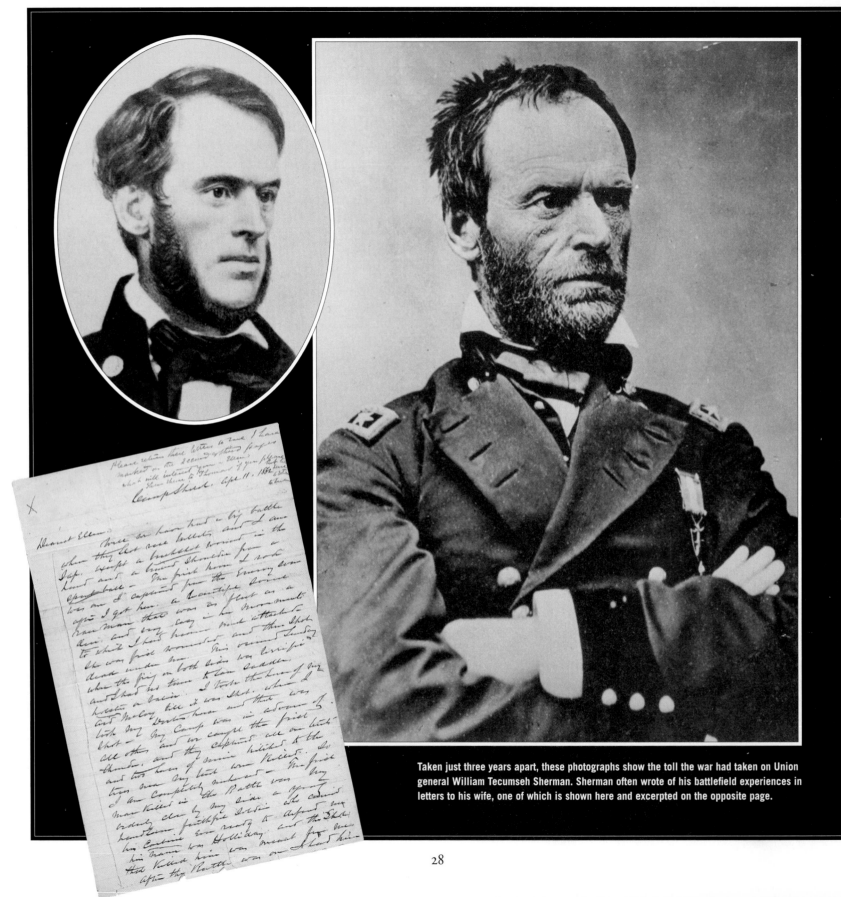

Taken just three years apart, these photographs show the toll the war had taken on Union general William Tecumseh Sherman. Sherman often wrote of his battlefield experiences in letters to his wife, one of which is shown here and excerpted on the opposite page.

28

Uppermost in Sherman's mind was not a Confederate assault but the fact that Buell's troops would be joining him any day. With their troops combined, the Federals would have an irresistible force for an assault on Corinth. Sherman had written to General Grant at Savannah only two days earlier: "The enemy is saucy [but] I do not apprehend anything like an attack on our position." So great was Sherman's confidence, so sure was he that his troops would soon be moving on Corinth, that no defensive positions had been prepared on the plateau.

Something that did worry Sherman was the condition of his troops. Few of them had adequate training, and even fewer had ever seen battle. Moreover, they had been on tenterhooks for days, and the 42-year-old West Pointer was finding the edginess of his volunteers irritating. When an elderly Ohio colonel named Jesse Appler reported a day earlier that his men had been fired on by a line of gray-clad soldiers at the front, Sherman had responded curtly. "Take your damned regiment back to Ohio," he told him. "There is no enemy nearer than Corinth!"

Appler had not been reassured, and on the morning of April 6 he took the precaution of deploying his troops in nervous anticipation of a Rebel assault. At about the same time, General Sherman arrived at the front to look for signs of enemy activity. Trotting out among the pickets 400 yards or so from his Shiloh headquarters, Sherman was scanning the distant woods with his field glasses when an officer ran forward, yelling, "General, look to your right!" Sherman whirled his horse. Confederate troops were looming out of the bushes no more than 50 yards away. "My God," cried Sherman, "we are attacked!" He threw up his right hand as if to protect himself. At that moment the Rebels opened fire. The orderly at Sherman's side tumbled from his horse, dead, and buckshot hit the general in the hand. "Hold your position," he shouted to Jesse Appler, "I will support you," and galloped off to get his troops into line.

The opening of the Rebel offensive had almost claimed the life of the Union camp commander. Even so, Sherman was unsure that he faced anything more

> *"The first man killed in the battle was my orderly, close by my side, a young, handsome, faithful soldier who carried his carbine ever ready to defend me. His name was Holliday and the shot that killed him was meant for me."*
>
> WILLIAM T. SHERMAN
> IN A LETTER TO HIS WIFE, ELLEN,
> FOUR DAYS AFTER SHILOH

than a Confederate reconnaissance party. But the general was not going to overreact to whatever the Rebels were doing. He had done that once before and been badly burned for it. If he repeated his mistake, the press would only call him crazy again.

Before serving under Grant, Cump Sherman had been stationed in Kentucky. There his overestimation of enemy numbers had brought him criticism. Under pressure, and suffering from asthma and severe headaches, he suffered a nervous breakdown. One newspaper reported at the time: "General Sherman, who lately commanded in Kentucky, is said to be insane. It is charitable to think so." Reappointed to field command after a three-month leave, Sherman was determined to redeem himself and to repay Ulysses S. Grant for having enough faith in him to give him command of the Union force at Pittsburg Landing.

Despite Sherman's hopes that the Confederates were not attacking in force, it quickly became clear that a major assault was under way. One who needed little convincing was the jittery Jesse Appler. Crying "Retreat and save yourselves!" he turned and ran for the rear, closely followed by his men. But most of the Union troops put up a stiff resistance, only falling back grudgingly before the sheer weight of the Rebel onslaught.

Like many Union troops, 16-year-old drummer John Cockerill had just begun breakfast when the firing started. Dashing to his father's tent, he grabbed a prized Enfield rifle while his father, a colonel of the 70th Ohio Regiment, mounted a horse, shouted a quick good-bye, and headed off to the front. Not sure what to do, young Cockerill took up a position behind Shiloh Church. The sound of the firing drew closer, and the battle began to close in all around him.

One Union colonel presented a ghastly sight as he galloped among his men, urging them to "Stand to it yet!" Already he bled from four wounds, in his hand, leg, neck, and torso. Then a shot hit him in the mouth and passed out the back of his head, killing him instantly. A soldier from Missouri screamed out in agony, his intestines protruding

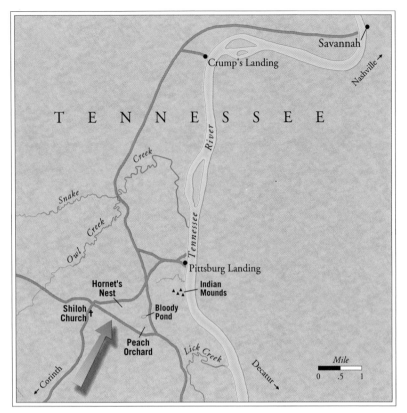

By April 5, 1862, a Confederate army *(red arrow)* had moved to within miles of the unsuspecting Union forces encamped on the west bank of the Tennessee River from Pittsburg Landing to Shiloh Church. Rebel hopes of surprising the enemy were fully realized: On the eve of the battle, Union commander Ulysses S. Grant, based at Savannah, Tennessee, told one of his officers, "I have scarcely the faintest idea of an attack being made upon us."

Confederate, it was the first time he had heard the distinctive shout. As he charged forward, it seemed to drive all sanity from him and his companions, and inspired them with wild enthusiasm.

Whooping their way through the abandoned front-line Union camps, the Rebels rifled tents for clothing and blankets, and acted as though the battle were already over. Some had not eaten for 24 hours and greedily helped themselves to the remains of interrupted Yankee breakfasts. One soldier, who burned his arm taking meat from the pot in which it was still cooking, remarked that either the Federals had been truly taken by surprise or they had the most dedicated army cooks on record.

Among the triumphant Confederates that morning was Sidney Johnston. He knew that his strongest talent as a commander was his leadership, and he had left Beauregard in the rear to direct reinforcements and supplies and ridden up to the front himself. Spotting one of his officers emerging from a tent with an armful of Federal loot, the general rebuked him sharply: "None of that, sir! We are not here for plunder." Then, softening before the man's dismay, Johnston picked up a small tin cup left by a campfire and said, "Let this be my share of the spoils today."

But despite such interruptions, the gray tide rolled irresistibly forward, taking heavy casualties, at times losing its momentum in dense undergrowth—but moving nevertheless. The Yankees driven before it streamed to the rear, some of them falling all the way back to the river's edge at Pittsburg Landing. Their retreat halted by the Tennessee, they cowered at the foot of bluffs standing high above the river. Some were raw recruits, others officers, others men separated from their fellows in the heat of battle. Such was the sight that greeted the army commander when he arrived on the field later that morning.

from a wound in his belly. "I feel as if my bowels are in boiling water," he cried to a chaplain who was bending over him. In desperation, the chaplain took out a penknife, spread the wound open, and pushed the intestines back in. Telling him to trust in Christ, he left the youth and moved on.

Amid the confusion of battle a private from Indiana caught a glimpse of something he had never seen before: "It was a gaudy sort of thing, with red bars. It flashed over me in a second that that thing was a Rebel flag. It was going fast, with a jerky motion, which told me that the bearer was on the double quick." Terrified, he turned and ran for the rear.

The frightened private was only one of thousands of men forced back toward the Tennessee River. A few dashed into their tents to grab favorite possessions. One picked up his Bible and put it in his pocket; should he be killed, he thought, his body could at least be identified from the book's inscription.

Behind the departing Yankees, the whole woods seemed to ring out with the Rebel yell. For one young

Ulysses Grant was breakfasting with staff officers at his headquarters in Savannah when the quiet spring morning was broken by the sound of dull thuds coming from the direction of Pittsburg Landing. The thuds could mean only one thing—a

Confederate attack. If Grant was surprised, he did not let his companions see. Setting down an untasted cup of coffee, he stood up and said, "Gentlemen, the ball is in motion. Let's be off."

While Grant's boat, the *Tigress,* got up steam, the general left orders for Buell's troops: When they got to Savannah they were to march along the east bank of the river to a position opposite Pittsburg Landing. Then he limped painfully to the *Tigress.* In a recent riding accident, his horse had fallen and pinned his leg to the ground, and the ankle had become so swollen that his boot had had to be cut off.

As the steamer was passing Crump's Landing on the west bank of the Tennessee River, Grant called out to Lew Wallace, the general in charge of the Union camp there, to ready his men and prepare to march. At about 8:00 a.m., the *Tigress* nosed into its mooring at Pittsburg Landing.

Grant was met by a chaotic scene, with crowds of Yankee soldiers who had fled from the Rebel attack milling about aimlessly and making so much

noise that the sounds of fighting on the plateau above were drowned out. With the help of an aide, Grant immediately mounted his horse and strapped a crutch to his saddle. Although he was hampered by his injury, the general was an excellent horseman and could still ride. He started immediately for the front, pounding up the steep bank with his staff in tow. When he gained the top of the bluffs, the roaring of muskets and artillery was so loud that Grant realized the Confederates must have launched a full-scale assault. He dispatched a messenger to tell Lew Wallace to bring up his troops as quickly as possible. In the meantime, Grant had to find Sherman.

It was 10:00 a.m. when Grant found him on the battlefield, and it was immediately apparent that his aggressive, hell-for-leather second in command had been in the thick of things and reveling in it. Sherman's stubby red beard was smeared with dirt, his hat brim had been ripped away, and his tie had worked around his neck so that it stuck out at the side. His dusty uniform had several bullet holes in it,

The Tennessee River would serve as a vital element in the Union efforts at the Battle of Shiloh. General Grant arrived at the scene of the fighting aboard his steamboat, the *Tigress,* shown at left moored between two troop transports at Pittsburg Landing. Other vessels carried Federal reinforcements to the battlefield and bore the wounded to safety. Gunboats drew close enough to bombard Confederate positions.

A SUMMONS TO SHILOH

Ann Wallace and William H. L. Wallace of Ottawa, Illinois, had known each other from the time she was a little girl and he was a young lawyer and family friend. When they had been married about 10 years, war separated them. Early in March 1862, Will, now a brigadier general stationed with Ulysses S. Grant's forces in Tennessee, wrote Ann that he had been ill for several days and longed to see her. "I feel as if I must go to you," Ann replied, "more so when I think of you sick." Desire turned to determination, and she boarded a steamboat headed south.

Early on April 6, Ann Wallace arrived at Pittsburg Landing, near the Union camp. As she waited impatiently for directions to Will's quarters, she heard gunfire in the distance. An officer approached her. She had come too late, he informed her, General Wallace had ridden into battle. Shiloh's bloodshed had begun.

Grim hours passed as a worried Ann helped tend the flood of casualties and awaited news of Will. Late in the evening, one of his men sought her out. For nearly six hours that day, General Wallace's division had helped hold a position called the Hornet's Nest. Finally, he ordered a retreat. While leading his soldiers down a dirt road, the general rose in his stirrups to take a cautious look at the woods to his side. He suddenly jerked and fell from his horse. A musket ball had struck him behind his left ear and emerged from his left eye socket. Though certain their commander was dead, his men tried to carry his body away but abandoned the attempt as the Rebels closed in.

Ann Wallace spent a sleepless night filled with despair. Then morning brought her unexpected joy. Federal troops recovering lost ground had found Will alive. But he was weak, his condition worsened by a cold and rainy night in the open. His staff transported him to Grant's headquarters in Savannah, where Ann kept a vigil at his bedside. "His pulse was strong and healthy," Ann later wrote, "we could not help but hope that he would recover." But infection soon set in. On April 10, Will Wallace died. Ann's long journey, begun in eager anticipation, had come to a painful end. Yet she would always be grateful that she had embarked upon it and spent those final hours with her beloved husband.

A solemn Ann Wallace *(left)* poses for a photograph about eight years after the death of her husband, General William H. L. Wallace, following the Battle of Shiloh. Ann brought Will's body back home for burial and arranged for the memorial photograph below, which shows her husband's portrait, his horse, and the American flag in front of the couple's home.

but he was unhurt except for the injury to his hand. He appeared completely at ease.

For more than an hour after his close shave early that morning, Sherman had fought a stubborn delaying action against the Rebels. But at 8:00 a.m. he saw something that scared him as much as it impressed him—the glistening bayonets of heavy masses of infantry. The full Confederate army was taking to the field, and it was, Sherman later observed, "a beautiful and dreadful sight."

As the battle had intensified, a calm fell upon the general that was an inspiration to all of those who saw him. His 21-year-old aide-de-camp remembered feeling that "it was grand to be there with him." And to the young drummer boy John Cockerill, who could see Sherman from his position at Shiloh Church, he was a hero: "The splendid soldier, erect in his saddle, his eye bent forward, looked a veritable war eagle, and I knew history was being made in that immediate neighborhood."

Astride his sorrel mare, Cump Sherman rode among his wavering troops, to all appearances oblivious of the firestorm that was bursting around him. Death seemed unable to touch him. As his staff officers approached to consult with him, they were seen to hunch low in the saddle in order to avoid being hit by the heavy firing. Sherman's horse was wounded, but he continued to ride her until a bullet intended for him hit her and sent horse and rider crashing to the ground. Quickly scrambling free of the carcass, he appropriated his aide's horse and continued to rally his troops.

Grant, too, was extraordinarily calm under fire. Realizing that he did not need to stay long with Sherman, he cantered off to continue his tour of the field. The battle boiled, but to the dismay of his staff officers Grant disregarded the danger. So fierce was the Rebel firing, in fact, that one young Yankee was convinced he could see the bullets in the air, like a swarm of black insects, and a member of the general's staff mistook the patter of bullets in the trees for rain. One projectile hit Grant's sword—which he hardly ever wore—and broke both scabbard and

blade nearly in two. He scarcely reacted to the near miss and continued his tour of the Union line.

As he rode by, Grant's appearance on the field of battle had a great effect on his men. One soldier noticed that he was relaxed, smoking a cigar, acting as if he were making a routine inspection. The general's confidence was infectious, and on seeing him the soldier immediately felt that the worst must be over. When one of his aides remarked that things were "pretty squally," Grant replied, "Not so bad. Lew Wallace must be here soon."

Toward the middle of the Union line Grant found his troops struggling to hold their position. Relentless Rebel assaults had driven the Federals back, but now they had found a more promising place in which to make a stand. Grant watched as the men, mostly farmers from Iowa and Illinois, began to deploy along an old wagon road, slightly sunken from use, that ran across high ground. The road was a natural bastion. On one side was a tangled wall of scrub oak and underbrush too dense for the enemy to maneuver in. On the other side, a stout split-rail fence separated the road from a large expanse of open ground with scattered stands of scrub oak. This area offered the only logical approach for anyone attacking the road. Grant rode over to General Benjamin Prentiss, whose soldiers and cannon occupied a crucial position in the center of the half-mile-long line the Federals had formed along the road. Grant had a simple order for him: Hold the position "at all hazards." Prentiss determined to take the words to heart.

The defenders of the sunken road did not have long to wait before the Rebels appeared before them. As they looked across the open area in front of the road, a long line of men in gray emerged from the woods beyond. Bayonets at the ready, they came on at a trot, and the Federals lay down and peered at them from beneath the bottom rail of the fence. The Rebels closed to about 150 yards before the Union gunners opened up. The effect was devastating. As the artillery fire struck it, the charging line waved like tall grain in the wind. But still the attackers came on. They were within 30 paces of the sunken road when the Union infantry jumped to their feet and fired a point-blank volley. The line buckled, the attack foundered, and a sickening collection of wounded and dead lay in its wake. One Confederate who stumbled back to his own lines gasped, "It's a hornet's nest in there." The name stuck.

For four hours, from about 11:00 a.m. until midafternoon, the Hornet's Nest became the focus of the battle as assault after assault—a dozen in all—rolled against the sunken road. The terror and the confusion would stay forever with both attackers and defenders in images that burned themselves into the memory.

One Southerner remembered an area in front of the sunken road so thick with scrub oak that it was "almost impossible for a man to walk through it." These woods became a deathtrap as both sides released "a perfect rain of bullets, shot, and shell." Excited troops accidentally shot their own fellows. And although the defenders' view of the attackers was often obscured by the heavy foliage, one Union officer recalled that "the groans and shrieks in the bushes told of the destructiveness of our fire." Anyone who came out alive felt that he was part of a miracle: "We still pressed on," wrote one Rebel. "I cannot imagine how I escaped being killed as I was in the front rank all the time."

A Confederate officer did manage to lead his men through the thickets to within 50 yards of the enemy lines. It turned out to be a deadly mistake. "A terrific and murderous fire was poured in upon me from their lines and battery," he remembered. "It was impossible to charge through the dense undergrowth, and I soon discovered my fire was having no effect upon the enemy."

Some of the bloodiest fighting on April 6 took place at an area known as the Hornet's Nest. Union artillery crews such as the ones shown at right fired off withering blasts every 30 seconds and, although they were greatly out-numbered, succeeded in holding up the Confederate advance long enough for Grant to form a new line of defense back at Pittsburg Landing.

But the Confederates still came on like "maddened demons," according to one Yankee. An artilleryman from Iowa remembered how the Rebels "hurled column after column on my position, charging most gallantly to the very muzzles of the guns." Another wrote, "It seemed almost barbarous to fire on brave men pressing forward so heroically to the mouth of hell." Then the woods caught fire, and what followed was hell itself. Choking wood smoke mingled with the powder smoke, and the stench of burning flesh filled the air. Screaming in pain and fear, wounded men unable to walk tried desperately to crawl away from the spreading flames.

A Northern artillery captain, his white horse spattered with blood, watched as a volley of musket fire halted yet another Rebel attack. He described the volley as "a sheet of flame and leaden hail that elicited curses, shrieks, groans, and shouts, all blended into an appalling cry." As the officer was putting two of his guns into position along the sunken road, he was amazed to catch sight of his 65-year-old father. Without telling his son about his plans, the father had signed up with a regiment back home in Ohio in the hope of being close to his boy. Father and son had the briefest moment to greet each other before having to return to their duties.

One Yankee forgot the proper loading drill and unwittingly fired off his gun before removing the ramrod. He realized his error only when he saw the rod quivering like an arrow in the body of a Rebel soldier. Elsewhere, shaken Federals drifted away from the line. One took shelter behind the trunk of a large tree. Another joined him, then another and another, until a line of huddled soldiers stretched back behind the tree. Beside them paced an officer, too distraught to do anything but walk up and down. A stunned Confederate fighting in his first battle saw a horse "galloping between the lines, snorting with terror, while his entrails, soiled with dust, trailed behind him."

A Federal soldier experienced in short order extremes of savage violence and moving tenderness: "I am lying so close to Captain Bob Littler that I could touch him by putting out my hand when a shell bursts directly in our front and a jagged piece of iron tears his arm so nearly off that it hangs by a slender bit of flesh and muscle." He was momentarily distracted from the bloody maelstrom as "a rabbit trembling with fear rushes out of the brush and snuggles up close to a soldier."

A battered Louisiana regiment received orders to charge once more and was told, "The flag must not go back again." Before a junior officer was able to finish communicating the order, the colorbearer was shot down. A moment later the regiment's colonel, with bullet holes in both cheeks and blood pouring from his mouth, came up to the officer and demanded the flag. "If any man but my color-bearer carries these colors, I am the man," he said. "I will see that these colors are in the right place." Grabbing the flag, he led another frontal assault. The fighting continued to rage on in the Hornet's Nest, but the outcome of the day would be decided elsewhere on the field.

Near the Hornet's Nest, Federal troops were drawn up in a peach orchard in full bloom, its clouds of soft pink flowers made hazy by the drifting smoke of battle. Sidney Johnston, who had been in the thick of the fighting all day, was positioned in front of the orchard, on the right of the Rebel line, where he had taken charge of some Tennessee troops reluctant to advance. He rode along slowly in front of them on his big bay, Fire-eater. His hat was off, his sword sheathed. Hooked on the little finger of his right hand was the tin cup he had picked up

THE LITTLEST SOLDIER

Among the youngest citizens to answer the call to arms was Ohio-born Johnny Clem, who at nine ran away to join the U.S. Army. The youngster soon impressed his older comrades with the courage he showed on the field of battle. But when newspapers began to carry stories of his exploits during the Battle of Chickamauga in 1863, Johnny gained a wider audience—and the hearts and minds of the Northern public. During the fighting a Confederate cavalry officer—who apparently made no exceptions for drummer boys, no matter how small—galloped toward Johnny, shouting, "Surrender, you little Yankee devil!" Armed with a sawed-off musket cut down to fit him, Johnny wounded the horseman. For this act he was awarded a sergeant's stripes and a silver medal. After the war he remained in the army. When John Clem retired in 1915 with the rank of major general, he was the last active serviceman in the U.S. military who had fought in the Civil War.

as his share of the spoils at the overrun Union camp. As he moved along the line he tapped the soldiers' bayonets with the cup and told them, "These will do the work. Men! They are stubborn. We must use the bayonet." When he reached the middle of the line, he turned to face the enemy. "I will lead you!" he yelled to his soldiers. One aide remembered thinking at the time, "It was inviting men to death, but they obeyed it. The line was already thrilling and trembling and rushed forward around him with a mighty shout."

The fire Johnston and the Tennesseans unleashed on the peach orchard sent the petals wafting down on the dead and dying lying beneath the branches. When he returned from the assault, the general had clearly been under heavy fire. His clothes were torn, and the sole of one of his boots had been cut almost in half by a bullet. But he was jubilant: "They didn't trip me up that time!" he shouted.

For the next half-hour Johnston issued orders and prepared to renew the attack. But when a member of his staff returned from delivering messages, he found the Confederate commander reeling in the saddle. Leading Fire-eater into a nearby ravine, the officer helped Johnston to the ground. No one had noticed until now that the general had been badly wounded.

Johnston's face was deathly pale. Frantically, the staff officer searched for a wound and finally found it: A bullet had entered the general's right leg in the bend of the knee, nicking an artery, and the blood was flowing into his high boot. The wound was what soldiers called a bleeder—serious, but not necessarily fatal. The officer poured brandy down Johnston's throat, and the general swallowed it down.

Another officer knelt over him and cried, "Johnston, don't you know me? Do you know me?" He seemed to smile faintly, but he made no answer. More brandy was poured into his mouth, but this time the liquid gurgled in his throat and spilled back out over his chin. The little tin cup that he had been carrying around all day dropped from his grasp. Johnston lost consciousness and at about 2:30 p.m. he died of loss of blood. In one of his pockets was a field tourniquet that might have saved him had anyone known how to use it.

With Johnston's death, Beauregard took command of the Confederate forces, and the course of the battle changed. On the right of the Rebel lines, where Johnston had been fighting when he was shot, the Federals were in disarray. A gap nearly three-quarters of a mile wide had opened up between the Union left and the Tennessee River, and it led straight to Pittsburg Landing. But in the confused lull that followed the general's death, the Confederates apparently failed to notice the opportunity the gap gave them to bypass the Federal line at the sunken road, cut off the troops there from the rest of the Union army, and move on Pittsburg Landing.

Beauregard now moved his headquarters to Shiloh Church, where Sherman had been headquartered. Sporting the same red artilleryman's cap he had worn at Bull Run, the general periodically stood on a tree stump to get a better view of the battle. From the stump he encouraged men on their way to the front, telling them they had whipped the Yankees and reminding them to "keep cool and shoot low." He was determined to crush the remaining Federal resistance at the sunken road. And to make sure he succeeded, Beauregard now turned to his artillery.

By 4:00 p.m., all available Confederate cannon were assembled into a single line: Sixty-two guns, hub to hub, were about to commence the largest artillery bombardment that the continent had ever seen. The Hornet's Nest exploded. Firing three to four times a minute, the cannon rained shells

Albert Sidney Johnston, shown at left in his prewar United States Army uniform, was the oldest general in the Confederate army. When he was fatally wounded at Shiloh on the afternoon of April 6 *(below),* he also became the highest-ranking casualty, Union or Confederate, of the Civil War. Recalled one officer who served with him in Tennessee, "The west perished with Albert Sidney Johnston and the Southern country followed."

down on the Yankees for more than an hour, turning the sky black with smoke and roaring, said one Union officer, like "a mighty hurricane sweeping everything before it."

In the face of this pounding, the troops at the two ends of the Federal line began to retreat toward Pittsburg Landing. Benjamin Prentiss's men still stood their ground at the center of the line, where for six hours they had done exactly what General Grant had ordered Prentiss to do, holding their position on the defensive line at all hazards. The Rebel fire had not broken his part of the line, but its flanks had been beaten back so far that what had been a line was now bent into the shape of a horseshoe. Surrounded on three sides and cut off from the rest of the Union army, Prentiss ordered his 2,000 remaining troops to surrender, but some of them refused to obey the order. When one soldier waved a white flag, an officer cut it down with his sword. An Iowa colonel who tried to escape with his men through a thicket cracked his head hard on a low tree branch; when he came to his senses a Confederate major was standing over him. "I think you will have to surrender," the Southerner remarked. The Yankee took out his watch and looked at it. It was 5:45.

Some of the troops falling back toward Pittsburg Landing were in good order, but for others it was a mad rout. With the collapse of the defense at the sunken road, Grant·had begun building a new defensive line closer to the little port, massing 50 or more guns in a shallow crescent to protect it. The general had ordered his cavalry to halt the stragglers, and every available body, including drummer boys, was put into the ranks. One officer from Illinois remembered: "The belligerent little drummers nearly all preferred to fight and were found along the line, gun in hand, as fierce as fighting cocks."

That same determination was shared by the Union commander. When asked if he intended to stall the enemy just long enough for the Federals to escape across the Tennessee River, Grant answered that retreat would be worthless: Rather than concede the field to the enemy, he would sacrifice so

many of his men in the fight that there would not be enough left to retreat.

In the meantime, in his headquarters at Shiloh Church, Beauregard was feeling satisfied with a day's work well done. Not that he could rest on his laurels: The crushing of the Hornet's Nest had exhausted his men, some of whom had been fighting for 12 straight hours and were simply fought out. In addition, units were scattered and disorganized, and many were low on ammunition. Nevertheless, Beauregard felt sure he would be able to rally his troops. Like their commander, they were buoyed by the Federal capitulation at the sunken road. It was a great victory. One young soldier believed that 10,000 Yankees had surrendered there, another that it could even have been the whole Northern army.

After his surrender at the sunken road, General Prentiss had been heard to predict happily that Don Carlos Buell's troops would arrive soon at Pittsburg Landing to reinforce the Federals. Beauregard shrugged off the prediction because he had received a report that Buell was marching in another direction, toward Decatur, Alabama. Nor was Beauregard unduly alarmed when, late in the day, Rebel units advancing on Federal positions near Pittsburg Landing had been repulsed. Today's win would be sealed tomorrow, and the Confederate general would add another triumph to those of Fort Sumter and Bull Run. That is, as long as the Union army had not withdrawn across the Tennessee by the morning. At about 6:00 p.m., with darkness approaching, Beauregard ordered the army to fall back for the night.

Far from retreating, the Federals were growing stronger. About the same time that Beauregard ordered a halt to the day's fighting, and contrary to the report he had put so much credence in, the first of Buell's units were arriving on the far side of the river after a three-and-a-half-hour march from Savan-

Although the bowie knives carried by so many Rebels were effective at close quarters, they were actually used more as camp tools than as weapons. The knife shown at left was stripped from the body of a dead Confederate on the field at Shiloh.

nah. They were led by General William Nelson, a six-foot-four, 300-pound blusterer known to his men as Bull. Nelson and 200 of his troops boarded the first steamer and began to cross the muddy waters of the Tennessee. The boat did not get far, however. Would-be Union deserters who had had enough of fighting were swimming for the far shore, and the vessel's captain stopped for fear of hitting them. But Nelson would have none of it and angrily ordered him on. Some of the men aboard the ship even sought permission to shoot at the swimmers.

On nearing the landing on the other side, Nelson mounted his huge black horse, jumped it over the ship's gunwale to the wharf, and rode into a mob of stragglers. "Damn your souls," he bellowed at them, swinging his sword. "If you won't fight, get out of the way of men who will!"

Soon after Nelson's arrival, Lew Wallace finally arrived with his men. He had been delayed by a mix-up over the orders Grant had sent him and by a time-consuming march down the wrong road. The last piece Grant had been waiting for was finally in place, and now he was confident that the Rebel prospects for victory were dimming.

A terrible night closed in over the battlefield. In the no man's land between the two armies lay the Union and Confederate dead and wounded. The injured who could not move screamed and groaned in the darkness. One young Yankee could hear them all too well. "Some cried for water, others for someone to come and help them," he recalled. "God heard them, for the heavens opened and the rain came." But what began about 10:00 p.m. as a cold drizzle was by midnight a torrential downpour, and flashes of lightning illuminated the battlefield. "Sickening sights fell before my eyes," a private from Mississippi wrote. "I saw a large piece of ground covered with dead heaped and piled upon each other. I shut my eyes." At another part of the field, the lightning showed semiwild hogs—ferocious razorbacks that were rounded up only once a year—feeding on the dead.

The injured who were able to move crept toward each other, huddling together for warmth and com-

General William "Bull" Nelson survived Shiloh, the bloodiest battle in the West, only to be shot and mortally wounded in a quarrel with a fellow Union officer in Louisville, Kentucky, six months later. "Send for a clergyman!" gasped Nelson moments before he died. "I wish to be baptized. I have been basely murdered."

fort. In an abandoned tent three youths—two of them Rebel and one Yankee—nursed their wounds and encouraged each other through the long night. By daybreak only one, a Rebel, was still alive. Scores of the wounded crawled to a small pond located near the sunken road to quench their thirst. Many died there, side by side, friend and foe alike. Their blood turned the water so rusty that the place became known as Bloody Pond.

Even the able-bodied faced an awful night. The storm, the screams of the wounded, and a constant barrage kept up by Federal gunboats on the river made it hard for the exhausted soldiers to sleep. One Confederate trying to escape the downpour crept under a blanket with another man. The next morning he discovered that he had passed the night next to a dead Yankee. A Wisconsin private was equally hard pressed for a place to sleep: "I put my blanket over my shoulder, stuck my bayonet in the ground, leaned my chin on the butt . . . and slept standing up." A drummer boy from Illinois managed to ignore the rain and slept soundly. To his horror, he awoke to find that he had been taken for dead and laid out neatly in a row of corpses.

It was a hard night for Grant. In the hope of sleeping in a real bed, he made his way to a log house near the river that had served for a time as a field headquarters. But it was being used as a hospital, and the sight of amputated limbs and the smell of blood were more than he could stand. He hobbled off, his swollen ankle still bothering him, and took shelter under a large oak tree. He settled down with a cigar clamped in his teeth, his hat pulled down over his face, and his coat collar turned up against the rain.

The fighting that day had changed his mind about the qualities of the enemy soldier. Up until then, Grant had believed that the ordinary Rebel infantryman possessed little love for the Confederate cause and would fight only halfheartedly for it. Shiloh cured him of that illusion forever. Over the course of the next three years he would experience time and time again the passion and the ferocity with which Southerners would fight.

Grant was still huddled under his oak tree at midnight when he was joined by William Sherman. He had gone out looking for the commander to urge a retreat across the river, but he now had second thoughts about mentioning it. Instead he merely observed, "Well, Grant, we've had the devil's own day, haven't we?"

"Yes," agreed Grant, puffing on his cigar. "Lick 'em tomorrow though."

Sometime during the night, a Confederate cavalry colonel named Nathan Bedford Forrest sent a detail out on patrol disguised in Union army overcoats. Forrest was used to taking the initiative. When the war started, he had put up posters in Memphis calling on anyone who wanted to kill Yan-

fighting. Still, the Rebel troops put up fierce resistance, some taunting their attackers with shouts of "Bull Run! Bull Run!" But the weight of Union numbers was telling. By 1:00 p.m. the Confederate defense was near collapse, and stragglers began heading to the rear.

Even after learning that Buell's reinforcements had indeed arrived, Beauregard continued to project an air of confidence. "The day is ours," he told a regiment of fellow Louisianans. "You are fighting a whipped army. Fire low and be deliberate." But his confidence turned out to be misplaced. As soon as officers rallied one unit, another would collapse. They had no fight left. Finally, at about 3:30 p.m., the Confederates started to withdraw in orderly fashion, back along the muddy roads toward

"Here is the place that was fought over…bits of leather belts, ammunition boxes, battered camp kettles, broken shovels, tin cups, knives, forks and spoons, playing cards, leaves of Bibles and hymn books, lie scattered in every direction."

UNION SOLDIER, THE BATTLE OF SHILOH

kees to join him. The report that his scouts brought back to him was alarming: They had made it all the way to some old Indian mounds overlooking the Tennessee River and had seen Buell's troops arriving at Pittsburg Landing. Forrest's immediate reaction was that the Confederates must attack that night in order to drive the Federals back to the river; the following day would be too late. He rushed off to deliver the bad news to Beauregard but was unable to find him. Forrest found another general and reported what the cavalry detail had seen, but the man was so little alarmed by the report that he merely instructed Forrest to keep a sharp lookout. The cavalryman stormed off and was, said one of his aides, "so mad he stunk."

At first light on Monday, April 7, the Federals began to advance, driving the front-line Confederate units steadily before them. Grant had 45,000 men now, about half of them fresh to the field, to face 20,000 Rebels worn out by the previous day's

Corinth, Mississippi. With them they bore the body of Albert Sidney Johnston.

Only a couple of miles into the retreat, the weary army halted and made camp. Grant might easily have fallen on the Rebels, but his men were also spent, so the Federals returned to the camps they had been forced out of the day before. One officer reentered his tent to find a young Union soldier near death. "As I raised his head and placed my canteen to his parched lips," he later wrote, "the last faint rays of the setting sun came struggling through the pines and illuminated, as with a halo, the face of that dying lad. With silence unbroken, save by the cries and groans of the wounded, came fainter and fainter the labored breath, and more feeble the clasp of the little hand. Suddenly arousing himself, in a whispered voice he said: 'Tell my mother where you found me, on the front line.'"

When a Union artilleryman got back to his tent, almost collapsing from exhaustion, there was a

Rebel lying dead on his blanket. The weary gunner simply rolled the corpse to one side, lay down next to it, and went to sleep.

Drummer boy John Cockerill, who had been in and around the fighting on both days of the battle, was in a state of mourning. A passing soldier told John that he had seen his father killed, shot from his horse. The distraught young man was in the empty camp of his father's regiment, the 70th Ohio, when it returned. He looked up to discover his father riding at the head of the troops. Dismounting from his horse, the elder Cockerill wrapped his son in "the most affectionate embrace that my life had ever known. . . . I realized how deeply he loved me." They spent the night in the father's bullet-riddled tent telling each other of their ordeals.

Earlier that day Sherman had sent out a force of 2,000 men toward Corinth in halfhearted pursuit of the Rebels. He had not gone far when he was surprised by the sight of 350 cavalrymen drawn up on a ridge who were guarding the Confederate retreat. They were led by Forrest, a man who trusted his instincts. As he stared down at the Yankee foot soldiers, his instincts were talking to him again. Sensing some uncertainty among the infantrymen, the colonel ordered an immediate charge against the larger Union force.

Bugles blaring, the Rebels thundered down on the stunned Yankees, firing their pistols and double-barreled shotguns and swinging sabers. Sherman watched in horror as Forrest, riding out in front of his horsemen, seemed to make straight for him. "I am sure that had he not emptied his pistols," Sherman recalled, "my career would have ended right there." But the Federals were re-forming to meet the assault, and their fire began to down some of the charging riders. The Rebels began to turn back, but not the aggressive Forrest. Too late, he realized that he was fighting alone.

To everyone there, it seemed certain that Forrest must perish. Yankees swarmed over him as his horse

NATHAN BEDFORD FORREST

The son of a Tennessee blacksmith, Nathan Bedford Forrest was a self-made man. Lacking any kind of military training, he enlisted in the Confederate army as a private when the war broke out, and within three months he had risen to the rank of lieutenant colonel.

After recovering from a serious injury suffered at Shiloh, Forrest went on to capture thousands of Union prisoners, carry off or destroy millions of dollars' worth of Union supplies and equipment, and trick, frustrate, or overwhelm Union commanders at every opportunity. William Tecumseh Sherman, who would call him "the most remarkable man our Civil War produced on either side," fully understood the importance of capturing Forrest: The man had to be hunted down and killed even if it "costs ten thousand lives and bankrupts the Federal treasury."

reared and kicked. "Kill him! Kill him and his horse!" they screamed. One soldier managed to jam his gun up against Forrest's left hip and shoot, almost lifting him out of the saddle and leaving a bullet lodged against his spine. But Forrest managed to keep his seat and turn his horse, slashing right and left with his saber to clear a path back through his assailants. Leaning down, he grabbed one Yankee by the collar, swung him up onto his horse's rump, and, using the man as a shield, galloped off. When Forrest was out of firing range, he flung the Yankee to the ground and rode back to join his amazed command on the ridge.

Forrest's cheating of death marked the last action at Shiloh, a two-day battle that resulted in more American casualties than all of the nation's previous wars combined. At the "place of peace," the North had suffered the loss of more than 13,000 men dead, wounded, or missing, the South 10,000. But these were not the only casualties. Reputations lay in tatters as well. For the first time Beauregard was openly criticized, and doubts were cast on the abilities of Albert Sidney Johnston. Grant, too, found himself reprimanded, both in the press and in Congress. The accusation that he had been unprepared for the Confederate attack at Pittsburg Landing stung him. And worse was to come, for he was subsequently removed from overall field command.

Grant was so humiliated that he thought about leaving the army. His name had become linked with Shiloh, a bloody near defeat that everyone wanted to forget. Recalling the harsh criticism that the press had hurled at him following his ill-starred service in Kentucky, Sherman was confident that Grant would be able to rebound from a similar experience and encouraged him to reconsider. He did. He would remain in the army. And in the following year the name Ulysses S. Grant would be linked to another place in the West—to a great victory, a triumph that everyone wanted to celebrate. His greatest victory of the war. Vicksburg. ◆

THE YOUNG NAPOLEON'S WATERLOO

Abraham Lincoln's appointment of George McClellan as commander of the Union army won universal praise that turned to frustration when the young general balked at fighting.

"If Gen. McClellan does not want to use the army," fumed Lincoln, "I would like to borrow it for a time, provided I could see how it could be made to do something." The president had good reason to be frustrated. In the wake of the disastrous Union defeat at Bull Run on July 21, 1861, Lincoln had called on George Brinton McClellan to rebuild the disorganized army and engage Confederate commander Joseph E. Johnston's army in northern Virginia.

Only 34 years of age, the ambitious McClellan proved to be an excellent administrator, quickly marshaling 192,000 troops into Union camps around the capital and christening his force "the Army of the Potomac." When newspapers dubbed him Young Napoleon, McClellan reveled in the comparison, noting proudly: "I don't believe that Napoleon even ever possessed the love and confidence of his men more fully than I do of mine."

But McClellan's early promise was soon clouded. He wildly overestimated Rebel strength, and he unashamedly refused to move against the enemy that he loudly and erroneously proclaimed far superior in numbers. He was also extremely protective of his men, and this reinforced his reluctance to take action. Stymied by a commander who refused to risk failure, the president half-seriously threatened to lead the army himself. The self-righteous McClellan did little to appease the president and bristled under Lincoln's constant prodding, queries, and visits—on one occasion leaving the president to cool his heels while he went to bed without a word.

Under a tremendous amount of political pressure by January 1862, Lincoln ordered the general to renew the Union assault on the Rebels. McClellan proposed instead to bypass General Johnston in Manassas and take Union forces by water to the peninsula located between the York and James Rivers east of Richmond; from there he would fight his way toward the Confederate capital. An exasperated Lincoln reluctantly agreed: "I don't care, gentlemen, what plan you have. All I ask is for you to just pitch in."

*"By some strange operation of magic I seem to have become THE power of the land. I almost think that were I to win some small success now, I could become **Dictator**, or anything else that might please me...."*

GEORGE McCLELLAN

General McClellan scrutinizes Confederate general P. G. T. Beauregard from a comfortable distance in the 1862 cartoon at left. For a portrait with his wife, Ellen *(above)*, McClellan struck a characteristically Napoleonic pose.

McClellan's 100,000-man army embarked from Alexandria, Virginia, just across the Potomac from Washington, on March 17, 1862. It took three weeks for all of the troops and matériel to regroup at the tip of the York-James Peninsula and start the advance toward Richmond. Progress was far slower than expected, for spring rains had turned the Peninsula into a nearly impassable mire. On the afternoon of April 5 the waterlogged force approached the Confederates' entrenchments at Yorktown, some of them built almost eight decades earlier during the Revolutionary War and recently refurbished. Major General John Bankhead Magruder commanded 11,000 lightly armed Confederates, whereas McClellan had the apparently overwhelming advantage of a great war machine.

Outgunned and outmanned, Magruder resorted to deception: His artillery fired at everything; his bands blared along the breastworks in the evening; and in daylight a column of men marched in a continuous circle, moving into and then out of the view of Union observers. The ruse worked, for the gullible McClellan thought that the marching men were streams of fresh troops arriving to reinforce Magruder's meager army. The Union general appealed for more troops. "It seems clear that I shall have the whole force of the enemy on my hands," McClellan reported to Lincoln on April 7, "probably not less than 100,000 men, and possibly more."

Barely able to contain his anger, Lincoln telegraphed McClellan, "It is indispensable that you strike a blow . . . you must act." The general ignored the president's entreaties, commenting arrogantly in a letter to his wife, "I was much tempted to reply that he had better come and do it himself." When he at last settled on a course of action, the cautious McClellan rejected an assault in favor of what he called the "more tedious, but sure operations of siege."

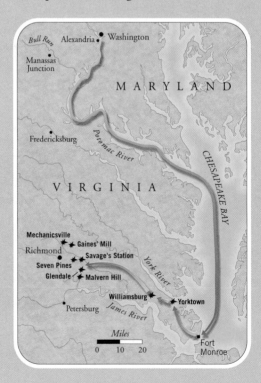

Avoiding the heavily fortified northern approach to Richmond, McClellan took his army down the Potomac and the Chesapeake Bay to the York-James Peninsula, then marched toward the Rebel capital.

Soldiers relaxing on a hillside look across the massive encampment of McClellan's army toward the Chesapeake. A flotilla of 400 vessels moved 121,500 men, 14,492 horses and mules, 1,150 wagons, 44 artillery batteries, and untold tons of matériel and supplies to the Peninsula.

The Union siege of Yorktown dragged on for nearly a month, giving Confederate commander Joe Johnston plenty of time to bring reinforcements down the Peninsula from his defensive lines in northern Virginia. The outflanked Confederate could hardly believe his good fortune. "No one but McClellan could have hesitated to attack," he crowed.

On the afternoon of Saturday, May 3, the Federal siege guns, some so heavy that it took teams of 100 horses to pull them into position, were finally ready for the bombardment. Johnston, however, did not intend to cooperate with McClellan's siege plans. Knowing that his position could not withstand bombardment from big guns, he engineered a stealthy nighttime retreat. Sunday, May 4, dawned on a Union army with no adversary. As the Federals occupied the deserted fortifications, McClellan boldly declared victory: "Our success is brilliant," boasted Young Napoleon, "and you may rest assured that its effects will be of lasting importance."

The next day the Army of the Potomac began warily following the retreating Johnston toward Richmond, and a skirmish at Williamsburg gave McClellan a small taste of victory. Johnston resumed his retreat, but at a slow pace designed to keep the enemy as far from Richmond for as long as possible. Then, on May 31 he suddenly turned on the plodding McClellan with fury. The bloody battle at Fair Oaks—better known by the Rebel name Seven Pines—raged inconclusively for two days before the Confederates withdrew, but the carnage shook McClellan's confidence. He wrote to Ellen, "I am tired of the sickening sight of the battlefield, with its mangled corpses and poor wounded." Union forces suffered 5,000 casualties, the Confederates 6,000, among them General Johnston.

> *"I am tired of the sickening sight of the battlefield, with its mangled corpses and poor wounded. Victory has no charms for me when purchased at such cost."*
>
> GEORGE MCCLELLAN
> AFTER THE BATTLE OF SEVEN PINES

Federals storm Rebel positions at Seven Pines *(above)*, where the wounded Joe Johnston *(left)* refused to leave the field until he retrieved the sword his father carried in the Revolutionary War.

With Johnston out of action, Confederate president Jefferson Davis quickly named General Robert E. Lee to lead the Army of Northern Virginia. McClellan was disdainful: "I prefer Lee to Johnston," he wrote. "The former is too cautious and weak under grave responsibility—personally brave and energetic to a fault, he yet is wanting in moral firmness when pressed by heavy responsibility and is likely to be timid and irresolute in action." That this assessment accurately described his own brand of leadership was an irony that was lost on George McClellan.

Lee, quite to the contrary, was a daring and brilliant commander who quickly set about his task of driving the Union army away from Richmond. On June 12 he sent 29-year-old General Jeb Stuart and a small cavalry force on a reconnaissance mission. Stuart's circuit around the entire Federal force served to further unnerve and humiliate McClellan, and it gave Lee the intelligence he needed to strike at the weakest point of the numerically superior Yankee army.

Beginning on June 25 and for the next week, Lee's forces attacked the Army of the Potomac in a series of ferocious battles that became known as the Seven Days. Again and again the armies clashed—at Mechanicsville, Gaines' Mill, Savage's Station, Frayser's Farm, and finally, on July 1, Malvern

At left, troops of the 55th and 60th Virginia under Robert E. Lee *(inset)* charge a Federal artillery position at Glendale on June 30, 1862, during the Seven Days' engagement. The repeated Confederate attacks drove McClellan's superior forces away from Richmond, but at a terrible price. "It was not war," Confederate general D. H. Hill said of the Seven Days' campaign. "It was murder."

Oblivious of the whiskey bottle placed on his cot by a prankster, an exhausted Lieutenant Colonel Samuel W. Owen sleeps in a Union camp after the Seven Days. Of 160,000 Federal soldiers sent to the Peninsula, 70,000 were wounded or killed or fell seriously ill. Yet the veterans remained intensely loyal to "Little Mac," as they affectionately nicknamed McClellan.

Hill. Four out of the five times the Union prevailed, yet in McClellan's mind the price of each victory was too high. His army steadily fell back down the Peninsula, away from Richmond.

The mighty Army of the Potomac had come within six miles of the capital, but it never attempted to attack the Rebel fortifi-

"It was thought to be a great thing to charge a battery of artillery or an earthworks lined with infantry.... We were very lavish of blood...."

A Confederate officer after the Seven Days' campaign

cations that were defending the city. McClellan maintained afterward that he had "failed to win only because overpowered by superior numbers." He continued to flood Washington with requests for reinforcements, but Lincoln had had enough. On August 3 the president ordered McClellan to withdraw and relieved him of command.

Lincoln and McClellan were photographed during their final meeting, which took place in the general's headquarters tent on October 4 after the Union victory at Antietam. McClellan's failure to pursue the Confederate army following the battle was the last straw for Lincoln. He sardonically called the Army of the Potomac "General McClellan's body guard."

On the heels of the Peninsular campaign came another debacle for the Union, when Lee pummeled John Pope's army in the Second Battle of Bull Run in August. Lee immediately took the war north, crossing the Potomac into Maryland and throwing Washington into panic. On September 2, Lincoln gave McClellan another chance, putting him in command of the Union army. Two weeks later, the armies clashed at Antietam in the bloodiest day in American history, with more than 25,000 casualties.

On September 17 the badly mauled Confederates fell back defeated, but again McClellan let them retreat to Virginia. In the hope of spurring McClellan into action, Lin-

"I have just read your dispatch about sore-tongued and fatigued horses. Will you pardon me for asking what the horses of your army have done since the battle of Antietam that fatigues anything?"

PRESIDENT LINCOLN TO GENERAL McCLELLAN

coln traveled to Antietam. "I came back thinking he would move at once," remembered the president. "But when I got home he began to argue why he ought NOT to move. I peremptorily ORDERED him to advance. It was nineteen days before he put a man over the river [and] nine days longer before he got his army across, and then he stopped again."

By then Lee had far outdistanced the timorous McClellan, but he continued nonetheless to ask for more men and supplies. On November 5 Lincoln relieved McClellan of command for the second and last time. McClellan believed until his death in 1885 that it was political backbiting and not his own incompetence that had wrecked his career.

Hat held high, McClellan gives his army a farewell salute on November 10, 1862, in a drawing by a witness to the emotional scene. His high degree of caution gave the South some of its greatest victories, yet he remained a hero to the men he led. "There is but one opinion among the troops," wrote General John Gibbon of McClellan's removal from command, "and that is that the Government has gone mad."

CHAPTER 2

GIBRALTAR OF THE WEST

"Grant will get Vicksburg before he quits."

U.S. CONGRESSMAN ELIHU B. WASHBURNE

Under a starlit, cloudless sky, blue-uniformed men and a sprinkling of women filled a motley collection of riverboats anchored on the west side of the Mississippi, about four miles above the port of Vicksburg. On the east bank, the lights of the bluff-top city sparkled and shimmered, some 200 feet above the river. In the magic of the warm spring evening, Vicksburg, Mississippi, did not look like what it was: a fortress that had defied the might of a Union army. Instead, it spread across the horizon like a glowing backdrop to a stage play, a drama that was about to come alive before the bobbing audience, as soon as the signal came to begin.

As 10:00 p.m. approached, the house lights of the city began to flicker and dim. Out on the water, a deeper black shadow, heavy and compact, began slipping stealthily downstream. Cannon muzzles poked out of the four-inch steel armor that covered the drifting bulk of the Federal ironclad *Benton,* flagship of Rear Admiral David Dixon Porter. In irregular file, 11 more naval vessels slipped silently downstream behind the *Benton*—six more heavily armored ironclad warships and five transports loaded with food and ammunition, decks stacked with grain sacks, piles of logs, and bales of hay and cotton to protect their boilers and crews from enemy fire. It was the night of April

16, 1863, and one of the most daring and decisive military operations of the Civil War had just begun.

Upriver, among the onlookers, a short, rumpled, mild-eyed man in a plain army coat watched the naval cavalcade from the deck of a river ferry, the *Von Phul*. With his wife, Julia, and three of his children at his side, General Ulysses S. Grant leaned against a rail on the downriver side of the vessel, his bearded face a study in serenity as he waited for the action to start. While Julia traded quiet pleasantries with the wives of some of the other officers, Grant clenched a cigar in his teeth and kept his thoughts to himself, as usual. Months of daring dreams and plans, written out painstakingly at his map-strewn desk in his floating headquarters ship, were focused on this moment. The fate of his army—not to mention his own already controversial career, even now hanging by a thread—had been cast upon the muddy waters of the Mississippi River, against the advice of his most trusted lieutenants. But if the weight of the moment bore down on the soft-spoken Ohioan, he gave no sign of it.

A few miles below Vicksburg, but still in sight of the town, one of the most energetic opponents of the naval operation was waiting anxiously aboard a small riverboat for the outcome. General William

Ulysses S. Grant, mastermind of the Union's victory over Confederate forces along the Mississippi, sits for a family portrait with his wife, Julia, and their children *(from left),* Nellie, Jesse, Fred, and Ulysses Jr. Fred, the eldest son, accompanied his father throughout the Vicksburg campaign.

Tecumseh Sherman, Grant's chief lieutenant, was, for all his misgivings, passionately aware of the stakes in this Mississippi gamble being orchestrated by his commander and close friend. For more than a year now, the Union and the Confederacy had been battling for control of the South's great river highways, and the place where that control had its center of gravity was the darkened city on the river, the genteel, heavily armed, strategically vital railhead and river port carved into the yellow clay bluffs looming over Sherman's head.

Victory. As he stood on the *Von Phul's* polished deck and stared into the darkness of the Mississippi, the thought of what he was trying to achieve rang constantly in Grant's highly organized, inscrutable mind. This awful, increasingly brutal war had to end, and the only way to accomplish it was to wrap the Confederacy in the steel and superior manpower of the mobilized North, cut off its economic lifelines, then roll back its armies until starvation, attrition, and military defeat forced the South to surrender. In effect, the Rebel states would have the life squeezed out of them. Critics had dubbed this strategy the Anaconda Plan and had written it off as an unnecessarily slow way of killing the Confederacy. The war, they declared, was never going to last that long.

Well, Grant thought, it had. Tens of thousands of young men on both sides had died or suffered hideous maiming wounds since the armchair strategists tossed off their criticisms of the plan. The same commentators who had confidently predicted that the conflict between the states would last only a few months were now clamoring for the drawn-out war to be over. And they blamed Grant as much as anyone for the fact that it wasn't.

A year earlier, the general mused, the Northern public had been staggered by the Federal casualties at the Battle of Shiloh. But Shiloh had marked one of the turning points in Union fortunes in the West, and ever since then they had continued, slowly and bloodily, to rise. Less than three weeks after the bat-

tle, the U.S. Navy, in a surprise offensive, had stunned the Southern population by capturing New Orleans. Union naval and land forces had pushed down the Mississippi from the north, taking Memphis two months after the near disaster at Shiloh, all the time moving toward the Federals advancing up from New Orleans. The Anaconda seemed ready to loop a huge coil around its prey.

But not yet. By late summer of 1862, Confederate forces in the East had rallied under the brilliant

This painting, entitled *The Union Fleet Passing Vicksburg,* recalls the fiery intensity of the April night when 12 Federal vessels attempted to run the fortress city's defenses. Despite a deluge of cannon shells from the Confederate batteries emplaced on the bluffs above Vicksburg, only one ship, the *Henry Clay,* was sunk.

state where rebellion still existed on January 1, 1863, would "thenceforward and forever" be free.

While the armies of the East battled it out, Grant was in Memphis studying his maps. At a time when most Northerners had their eyes fixed on the Confederate capital of Richmond, Grant looked south down the Mississippi—and confronted the challenge of Vicksburg. If the Anaconda was ever to claim its victim, he knew that he had to capture the citadel that no less a figure than Jefferson Davis had labeled the Gibraltar of the Mississippi, "the nailhead that held the South's two halves together."

Davis's description had never been more true. The importance of this elegant city of some 3,500 white citizens and about 1,500 blacks, perched on its high bluffs above the Mississippi, had only grown with the loss of New Orleans. Vicksburg was the economic heart of the sprawling Confederacy, a pump that took sorely needed foodstuffs, European weaponry, and other matériel flowing through Louisiana from Texas and Arkansas and moved them east along the Southern Mississippi Railroad.

Abraham Lincoln, too, well understood the importance of the city. As a young man, he had traveled down the Mississippi by flatboat, and undoubtedly spent time at the very docks where the lifeblood of the Confederacy now poured eastward. "Vicksburg is the key," he had told his advisers. "The war can never be brought to a close until that key is in our pocket."

But it would not be taken easily. Before the fall of New Orleans, the city of handsome mansions ranged below a turreted church and a Greek Revival courthouse flying a Confederate flag had only a token garrison. The appearance of Union warships downriver rapidly changed that situation. Gray-coated soldiers poured into Vicksburg, and heavy cannon began to bristle from the tall bluffs, until they eventually studded a corridor more than a dozen miles long.

Vicksburg's location made it a natural fortress. From its perch on bluffs that edged the river and rippled eastward in rolling hills, it commanded the

direction of Robert E. Lee and had smashed a Union army in a second battle at Bull Run, Virginia. Then Lee in a daring move invaded the North: Washington was apparently threatened, and the Union was once again on the defensive. But after September 17, when the two sides collided at Antietam Creek, Maryland, Lee's bloodied and decimated army limped back to Virginia. Five days later U.S. president Abraham Lincoln issued the Emancipation Proclamation, giving notice that all slaves held in a

FIVE MINUTES TO FREEDOM

"I have a right to rejoice; an' so have you; for we shall be free in jus' about five minutes."

GEORGE PAYNE, FORMER VIRGINIA SLAVE, WASHINGTON, D.C., DECEMBER 31, 1862

The Union's show of strength at the Battle of Antietam on September 17, 1862, gave President Lincoln the opening he had been waiting for to issue his initial draft of the Emancipation Proclamation. Five days after the battle he made public his vow to abolish slavery in any state or part of a state still in rebellion on January 1, 1863. If the rebellion continued, Lincoln would wield abolition as a weapon of war.

Although the president ardently believed that "if slavery is not wrong, nothing is wrong," the proclamation had more to do with military and economic advantage than moral justice. Freeing slaves would be likely to disrupt the Rebel economy and provide new recruits for the Union army. Lincoln also hoped that transforming the war from a struggle to preserve the Union into a crusade for freedom would appeal to the strong antislavery sentiment in Great Britain and prevent British intervention on behalf of the South.

Lincoln's strategy would prove a success, but it was tinged with hypocrisy. He feared inflaming secessionists in the border states, which had remained part of the Union, and the proclamation did not apply to slaves held in those states. Black leaders such as Frederick Douglass acknowledged the act's limitations, but they saw it as the turning point in the conflict between slavery and freedom.

On New Year's Day 1863, black men and women and white abolitionists in various parts of the country gathered to celebrate Lincoln's signing of the proclamation. But as the morning wore on with no word from Washington, people began to fear he had changed his mind. Douglass, who was waiting with friends at Boston's Tremont Temple, noted that "a visible shadow seemed falling on the expecting throng." Suddenly a man rushed up. "It is coming," he shouted, "it is on the wires!" The Boston crowd burst into cheers and a song of thanksgiving. "Sound the loud timbrel o'er Egypt's dark sea," they sang, "Jehovah hath triumphed, his people are free."

On a Sea Islands plantation, slaves listen to a Federal agent reading the Emancipation Proclamation, which declared that they were to be "forever free."

river and the low, watery terrain to the north and on the Louisiana shore opposite. Over the centuries the Mississippi had frequently changed its course, cutting its meandering way through the rich alluvial soil and creating a 40-mile-wide strip filled with crescent-shaped lakes marking former riverbeds, swamps, and sluggish, shallow bayous. Once the Confederates augmented such natural defenses, nothing less than a full-scale naval and land assault, led by an implacable commander, would carry the day.

Ulysses S. Grant was as implacable as they came. Hands jammed into the pockets of his rumpled uniform, the ever-present cigar in his mouth, he listened while his staff officers talked about Vicksburg. The general was under political pressure for a quick result, however, and in late December 1862, he began a series of actions against the city. Grant ordered William Sherman to ferry troops down the Mississippi from Memphis to the Yazoo River some 10 miles above Vicksburg, travel up the Yazoo, then debark and occupy an area of high bluffs from which they could attack the city. However, a Rebel spy was watching as the Union fleet of 81 ships, their decks packed with riflemen, swept past him on the water. His fingers were soon tapping out a warning on a private telegraph wire to the garrison at Vicksburg. When the Federals arrived, the Rebels were waiting for them and repulsed the attack.

For two and a half months, as the raw, wet winter wore on, Grant tried every scheme he could think of to bring his army around the Vicksburg defenses. The most dramatic was an attempt to dig a canal across a sharp, narrow bend in the river opposite Vicksburg, where the Union had begun establishing a foothold the summer before. But the work was so difficult and slow—"a pure waste of human labor," Sherman wrote his wife—that Grant finally called it off. Then he put troops aboard steamers and tried to float them down a chain of waterways in Louisiana that took a roundabout course south that joined to the Mississippi below Vicksburg, but the transports got stuck in the shallow, boggy channels. On the east side of the river, his engineers blew up a huge levee to

THE BATTLE OF NEW ORLEANS

In the spring of 1862, Union naval captain David Glasgow Farragut (above) and his fleet set out to capture New Orleans. The 60-year-old Farragut, who had sailed with the navy since age nine, knew they faced a difficult mission. Two forts and several vessels guarded the city. But victory would give the North control of the mouth of the Mississippi and a base for operations upriver.

Hoping to cripple the forts and then sail on to the city, Farragut opened his bombardment on April 18. By Easter Day, April 20, neither fort had surrendered. Against the advice of his officers, the captain ordered a dangerous night run past the enemy guns. In the ensuing two-hour battle with the forts and Confederate ships, Farragut felt "as if the artillery of heaven were playing upon the earth." But his armada prevailed, and five days later Union flags flew above New Orleans.

reopen a dammed-up waterway linking the Mississippi to the upper Yazoo River. Once again the Federals were stymied. Alert to the enemy vessels steaming toward Vicksburg, Confederates felled giant trees across the route, making forward motion extremely slow. When the Union forces came under fierce enemy fire from a small fort midway to Vicksburg, they gave up and beat a muddy retreat.

The rising press criticism of Grant's failure to make progress might have ended another's career. In a letter to a member of Lincoln's cabinet, a reporter for the *Cincinnati Gazette* wrote, "Our noble army of the Mississippi is being wasted by the foolish, drunken, stupid Grant. He can't organize or control or fight an army. I have no personal feeling about it; but I know he is an ass." Grant remained silent in the face of such personal and professional attacks, which were ignored in the White House. When asked why he didn't fire the general, President Lincoln replied, "I believe I am the only friend Grant has, and I think I will try him a little longer."

By now Grant was nursing a bolder plan. Because Rebel defenses were concentrated at Vicksburg, he was confident that his army could march down the west bank with little or no opposition. He could then ferry the troops across the river south of Vicksburg and march back up behind the city's defenses—risking everything on a single roll of the dice.

Of course, carrying out such an operation was easier said than done. The west bank was boggy and would get worse when chewed up by thousands of tramping feet and the wheels of countless supply wagons. And to get across the mile-wide Mississippi at any downriver point, Grant would need boats, supplies, and huge amounts of ammunition. How could he get them downstream? The daring voice inside him that always urged Grant to strike harder, faster, and more decisively than his enemies was whispering the way: Have Admiral Porter's fleet run the gantlet of the Vicksburg batteries.

As early as January 1863 Grant had suggested such a plan to Sherman, who opposed it outright. When Grant tried the idea out on Porter, he got a

much better response. The naval commander made one thing clear, however: Once his heavy, ungainly ships had steamed down the Mississippi, they would not be coming back upriver; the current would slow them down and make them easy targets for Confederate gunners along the shore.

On February 22, as his staff officers and a few female guests held a party on his headquarters ship at a small dock north of Vicksburg, Grant retired to his private office and hunched over his maps. He sat for hours, scribbling innumerable notes in the quick, flowing manner that his subordinates had come to know as the sign that his meticulous mind for detail was moving at full throttle. One of his senior officers eventually stepped into the room with a drink in his hand and urged Grant to have a sip and join the party. Grant declined. "You know your whiskey won't help me to think," he said. "Give me a dozen of the best cigars you can find, and I think by the time I have finished them I shall have this job pretty nearly planned." Soon he sprang his idea on a full council of his top generals. Sherman and the others continued to be opposed. But Grant could see no other idea worth pursuing. He intended to go ahead.

The map reading was over, the planning done. As Grant and his family stood on the *Von Phul*'s deck on the evening of April 16, the faintest sounds of revelry floated upstream toward them. The Confederate officers of Vicksburg were holding a party in the town. As they danced and traded compliments with the young Southern ladies in their ringlets and silk finery, the Rebels were unaware that the festivities were about to be rudely interrupted.

Aboard the *Benton*, Admiral David Porter ran through his own checklist of preparations once more.

More than 2,000 slaves from nearby plantations were pressed into service by the Union army in January 1863 to complete a canal across the mile-wide DeSoto Peninsula opposite Vicksburg. Started the previous summer, the canal was to connect the two legs of a hairpin bend in the Mississippi and provide a safe bypass for Union vessels. The project was abandoned after the river overran the canal's banks and Confederates began firing across the river at the workers.

His warships loomed larger than usual in the water because each one had a coal barge lashed to its right-hand side. The side facing Vicksburg was left free to return fire from the city's guns. To quell the loud noises of the ships' steam engines, technicians had muffled the exhaust pipes, and commanders were ordered to move at the slowest speed possible to avoid the clank and roar of full operation. Like Grant a stickler for detail, Porter ordered all shipboard pets to be taken ashore. Only the dimmest of stern lights were to be shown. But for all those precautions, Porter was sure that the stealthy passage would not go unnoticed by the Rebels. He ordered that men should stand ready belowdecks on each vessel with cotton wads to plug any holes in the hull should Confederate artillery find its mark. The ships began their muffled parade.

scramble to arms. "We could hear the gallop of couriers upon the paved streets," she wrote, "the rapid firing from the boats, the roar of the Confederate batteries, and, above all, the screaming, booming sound of the shells, as they exploded in the air and around the city."

Down on the river, an officer who was aboard a Union transport was watching the chaos that spread throughout Vicksburg: "We see the people in the streets of the town running and gesticulating as if all were mad. Their men at the batteries load and fire and yell as if every shot sunk a steamboat. . . . Down the river it is a sheet of flame. It was as if hell itself were loose that night on the Mississippi River." And through all of the commotion Grant remained silent, smoking a cigar, an intense light in his eyes.

"The Mississippi River may go through our canal or decline to....The canal is simply ridiculous, improperly located in the first place, and not properly cut in the second."

GENERAL WILLIAM TECUMSEH SHERMAN

The Union spectators held their breath as the dark shapes floated past the Vicksburg docks, right under the muzzles of a dozen Confederate guns the Yankees had dubbed the Twelve Apostles. Then, high up on the bluffs, there was a flash of light, then another—and the crack of cannon shot reached the watchers. The fleet had been discovered.

With no further need for silence, heavy flat booms roared back from the warships, as huge licks of flame poured out of the guns along their sides. Suddenly, curtains of orange light sprang up on the Union-controlled side of the river, throwing the vessels into a harsh glare. Confederate pickets stationed on small boats in the river had rowed to the western bank and set fire to several abandoned houses there to give the Vicksburg gunners a better target. To 12-year-old Fred Grant, standing next to his father on the deck of the *Von Phul,* it looked as if the whole river were lighted up by sunlight.

Roused from her bed by the noise, one townswoman rushed to the window and watched the city

As the general watched, the Federal ships took hit after hit before they slipped out of cannon range to the south. Behind them, they left one large addition to the glare, a transport that was burning to the water line. "Our men are all dead men," a nurse aboard Grant's ship was heard to say. "No one can live in such a rain of fire and lead." But casualties turned out to be light, only a handful of men wounded in the run and none killed. The first part of Grant's great gamble had paid off handsomely. Waiting aboard his small riverboat downriver, a cheerful William Sherman halloed a welcome to each of the ships as they passed.

When the fires on the Louisiana shore died down and the smoke of gunfire drifted away, a welcome quiet settled over the Mississippi. "The stars looked down tenderly upon Union and Rebel alike," thought Julia Grant, "and the frogs began again their summer songs." The first stage of the operation had been completed. Now the army had to be moved down the west bank of the river and reunited with

After months of failed attempts to breach Vicksburg's defenses, Grant's army marched down the Union-held west bank of the Mississippi to a point below the city. After crossing the river at Bruinsburg, Grant moved east and captured Jackson, the state capital, then doubled back to approach Vicksburg from the rear and lay siege to the city.

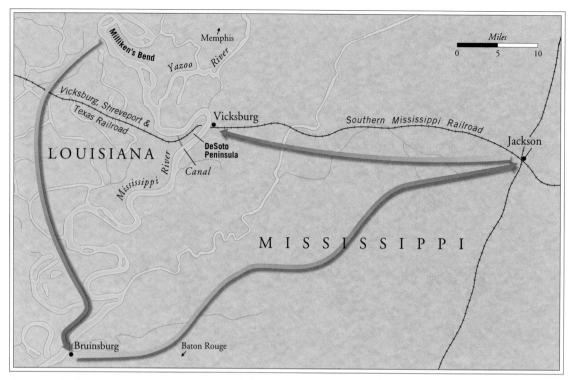

the navy before both crossed south of Vicksburg. Then Grant would be in a position to mount an attack on the city from the rear.

The troops' passage down the west bank of the river turned out to be, in its own way, as hellish as the ordeal of shot and fire. The soggy ground was churned into a soup that reached to the soldiers' knees, and as many as 18 horses were needed to pull each field gun. While man and beast struggled to move a single gun, the stalled weapons sank deeper into the ooze under their own weight. Water was everywhere, and midwestern farm boys listened nervously to the sounds of alligators croaking in the bayous. "We are all dirty as hogs," one soldier from Iowa reported, "we are all lousy." His commanders agreed with the assessment. Declared a Union general, "A worse march no army ever made in the history of military operations."

Yet no matter how slowly, the army was at least moving. The strange and varied assortment of clerks, farmers, engineers, tradesmen, blacksmiths—all the walks of life that made up the volunteer army—proved equal to any task the sucking ground threw up for them. As his men slogged and toiled—laying log roads, putting together pontoon bridges—Grant rode quietly back and forth among them, unsnarling traffic jams, dismounting to sink into the muck along with the troops. "There was no nonsense, no sentiment," wrote one officer of his leader, "only a plain businessman of the republic, there for the one single purpose of getting that command across the river in the shortest time possible." Grant, he noted with wonder, "seemed wrought up to the last pitch of determination and energy."

As he made his way south, the Union commander knew that he had to keep the enemy guessing about his intentions. All of his laborious and failed efforts at landing forces north of Vicksburg had had the effect of convincing the defenders that the real threat would come from that direction. While the long snaking lines of troops headed downriver on the west bank beyond view of the Vicksburg garrison, Grant ordered another raid on the impregnable bluffs above the city. The gray-capped heads continued to point north. Grant and his army slipped across the Mississippi 30 miles below Vicksburg.

On the morning of April 30, files of mud-splashed soldiers began tramping into formation at a boat landing at Bruinsburg on the east bank of the Mississippi. Only the most basic necessities could be taken ashore; soldiers were forced to abandon anything that might slow their attack on the enemy. Officers were not even permitted to take their horses or tents, and Grant himself took nothing more than a toothbrush and a comb. Bone weary, anxious, and with a head that was spinning with details on how to proceed next, Grant was suddenly filled with an almost ecstatic sense of relief. "I was now in the enemy's country, with a vast river and the stronghold of Vicksburg between me and my base of supplies. But I was on dry ground on the same side of the river with the enemy. All the campaigns, labors, hardships and exposure . . . previous to this time that had been made and endured were for the accomplishment of this one object." The warrior was now ready to make war.

War was, in fact, a kind of relief to Ulysses S. Grant. Its organizational complexity and horror, its stark risks and triumphs, stood in epic contrast to the humdrum failure of much of his earlier life. The modest, appealing man, who had become used to ordering thousands of men into battle to face their death, did not fare well when faced with the challenges of ordinary life. This quiet, unassuming figure with a kindly, blue-eyed stare could think in

The Union tinclad gunboat *Rattler* served as flagship in the unsuccessful 1862 Yazoo River campaign against Vicksburg. The Union navy relied heavily on such vessels to maintain its hold on the Mississippi River and its tributaries.

the boldest military terms yet had almost none of the sense of hierarchy that went with the ordinary military mind. He once told colleagues that he felt qualified to command a cavalry brigade; there was a point, not long previous, when even that seemed to his peers to be beyond Grant's capacities.

Inability to live up to others' expectations had dogged Grant from his early years growing up in a small town in Ohio, where his father, Jesse, was a prosperous and politically ambitious tanner, his mother, Hannah, a severe, reserved woman of few words, a tendency her son soon mimicked. If he hoped that his eldest boy—originally named Hiram Ulysses Grant—would join him in the family business, Jesse was soon disappointed: Young Ulysses hated the enterprise. He led a country boy's existence, albeit a comfortable one, did moderately well in school, and showed only one significant talent—for dealing with horses. When Ulysses turned 17, his father, who had been elected mayor, used his political clout to win him a cadetship at West Point.

Grant was hardly an impressive candidate soldier. When he arrived at West Point he was an immature five feet one inch tall and weighed 117 pounds. One of his schoolmates recalled him as "delicate." His appearance was unmemorable—and so, apparently, was his name. Always called Ulysses at home, he began signing himself U. H. Grant. But on the West Point registry his name somehow became U. S. Grant. Perhaps he found the new middle initial a reminder of his mother's maiden name, Simpson. In any event, he would be U. S. Grant for the rest of his life.

Grant's performance at the academy was good but it was not outstanding. He complained of the cadets' tight pants and of the pomposity of his peers; he spent most of his time reading novels and he took a drawing course; and he developed a lifelong distaste for enthusiastic conquerors like Napoleon. Apart from his senior year roommate, Fred Dent, he made few friends. But he was captivated by Dent's romantic, strong-willed sister, Julia, and soon asked her to marry him. The marriage would have to wait for four years, however, while he served at army posts

"One of my superstitions had always been when I started to go anywhere, or do anything, not to turn back, or stop until the thing intended was accomplished. I have frequently started to go to places where I had never been and to which I did not know the way, and if I got past the place without knowing it, instead of turning back, I would go until a road was found turning in the right direction, take that, and come in by the other side."

ULYSSES S. GRANT

in Louisiana and Texas, and with the U.S. expeditionary force in Mexico.

As an infantry lieutenant, Grant distinguished himself during the Mexican War, which lasted from 1846 to 1848. In his first battle he charged through heavy enemy rifle and artillery fire, feeling no fear until a cannonball blew the head off an enlisted man near him. "There is no great sport in having bullets flying about one in every direction," he wrote Julia about his experiences, "but I find they have less horror when among them than when in anticipation." Grant's boldness earned him a mention in dispatches. More important, he discovered that he possessed the true warrior's gene: a calmness and steadiness when faced with violent action. He also found that he preferred to act rather than be acted upon.

After the war, Ulysses and Julia were married, and in October 1848 they moved to a posting in Detroit. Three years later he was transferred to the Pacific Coast. Julia was pregnant with their second child, and he told her that the trip across the Panamanian isthmus was too dangerous for her to make. She returned to her family in Saint Louis. At remote Fort Humboldt in northern California, Grant's loneliness for Julia and his family was intense. He begged for a transfer and was denied. He began to drink.

To those who knew him, Grant's affair with the bottle was an aberration, not an ingrained flaw. One acquaintance, who described him as a man of unusual self-control, claimed that Grant's drinking did not reflect on his character. Another said that Grant only went on occasional sprees. In any event, his private habits did not seem to affect his peers' view of his skills or hamper his career, and in April 1854 he accepted promotion to the rank of captain. Then he tendered his resignation. He was soon back with his beloved Julia, penniless and without a job.

Grant turned to farming, working a plot of land in Missouri that was owned by one of his brothers-in-law. He built a house, appropriately named Hardscrabble. "Every day I like farming better," he wrote his father in 1856, "and I do not doubt but that money is to be made at it." He was wrong. That winter, he sold firewood on the streets of Saint Louis to survive. The next spring, a time of nationwide depression, his crops failed. He pawned his gold watch for $22 and eventually gave up the farm. After working for less than a year as a real-estate agent and rent collector, he moved the family to the Illinois town of Galena, a busy river port hard by the Mississippi. His father had moved there from Ohio in the early 1840s, and Grant took a job as a clerk in the family's leather store.

By this time, war between the states was brewing. Grant was well aware of it, even as he spent quiet but tedious months in remote Galena. Soon the skies glared red over Fort Sumter, and Grant was ready to rejoin the army. He told his father: "We are now in the midst of trying times when everyone must be for or against his country, and show his colors too, by his very act." The only West Pointer around, he was chosen to chair a town meeting in Galena—and never returned to the leather store again. He helped organize a company of volunteers and waited to be called back to duty. When the call came, he left to take command of an Illinois regiment of infantry.

Grant's informality made him something of an oddity among army officers, and so did his lack of social graces. He had almost no conversational skills: "When he has nothing to say, he says nothing," said one observer. One of his first orders to his new troops was not an inspirational speech but the command "Men, back to your quarters." When he did have something to say, however—as when issuing orders for battle—he proved to be fluent, economical, rapid, and clear. His style of command was a curious one. He did not like to waste energy: When he had nothing to do, he did nothing, and appeared indolent. He liked to give subordinates wide latitude by issuing orders in general terms, without specifics. But he also understood the countless details necessary to make an army work, and when it came to planning an actual campaign, he would soon enough demonstrate his abilities as a leader of men.

None of those qualities were yet apparent to the Union soldiers who first met the small man in the faded army overcoat. Being back in uniform exalted

A clean-shaven Grant *(left)* was photographed in the early 1850s shortly before resigning his captain's commission. He had little success earning enough to support his wife and children, and in 1860 he was forced to seek employment in the Grant family's Galena, Illinois, leather goods store *(below)*.

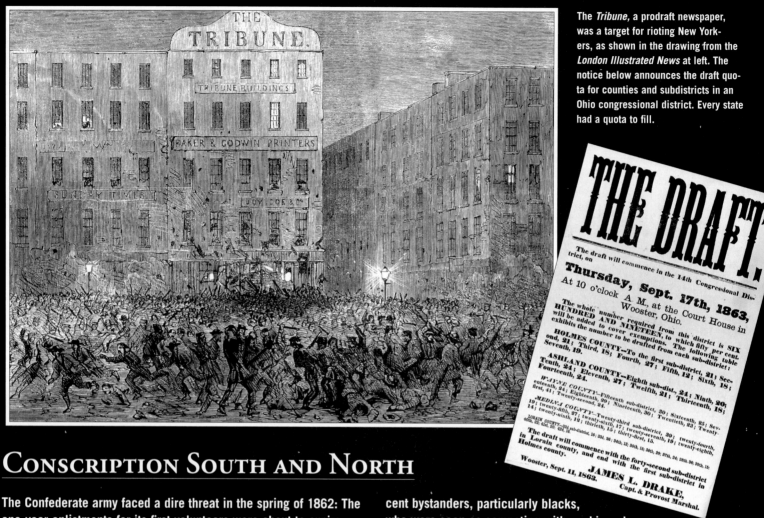

The *Tribune,* a prodraft newspaper, was a target for rioting New Yorkers, as shown in the drawing from the *London Illustrated News* at left. The notice below announces the draft quota for counties and subdistricts in an Ohio congressional district. Every state had a quota to fill.

THE DRAFT.

The draft will commence in the 14th Congressional District, on

Thursday, Sept. 17th, 1863,

At 10 o'clock A. M., at the Court House in Wooster, Ohio.

The whole number required from this district is SIX HUNDRED AND NINETEEN, to which fifty per cent. will be added to cover exemptions. The following table exhibits the number to be drafted from each sub-district:

HOLMES COUNTY—To the first sub-district, 21; Second, 21; Third, 15; Fourth, 27; Fifth, 12; Sixth, 18; Seventh, 19.

ASHLAND COUNTY—Eighth sub-dist., 24; Ninth, 20; Tenth, 24; Eleventh, 27; Twelfth, 21; Thirteenth, 18; Fourteenth, 24.

WAYNE COUNTY—Fifteenth sub-district, 24; Sixteenth, 24; Eighteenth, 29; Nineteenth, 30; Twentieth, 23; Twenty-first, 41; Twenty-second, 24.

MEDINA COUNTY—Twenty-third sub-district, 39; twenty-fourth, 19; twenty-fifth, 27; twenty-sixth, 17; twenty-seventh, 19; twenty-eighth, 14; twenty-ninth, 15; thirtieth, 15; thirty-first, 15.

LORAIN COUNTY—32d sub-district, 16; 33d, 36; 34th, 15; 35th, 15; 36th, 29; 37th, 34; 38th, 36; 39th, 15; 40th, 22; 41st, 20; 42d, 16.

The draft will commence with the forty-second sub-district in Lorain county, and end with the first sub-district in Holmes county.

Wooster, Sept. 11, 1863.

JAMES L. DRAKE, Capt. & Provost Marshal.

Conscription South and North

The Confederate army faced a dire threat in the spring of 1862: The one-year enlistments for its first volunteers were about to expire. To protect the Southern cause, the Confederate Congress extended those enlistments for the war's duration, and it also instituted the first draft in American history. The law required all able-bodied white men between the ages of 18 and 35 to serve for three years.

Many Rebel volunteers found the draft an offense, charging that "a soldier was simply a machine, a *conscript,*" without pride or valor. And draft exemptions enraged the poor: Men with means could pay for substitutes, and anyone owning at least 20 slaves was excused outright. Almost half of those drafted refused to join.

In the North, the first Federal conscription ignited several bloody riots. The worst was in New York City, where a white mob took to the streets on July 13, 1863, to stone and burn a local draft office. The rioters went on to ransack homes and shops and assault innocent bystanders, particularly blacks, who were seen as competing with working-class whites for jobs. Gangs burned an orphanage for black children and lynched at least two black men. Several state militia units came to aid the outnumbered local police that night, but it took still more troops to bring the mob under control. By the time the rioting ended on July 16, 119 people were dead and 306 injured.

The Union draft proved a disaster: Out of 292,441 men called, only 35,883 eventually became soldiers. The rest failed to report, got physical exemptions, bought their way out for $300, or paid for substitutes, many of them ill qualified. The Yankee conscripts were, in the opinion of General George Meade, "mostly worthless." Perhaps the only positive result of the draft was an unintentional one: The number of volunteers rose as some men raced to avoid the stigma of being a draftee.

Grant, but his first assignment was mundane enough. He was ordered to march into Missouri and help keep it from joining the Confederacy. As the size of the Federal army grew, however, he quickly rose in rank to brigadier general.

Grant's potential as a gifted officer had first been spotlighted when he forced the surrender of two Rebel river strongholds in western Tennessee, Fort Donelson and Fort Henry, in the winter of 1862. But Grant had been deeply chagrined—and his newborn reputation badly damaged—by the next major action he commanded. Only two months later, at the Battle of Shiloh, he had been overconfident and careless, allowing the enemy to take the initiative and launch a surprise attack. The battle was a hideous lesson that rose up frequently in Grant's mind. It did so again as he stood on the Mississippi's east bank, below Vicksburg, and contemplated his next move. This time he would keep an iron grip on the initiative.

Leading the defense of Vicksburg was General John Pemberton, who regarded the city's security as a sacred trust. A Pennsylvania native of Quaker ancestry, Pemberton was, perhaps, an unlikely soldier of the South. He was a West Pointer and after graduation had been stationed in Virginia, where he met and married a woman from a prominent Norfolk family. He fought in Mexico, where he was wounded twice, and won a promotion to captain. When the Civil War came, two of his brothers enlisted in the Union army, but Pemberton resigned his commission and headed for Richmond. Some citizens of Vicksburg would later question his loyalty to their cause, but the northern-born general's commitment was never doubted by any Confederate leader. Like Grant, he had the full support of his president.

John Pemberton had two masters, however. One was President Davis, the other General Joseph Johnston, recently arrived from Virginia to take charge of the western theater of the war. Johnston was a man of decided opinions, a seasoned veteran with a sense of strategy that might be the equal of Grant's. While Davis, the politician, wanted Vicksburg defended at

all costs, Johnston, the military man, knew that armies, not cities, were the key to winning wars. He wanted the troops in Vicksburg to march out of the city and destroy the invading Northern army. "Success will give you back what was abandoned to win it," he wrote Pemberton, fearing that the city's garrison would be bottled up forever behind its defenses.

Abandon Vicksburg! To Pemberton this was unthinkable. Grant, who had served with Pemberton in Mexico, had guessed as much. He knew the Pennsylvanian to be "scrupulously particular in matters of honor and integrity"—and perhaps, by temperament, conservative and inflexible. Keeping him pinned more or less in place was key to the plan still building in Grant's mind. The Union commander knew that he was committing himself against an enemy that would substantially outnumber him if Pemberton and Johnston could unite their forces. But if Grant acted quickly he could engage them one at a time and, he felt confident, emerge the victor from both engagements. Within two days of landing on the east bank of the river, Federal troops sent a small Rebel force that had come out to meet them running back to Vicksburg. Grant's beachhead was now secure, and to celebrate he climbed aboard his headquarters steamer and took his first bath in a week. He also received visitors. One of the first to turn up was a shocker: his son Fred.

A bright, likable boy bent on adventure, Fred had crossed the Mississippi with Grant aboard one of Admiral Porter's gunboats. But he had been asleep when the Union forces went ashore. When he awoke he found that his father was gone. Grant had left orders with an officer that Fred was not to leave the ship, but the young adventurer was not to be denied. He asked for permission to go ashore for a little rabbit hunting, and, permission granted, set off after the Union forces as soon as he could slip away unnoticed. He had equipped himself for the occasion with the sword and sash that his father seldom bothered to use.

Along the way, Fred picked up a traveling companion, Charles Dana, a special commissioner for the war department and former newspaperman at the *New York Tribune*. Dana had been sent west to keep an eye on Grant. For although Grant had the backing of Abraham Lincoln, he did not enjoy the confidence of all of the president's cabinet members. Secretary of War Edwin Stanton was one of the skeptics, and he had ordered Dana to report back regularly on, among other things, the oft-repeated rumors about the general's drinking. Grant's staff had been angry about Dana's assignment, and some officers even wanted to toss him into the Mississippi. But Grant had welcomed him, answered all his questions, and invited him to dine at his mess. In this way, Dana had gotten to know him well, and he liked what he saw.

"Grant was an uncommon fellow," wrote Dana, "the most modest, the most disinterested, and the most honest man I ever knew, with a temper that nothing could disturb and a judgment that was judicial in its comprehensiveness and wisdom. Not a great man, except morally, not an original or brilliant man, but sincere, thoughtful, deep, and gifted with courage that never faltered. When the time came to risk all, he went in like a simple-hearted, unaffected, unpretending hero, whom no ill omens could deject and no triumph unduly exalt."

Grant was risking it all now, below Vicksburg, moving so quickly that Dana had been unable to keep up with him when the first Union forces crossed over to the east bank of the Mississippi. Dana had managed to get across the river later and met up with the general's son. Together, they set off after the army.

By the time Dana and Fred caught up with Grant, they were riding a couple of huge artillery horses. Dana had acquired a dilapidated bridle and saddle for his mount, but his young sidekick was making do with a piece of clothesline and a saddle without stirrups. Although concerned for the boy's safety, Grant was pleased at Fred's enterprise and allowed him to travel with him for the rest of the campaign.

Grant had arrived on the east side of the river knowing that he would have to act fast to prevent the army commanded by Johnston, which was marching down from Tennessee, from joining with Pemberton's. Johnston had already moved his

Two cooks, former slaves, sit outside their tent at a Union army outpost in Culpeper, Virginia.

A STAKE IN THE WAR'S OUTCOME

From the Civil War's beginning, many northern blacks had volunteered to fight for the Union but were rebuffed. In 1861 black men in Cincinnati tried to form a company for the defense of the city, but the police told them to keep out of what was a "white man's war." The widespread sentiment among white Americans was that black men could not be made into soldiers. Even President Lincoln doubted their fighting ability, saying in September 1862: "If we were to arm the Negroes, I fear that in a few weeks the arms would be in the hands of the rebels."

The prejudice did not extend to support roles. In 1861 a black newspaper reported on the work situation in the District of Columbia: "Five hundred men find employment each day in the Quartermaster's department. Barbers and hackmen are doing a thriving business. Three or four thousand men are employed at cutting wood." But such limited opportunities to serve were unacceptable to black leaders like Frederick Douglass, who wanted to use the war to raise the status of his race. He campaigned for combat roles, writing to President Lincoln in 1861: "Men in earnest don't fight with one hand, when they might fight with two."

Yet Douglass might have failed if not for an increasingly serious manpower shortage:

"Once let the black man get upon his person the brass letters, U.S.; let him get an eagle on his button, and a musket on his shoulder and bullets in his pocket, and there is no power on earth which can deny that he has earned the right to citizenship."

FREDERICK DOUGLASS

Dressed in castoff Federal uniforms, black teamsters wait for work at City Point, Virginia, a large Union supply depot. They were among the thousands of ex-slaves who flocked to Union lines and were accepted as "contraband of war" for service in support roles such as carpenter, musician, nurse, and laborer.

This recruiting poster shows a black regiment with its white officer. Many blacks resented their severely limited opportunities for advancement within the Union army and threatened not to enlist, but Frederick Douglass urged them to accept the situation and fight. "To say we won't be soldiers because we cannot be colonels is like saying we won't go into the water till we have learned to swim. A half a loaf is better than no bread."

By 1862, with the war going badly for the North, white volunteers were becoming scarce. In July, Congress passed two laws that aided black enlistment. Though officially frowned upon, abolitionist officers in the Union army organized provisional black units in South Carolina, Kansas, and Louisiana, where they enjoyed some success in minor skirmishes. These results, coupled with the issuance of the Emancipation Proclamation, led to Lincoln's about-face in March 1863: "The colored population is the great *available* and yet *unavailed of* force for restoring the union."

The man-hungry war department organized 14 black regiments under the command of white officers in the next five months. From the start these regiments fought commendably. After the first engagement in May 1863 at Port Hudson, Louisiana, a white officer declared: "You have no idea how my prejudices with regard to Negro troops have been dispelled by the battle the other day." At Milliken's Bend, northwest of Vicksburg, Captain M. M. Miller reported in June: "I can say for them that I never saw a braver company of men in my life." In July, at Fort Wagner, near Charleston

harbor, the 54th Massachusetts won everlasting glory for its valiant, yet ultimately futile, attack in which the regiment suffered 40 percent casualties.

These reports fueled the fire of black enlistment, which eventually totaled 166 regiments with 180,000 men. The feelings of many were expressed in 1863 by Christopher Fleetwood, a free black from Baltimore: "This year has brought about many changes that at the beginning were or would have been thought impossible. The close of the year finds me a soldier for the cause of my race."

Supporting himself with a cane, Sergeant William H. Carney of the 54th Massachusetts holds the regimental flag he saved from capture during the assault on Fort Wagner in South Carolina. The *New York Tribune* praised the heroism of the 54th, saying: "It did not falter. It made Fort Wagner such a name for the colored race as Bunker Hill has been for ninety years to the white Yankees."

The Congressional Medal of Honor was awarded to 23 black soldiers who fought in the Civil War. Shown here, front and back, is the medal received by William Carney.

headquarters and a small advance force to the state capital of Jackson, 40 miles east of Vicksburg. Grant's instincts told him that the place to strike was between Vicksburg and Jackson instead of heading straight for Vicksburg.

Rather than try to maintain a supply line back to Bruinsburg, Grant decided to abandon the lumbering supply trains that would hamper his movements in hostile territory. He would cut loose from his base there and live off the land. Fortunately, this part of Mississippi was rich farming country, with plenty of chicken, mutton, ripe strawberries, turkey, duck, and sundry vegetables. Gathering every farm wagon, oxcart, and buckboard he could find, Grant ordered his troops to prepare five days' rations, then launched the army inland. They ate well along the way, and young Fred noted that the free-foraging troops ate even better than the staff at his father's own mess.

Meanwhile, John Pemberton's confusion was mounting. He knew that Grant had begun to move away from the Mississippi, but he could not believe that he would continue in that direction. What army commander would move for long away from access to his supplies? At the same time that he was trying to figure out what Grant was up to, the Confederate commander was having a hard time deciding on his own course of action. Torn between the conflicting advice of Jefferson Davis on the one hand and Joe Johnston on the other, he tried to accommodate both: He ordered two-thirds of his troops to a point midway to Jackson and kept the rest inside Vicksburg in case the Union commander made a dash at the city. But by hedging his bets in this way, Pemberton would not have enough soldiers to beat the Yankees in the field. He had handed the initiative to his opponent.

Suffering from no such indecision, Grant and his unencumbered army advanced at a fast clip on Jackson from the southwest, forcing the Rebels to evacuate the town and retreat to the north on May 14. Not far behind the first Union troops into the capital was Fred Grant, resplendent in his father's sword and sash. Spotting a large Confederate flag raised above the statehouse, the boy raced toward the building, only to be beaten to the prize by a mud-spattered staff officer. Disappointed, Fred turned elsewhere for trophies. As he roamed through the building he saw a pipe, still lighted, lying on a desk and jumped to the conclusion that it belonged to the governor. "I confiscated it," Fred later wrote, "ostensibly for the national service, but actually for my own private use."

That night Fred joined Grant and other Union officers at the Bowman House, the city's finest hostelry; father and son occupied the same room General Johnston had used the night before. The next morning one of Grant's party went to settle accounts with the hotel landlord. "What's our bill?" he asked.

"Ninety dollars," replied the man. But when he was offered a Confederate $100 bill, the landlord's face dropped.

"I didn't know you were going to pay in that money, or I should have charged more."

"Very well, charge whatever you like," the Federal replied. The bill was finally settled for $200—Confederate. But the landlord's problems were far from over. Rebel soldiers later burned down his hotel because he had refused to accept Confederate currency at the same rate as greenbacks.

Only two weeks had passed since the Mississippi crossing. The pace had been hectic and the heat was oppressive, but slowing down was not on Grant's mind. He left orders for the destruction of the rail lines at Jackson, then set off west toward Vicksburg. Contrary to Grant's expectations, the vacillating Pemberton and the force he had moved out of the city were not headed in John-

PRIVATE CASHIER'S LITTLE SECRET

Albert D. J. Cashier *(above)* of the 95th Illinois endured camp life for three years and fought in some 40 battles. Except for his small stature and hairless face, he seemed much like any other soldier. There was, however, one difference: Albert Cashier was a woman.

Hundreds of women such as Cashier, whose real name was Jennie Hodgers, cut their hair and donned male garb to join the Union and Confederate armies. Cursory medical examinations, ill-fitting uniforms, and the presence of preadolescent boys in the ranks aided in the deception. These women risked their lives for many reasons, ranging from feelings of patriotism to a desire for greater personal freedom. Several were discovered and dismissed. Others fell in battle, their identities revealed only after death. The lucky ones, like Hodgers, survived the war, secret intact.

Hodgers's secret was discovered in 1911 by a doctor who examined her following an auto accident. Despite this revelation, upon her death in 1915 she was buried with full military honors, and her tombstone was inscribed "Albert D. J. Cashier, Company G, 95th Illinois Infantry."

ston's direction. Instead, he had moved south from Vicksburg to attack the Union rear in order to cut off Grant's supply lines and abort an assault on the city. However, Pemberton soon received a report that Grant's army was marching toward Vicksburg, and it had no rear to attack. It was unthinkable for an army to move without supply trains, and yet it was happening. Pemberton realized with horror that he had no choice but to confront Grant head-on in battle.

The two forces encountered each other on May 16 about 20 miles east of Vicksburg. Grant got the upper hand and drove the Rebels back in the direction of Vicksburg. There were waves of cheers as Grant rode among his victorious troops after the battle. A Union corporal who was watching the general's progress noted his reaction: "Speechless and almost without a bow, he pushed on past, like an embarrassed man hurrying to get away from some defeat. Once he stopped near the colors, and, without addressing himself to anyone in particular, said: 'Well done!' "

Jubilant, the Federal army set off in close pursuit of the Confederates—too close, in the case of Fred Grant. The youngster had gotten so near to the fleeing Rebels that he had been nicked in the leg by an enemy sharpshooter. "I am killed!" wailed Fred to a Union officer. Suspecting that the wound was somewhat less than fatal, the officer recommended that Fred wiggle his toes to check that they were all right, then man and boy beat a hasty retreat.

While Fred was recovering from his mishap, his father took a ride with Cump Sherman to the bluffs along the Yazoo River north of Vicksburg that he had tried to capture back in December. Looking across to the city in the distance, Sherman turned in his saddle and faced Grant. "Until this moment," he declared, "I never thought your expedition a success. I never could see the end clearly till now. But this is a campaign; this is a complete and successful campaign whether or not we take the town." But Grant fully intended to take the town—and its army, too.

Back in Vicksburg again, General Pemberton took comfort in the strength of the earth ramparts that surrounded him. It was true that he had been beaten in the field, but within the city there were many fresh troops, and now he felt himself to be in a very strong position indeed. Moreover, Jefferson Davis himself had ordered the Confederate commander to "hold Vicksburg at all hazards," and John Pemberton was not one to take such an order lightly.

Pemberton's defenses were, in fact, a study in the art of fortification. Running from the high ground half a mile to its north, along a string of hills, bluffs, and ridges to a point three miles below the town, an arc of huge earthworks loomed over the countryside. Strong forts overlooked each of the six roads that entered Vicksburg, while redoubts, smaller forts, and battery positions studded the entire line. The remaining stretches of rampart were peppered with rifle pits and trenches; outside, a ditch eight feet deep and 14 feet wide would assist in foiling any attackers and would leave them exposed to slaughter. A thicket of sharpened tree trunks and interlaced branches known as an abatis completed the outworks. All told, 102 cannon poked out of the defensive wall, their numbers augmented by so-called Quaker Guns, which were nothing more than logs that had been painted black to make them resemble artillery pieces. The first Yankees to arrive at the scene quailed at the challenge ahead. "The approaches to this position were frightful," wrote one officer, "enough to appall the stoutest heart."

Row after row of well-emplaced cannon, like the four-gun Confederate battery shown at left, proved impervious to the Union naval gunfire that battered Vicksburg and its defenders from morning till night during the six-week-long siege.

Pemberton's faith in the city's defenses seemed well founded. On May 19 Grant hurled his troops against the fortress, only to have them repulsed, with heavy losses. He tried again May 22, with the same result. Calm as ever, Grant had watched it all, sitting on horseback and whittling a stick as his troops were beaten back. Two unsuccessful attempts were enough to show Grant that the fortress would have to be conquered by different means— the long, slow starvation of a siege. "We'll have to dig our way in," a newspaper reporter heard him say quietly.

Through the long days of the southern spring, Grant watched as his engineers went to work, throwing a cordon of steel and earthworks around the well-defended city. With Union gunboats steaming up and down the river and a system of trenches north, east, and south of Vicksburg, Grant had the Rebels in a choke hold. He began to edge his trenches toward the Confederate lines. "The soldiers worked at digging zigzag approaches to the rebel works," one of his engineer officers recalled. "When entrenchments were safe and finished, still others, yet farther in advance were made, as if by magic, in a single night."

The Federal troops hunkered down in muddy trenches and the Rebels dug in behind their earthen ramparts were so close that they could easily hear one another, and they yelled jokes and taunts back and forth across the pockmarked no man's land separating them. At times, the contact was even closer, with one Union captain reporting that "our pickets often had a cup of coffee or a chew of tobacco with the Rebel pickets at night." As had happened before in this war between brothers, the nearness of the enemy troops at a time when there was no immediate fighting fostered a kind of camaraderie. In the stillness of those balmy evenings, as figures rose from the trenches and met in no man's land, the drummer boy of an Iowa regiment would creep out and look for one particular shadowy figure—his brother, who was serving with a Confederate unit. The two young men, divided and brought

Despite his Pennsylvania Quaker heritage, Confederate lieutenant general John C. Pemberton *(above, left)* was an ardent supporter of Southern rights, perhaps in part because of his marriage to Martha Thompson *(above, right),* a native of Norfolk, Virginia. Pemberton was assigned the task of strengthening Vicksburg's fortifications and keeping the city out of Grant's hands. After months of repulsing Union attacks and enduring a lengthy siege, the Confederate defenders reached the breaking point. On July 1, 1863, Pemberton sent a dispatch to his division commanders stating, "Unless the siege of Vicksburg is raised, or supplies are thrown in, it will become necessary very shortly to evacuate the place. I see no prospect of the former, and there are many great, if not insufferable obstacles in the way of the latter." Blamed for the loss of the city, Pemberton never again received an assignment commensurate with his rank. He finished out the war as a lieutenant colonel of artillery.

together by the bloody conflict, would link arms and stroll slowly through Vicksburg's shattered suburbs talking of home and relatives far away.

Sometimes they and others would converge on an abandoned house where a deep well still produced good drinking water. Like patrolmen on an eerie night beat, groups of men would meet and talk, and often argue vehemently about politics. But in a strange, self-protective gesture, whenever the disagreements grew too heated, the rival soldiers would pull aside from each other, "to avoid a fight on the subject," as one of them said.

And as the sun rose, Porter's gunboats would nose from their docks onto the Mississippi to pound the beleaguered city, while Grant's artillery, 200 guns in all, bombarded Vicksburg from its three landward sides. For the defenders, there was little to do but endure—and dream of a relieving force that never came.

To the civilian population of Vicksburg—mainly women, children, and slaves—the fight had at first seemed distant. But the shelling soon brought it closer to home, especially when cannon fire aimed at enemy fortifications started to fall on the city itself. Under the pressure of the unrelenting bombardment, the citizens abandoned their graceful, vulnerable wood houses and moved into caves dug in the soft yellow soil of the bluffs.

Black laborers charged $30 to $50 to dig a cave, depending on size. Those who could afford to move on to bigger caves rented out their earlier dwellings, charging around $15 per month. Twenty-seven-year-old Mary Loughborough described the T-shaped dwelling in which she and her young daughter lived: "In one of the wings, my bed fitted; the other I used as a kind of drawing room; in this the earth had been cut down a foot or two below the floor of the main cave; I could stand erect there," she wrote. "We had our roof arched and braced, the supports of the bracing taking up much room in our confined quarters. The earth was about five feet thick above."

Dressed in uniform regalia and holding the reins of his pony, young Fred Grant chats with Charles Dana, a war department official, at his father's Vicksburg field headquarters in this sketch by Theodore Davis. In the background, General Grant scans a recent dispatch.

Some caves were even grander. One woman described her dwelling as "far more pleasant than most people imagine. A hallway ran the entire length of the four bedrooms arranged on either side. Beyond the hall was a large square room used as a dining room and from this a continuation of the hall that led to another entrance." Small caves were often occupied by one family, while larger ones were shared by several. Sometimes people stayed in their aboveground homes until the bombardment drove them to the caves; others lived in the caves only at night; and some took up more or less permanent residence underground. In such havens, the citizens of Vicksburg sought shelter from a war that had come to their very doorstep.

For a month and a half the Union army laid siege to the city, which became so honeycombed with caves that the Yankees began to call it Prairie Dog Village. It was a grim and terrifying time for the citizens. "I shall never forget my extreme fear during the night and my utter hopelessness of ever seeing the morning light," Mary Loughborough wrote of one bombardment. "Terror stricken, we remained crouched in the cave, while shell after shell followed each other in quick succession. I endeavored by constant prayer to prepare myself for the sudden death I was almost certain awaited me."

Loughborough found herself waiting for the whistle and hiss of the shell that could spell instant death. "As it neared, the noise became more deafening," she recalled, "the air was full of the rushing sound; pains darted through my temples; my ears were full of the confusing noise; and, as it exploded, the report flashed through my head like an electric shock, leaving me . . . cowering in a corner, holding my child to my heart."

The sense of isolation within the city was complete. Wrote one woman, "We are utterly cut off from the world, surrounded by a circle of fire. Would it be wise, like the scorpion, to sting ourselves to death?" In anger and exasperation, she voiced a general belief that the Union bombardment was designed to "wear out the women and children and sick," and so force Pemberton to surrender. The Yankees, she added, underestimated the strength of Southern womanhood.

But that strength was sorely tested. The shelling continued until, as one resident wrote, "There was scarcely a building but what had been struck by the enemy's shells, while many of them were entirely demolished. The city had the appearance of a half-ruined pile of buildings." No place was safe. A doctor recalled, "The wounded are killed in the hospitals, surgeons wounded while attending to their duties." He himself narrowly escaped death when a shell scored a direct hit on the main floor of the city hospital.

Often oblivious of the dangers, the children seemed to think of cave life as an adventure. "It was curious to see how well trained the little ones were," wrote Lida Lord, herself a young child during the siege. "At night, when the bombs began to fly like pigeons over our heads, they would be waked out of a sound sleep, would slip on their shoes, and run, without a word, like rabbits to their burrows."

At other times, the horrors of the bombardment were all too real to the youngsters. One day Lida's mother, Margaret, tried to comfort her daughter as the shells shook the ground above them. When Lida began to cry, Margaret Lord told her, "Don't cry, my darling. God will protect us."

"But momma," sobbed the young girl, "I'm so afraid God's killed too!"

Lida recalled how close her little brother, Willie, came to tragedy. Stooping down to pick up a used bullet, he only just escaped being hit by an artillery shell that passed so close over his back that it

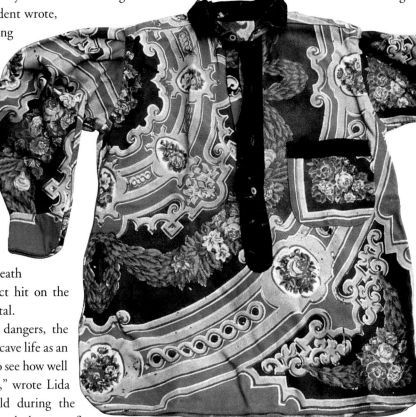

This wildly patterned shirt was worn by a Confederate soldier captured at Vicksburg. An example both of ingenious improvisation and of the South's inability to clothe its troops adequately, the garment was made from a wool tablecloth and trimmed with a black velvet collar and placket.

scorched his clothing. One day Willie himself watched a mother chase after her young son outside a nearby cave, the child laughing and running as if they were playing a game. The woman finally managed to catch up with the youngster, but just as she reached out to take hold of him, an exploding shell ripped away her arm.

In her diary, Mary Loughborough chronicled the tragedies. "A little girl, the daughter of a Mrs. Jones, was sitting at the entrance of a cave, when a Parrott shell entered the portal and took her head off." The screams of women, she continued, "were the saddest I ever heard." A little black child, playing with an unexploded shell, accidentally detonated the weapon: "The terrible explosion followed, showing, as the white cloud of smoke floated away, the mangled remains of a life that to the mother's heart had possessed all of beauty and joy."

That same day Loughborough wrote of a young girl who had ventured back to her home aboveground during a lull in the bombardment. But on her way back to her cave "an explosion sounded near her—one wild scream, and she ran into her mother's presence, sinking like a wounded dove, the life blood flowing over the light summer dress in crimson ripples from a death-wound in her side, caused by the shell fragment."

Still, the people continued to hold out the belief that they would be relieved. The magic name of Joe Johnston was on everybody's lips. "If we can only hold this place 'til Johnston can come to our aid from outside," prayed Emma Balfour. On June 28, Margaret Lord wrote in her diary, "Still in this dreary cave. Who would have believed that we could have borne such a life for five weeks? The siege has lasted 42 days

Union troops dug these hillside shelters to protect themselves from Confederate artillery fire during the Vicksburg siege. The residents of the white frame house fled to safer quarters in a cave.

William Rufus Terrill *(left)*, who fought for the Union, first won acclaim as an artillery officer at Shiloh. "Wherever Captain Terrill turned his battery, silence followed on the part of the enemy," wrote one witness. His Confederate brother, James *(below)*, distinguished himself as the commanding officer of the 13th Virginia Infantry Regiment in the Army of Northern Virginia.

BROTHER AGAINST BROTHER

No story of the Civil War's often ruinous effects on families is more poignant than that of a Virginia household whose two sons, William Rufus Terrill and James Terrill, chose to fight on opposite sides.

James followed his home state when it seceded, while William, a graduate of West Point, remained faithful to his oath as a United States officer. This decision outraged his father, who wrote William, "Can you be so recreant and so unnatural as to aid in this mad attempt to impose the yoke of tyranny upon your kith and kin? Do so and your name shall be stricken from the family records."

Whatever anguish he must have felt over this rift, William proved a brilliant officer, distinguishing himself at the Battle of Shiloh in April 1862. Promoted to brigadier general, he was killed at Perryville, Kentucky, later that same year. Confederate colonel James, also nominated to the rank of brigadier general, fell in battle in 1864, the day before he was confirmed by the Confederate Senate. After the war, the family erected a memorial to the brothers on which is carved "God Alone Knows Which Was Right."

and yet no relief—every day this week we have waited for the sound of Gen. Johnston's guns, but in vain."

As the siege wore on, the rest of the Confederacy grew increasingly desperate about the plight of its western citadel. Stories abounded about the horrors within Vicksburg. Diarist Mary Chesnut, in faraway Richmond, was told about a three-year-old child who was struck by a shell. "There was this poor little girl with her touchingly lovely face, and her arm gone." Mark Twain heard about a man who was shaking hands with a friend when an exploding shell left him grasping a severed hand.

Terrible as were the injuries from the constant Union shelling, now another enemy was making its presence felt, one that could not long be resisted. Creeping past the Confederate soldiers and through the defenses, into the city and down into every cave, was the ally that Grant had relied on from the beginning. The Yankees called it General Starvation.

Early on in the siege, the city's uniformed defenders had been put on short rations, and by June 4 the whole town had gone on rationing. Coffee was one of the first things to run out. In place of flour, soldiers and civilians alike began trying to make bread out of ground peas. It was hard and awful tasting. Meat—at least beef—also disappeared, and strange substitutes were tried. One day an army chaplain saw soldiers butchering what he at first thought was a cow. Not until he took a closer look did he notice that the carcass had "a head with long ears." It was a mule. Mule flesh was soon selling for $1 per pound to civilians, and given free to soldiers who wanted it. One of Pemberton's men pronounced it "coarse-grained and darker than beef, but really delicious, sweet and juicy." Wags printed an alleged menu from the fictitious Hotel de Vicksburg, which featured Mule Tail Soup, Mule Salad, and Muletongue Cold a-la-Bray.

People also ate horse meat, and rumor had it that some soldiers had sampled rat meat and declared it to be a delicacy. According to one Vicksburger, fried rats had a flavor "fully equal to that of squirrels." As

Generals Grant and Pemberton meet just a few hundred feet from the Rebel lines to discuss terms of surrender for Vicksburg. The northern-born Pemberton chose the surrender date himself: "I know my people . . . and their national vanity. I know we can get better terms on the Fourth of July than on any other day of the year."

the hunger worsened, observers noticed that the city's dogs, which had howled during bombardments earlier in the siege, were all but gone. Cats had disappeared too.

Suffering from hunger, diarist Mary Loughborough watched the effect of the reduced rations on her two-year-old daughter. "My little one had swung in her hammock," she wrote, "reduced in strength, with a low fever flushing her face." A soldier brought the child a jaybird, which she played with for a time before she turned away in weariness. "Miss Mary," said Loughborough's servant, "she's hungry. Let me make her some soup from the bird." At first Loughborough refused the request. Then she relented. The servant left with the little bird and reappeared a short time later with a cup of soup and a plate with a few bits of white meat.

Another mother, irritated by her young daughter's immature behavior, had grabbed the child and prepared to spank her. "Oh, I cannot, my poor little half-

starved child," she cried, as she felt the thinness of her daughter's arm. "It is not naughtiness, it is hunger."

Time was now running out for the defenders. The summer was upon them. Drinking water was short, and diseases like malaria and dysentery were spreading. The expectation that Johnston was going to come to the besieged city's rescue had evaporated, and a rumor began to spread that General Grant was planning another full-scale assault and had picked July 4 as the date.

In actuality, General Johnston, who was encamped 50 miles northeast of Vicksburg, was preparing to march on the Union rear in the hope that Pemberton would join him and give battle. It was too little, too late. Events in the city had outpaced everyone's plans.

On the morning of July 3 Mary Loughborough watched as three Confederate soldiers rode past her cave and on toward the Union lines. One of the men bore a white flag. All along the lines the firing began

Just days after the city's surrender, a collection of Confederate field guns seized by Grant's forces packs a vacant lot behind a Methodist church in Vicksburg.

to stop, and Loughborough found the sudden calm "absolutely oppressive." Two hours later she saw the men return. Then, around 3:00 p.m., General Pemberton rode out to meet with the Yankees. It could mean only one thing. The Rebels had surrendered.

Independence Day 1863 dawned hot and hazy. Slowly at first, the civilian cave dwellers began to emerge into the sunlight, an army of refugees within their own city. Under loads of blankets, cooking utensils, and furniture, they made their way back to the aboveground homes that they had had to abandon—or to what was left of them. A strange quiet had fallen over Vicksburg, whose fortifications

behind the house, and a group of blacks there happily provided him a drink.

When the uncomfortable meeting was over, Grant's staff officers gave vent to their anger. But their leader laughed it off. "Well, if Pemberton can stand it," he said, "under the circumstances, I can!" Then he rode on down to the city docks to greet Admiral Porter, whose ships fired off broadside after broadside to commemorate the victory.

Next, Grant made his way back through the city, nodding at crowds of smiling blacks and at sullen whites, most of whom seemed not to know him. Pausing at the city's courthouse, he looked up to the Stars and Stripes that now hung from the flagpole. Moving

"The enemy are now undoubtedly in our grasp. The fall of Vicksburg and the capture of most of the garrison can only be a question of time."

ULYSSES S. GRANT, MAY 24, 1863

were now showing white flags. Then the city's haggard defenders, colors flying and in perfect formation, began to march out of the battered ramparts toward the Union positions. The Yankees stood in equally stiff array as their enemy stacked arms, laid down flags, and returned to their own lines.

Soon the civilians heard the tramp of other marching feet and a military band playing "Yankee Doodle." Then they saw Ulysses S. Grant himself, the victorious Union general, riding into the city past the now-silent guns, ready to claim his spoils.

But Grant had not come to lord it over what he considered a valiant foe. Accompanied by Fred, he went with his staff to call on Pemberton at a house that the Rebels were using as their headquarters. Pemberton and some of his officers were sitting on the porch when Grant arrived. The Confederate general did not rise as Grant mounted the steps toward him. No one offered him a seat. When the Union commander asked for a glass of water, Pemberton, without getting up, pointed silently toward the rear of the house. Grant was unfazed. He found a well

on, he passed men in blue and gray who, freed of their antagonism, were mixing freely—talking about their experiences, looking for kin, and, in the Union case, sharing their rations with men they had so recently been trying to starve out. Grant took it all in as he moved back out through the Vicksburg defenses and on to his own headquarters east of the city.

At Vicksburg the war was over. It had taken more than a year, but the link between the eastern part of the Confederacy and the westernmost states had been broken forever. News of the city's fall was greeted with shock in the South and jubilation in the North. Again Ulysses S. Grant had shown that he was one Union general who could win decisively. In the days ahead, his military soul mate, William Sherman, would return from harassing Joe Johnston's army on its retreat back into Tennessee, and the two generals would plan the next phase of their extraordinary collaboration. In Washington, Abraham Lincoln wrote, "The Father of Waters again goes unvexed to the sea." The Fourth of July would not be celebrated by the white citizenry of Vicksburg for the next 78 years. ◆

THE SOLDIER'S LIFE

In the spring of 1861, Frank Peak of Arkansas couldn't wait to begin his life as a soldier: "So impatient did I become for starting that I felt like ten thousand pins were pricking me in every part of the body, and I started off a week in advance of my brothers." In the South and the North, thousands of farm boys and city men like Peak rushed to enlist for what they expected to be a brief war. But as the years dragged on, the hardships of campaigning and the boredom of camp cooled the ardor of most. Admitted one Georgia soldier: "I had been itching for a long time to get in a fight, but don't believe there is any fun in it. At any rate, I would as soon be somewhere else."

Chief among their complaints was the food. W. H. Andrews of the 1st Georgia Regulars wrote: "Have always heard it said, touch a man's pocket and touch his soul. But if I wanted to find a soldier's soul, I would touch him on the stomach." Standard daily rations were generous: 12 ounces of bacon or pork, fresh or salted (salt pork was nicknamed sowbelly), or 20 ounces of fresh or salted beef; one pound of hard bread (hardtack), 22 ounces of soft bread or flour, or 20 ounces of cornmeal. These were supplemented with beans or peas, rice, potatoes, salt, vinegar, coffee, and sugar. But soldiers often received less-than-standard rations, especially the Confederates toward the end of the war. And inexperienced warriors sometimes caused their own hunger: Before a long march, soldiers were issued three days' rations and ordered to cook and carry them, but some ate all their food at once.

The meat was often rancid, especially in the South, where salt was almost unobtainable and transportation poor. The flour-and-water hardtack biscuits, such as the ones pictured opposite, were consumed in large quantities by Union troops, but they often contained weevils. "All the fresh meat we had come in the hard bread . . . and I preferring my game cooked used to toast my biscuits," quipped one Union soldier.

Soldiers also grumbled about the heavy loads they carried: "If there is anything peculiarly attractive in marching from 10 to 20 miles a day under a scorching sun with a good mule load, and sinking up to one's knees in the 'Sacred Soil' at each step, my mind is not of sufficiently poeticle nature to appreciate it," J. G. Fraser wrote to his family. On his back the infantryman carried between 40 and 50 pounds of gear, including his musket, bayonet, ammunition, rations, extra clothing, blanket, half a pup tent, and a rubberized blanket, or ground cloth. Few Confederates had tents or ground cloths, so their load was lighter.

Inadequate clothing was another hardship, especially among Confederate soldiers; wool was the sturdiest fabric with which to make uniforms, and the South had few woolen mills. "In this army one hole in the seat of the breeches indicates a captain, two holes a lieutenant, and the seat of the pants all out indicates that the individual is a private," declared infantryman Sebron Sneed of Texas. Shoes wore out quickly and were difficult to replace, as one Georgia soldier recorded: "Gen. Lee has issued an order giving the green cow hides to the soldiers to make mocassins out of by turning the hair side in next to the foot.

Have seen several soldiers with them on. Don't imagine they feel much like shoes, but they are better than going barefooted."

Between battles soldiers spent their time drilling, cleaning equipment, standing guard, cooking, and mending. Playing cards, making music, snowball fighting, writing letters, playing baseball, gambling, reading, and looking for liquor also filled the weeks spent in winter camps between campaigns. Playing tricks was another favorite pastime; as one soldier noted in his diary: "It is right amusing to be awake sometimes in the wee small hours of the night and listen to the different noises being made in camps by the soldiers. In one part . . . you can hear a rooster crow. Over in another direction you will hear a turkey gobble . . . a dog barking or a cat squalling . . . the lowing of a cow, a mule braying . . . . anything for mischief to create a laugh. If it was not for the devilment going on in camps, we would all die with the blues."

Many men were tempted to desert. But the majority stuck with it. Explained Alabama soldier John Cotton to his wife in 1863: "I want to come home as bad as any body can . . . but I shant run away. . . . I don't want it throwed up to my children after I am dead that I was a deserter." And Day Elmore, who joined the army at 17, distinguished himself at Murfreesboro, was wounded at Chickamauga, and was captured and imprisoned for a time, wrote his father back in Illinois about his decision to reenlist: "I can not Express my self so I will only say that my whole soul is wrapt up in this our countrys caus I ought to be at school but I feel that I am only doeing my Duty to my self and you, Pa."

SOWBELLY, HARDTACK, AND BEANS

Crushing the beans with rocks or rifle butts, soldiers brewed coffee in individual boilers *(above)* hung over a fire. Yankee F. Y. Hedley made his "strong enough to float an iron wedge."

At the camp bakery a Union soldier carries fresh loaves of bread, a welcome change from hardtack.

"The Negroes are selling all the oysters they can get to our men.
The soldier takes the tin cup and dips it into the tub or bucket of oysters,
fills it full and then drinks the oysters as if he was drinking water."

Yankee soldier writing from Savannah, Georgia

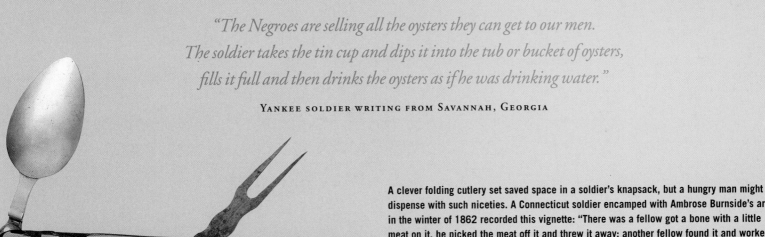

A clever folding cutlery set saved space in a soldier's knapsack, but a hungry man might dispense with such niceties. A Connecticut soldier encamped with Ambrose Burnside's army in the winter of 1862 recorded this vignette: "There was a fellow got a bone with a little meat on it, he picked the meat off it and threw it away; another fellow found it and worked away on it awhile and threw it away; well, there were four men who picked that old bone."

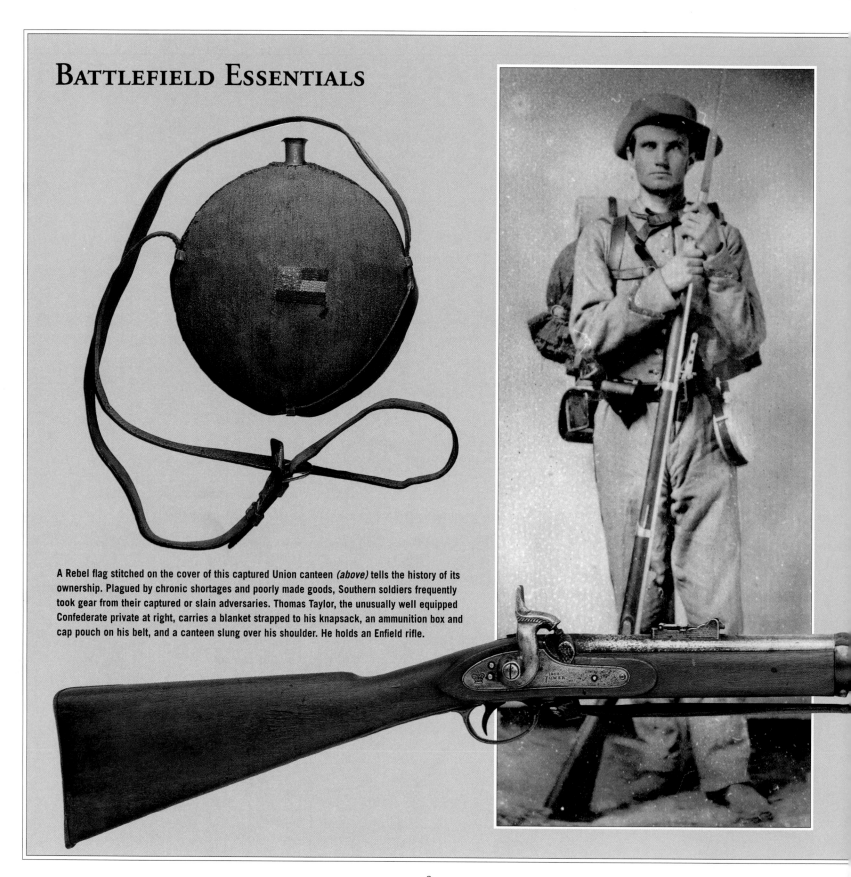

BATTLEFIELD ESSENTIALS

A Rebel flag stitched on the cover of this captured Union canteen *(above)* tells the history of its ownership. Plagued by chronic shortages and poorly made goods, Southern soldiers frequently took gear from their captured or slain adversaries. Thomas Taylor, the unusually well equipped Confederate private at right, carries a blanket strapped to his knapsack, an ammunition box and cap pouch on his belt, and a canteen slung over his shoulder. He holds an Enfield rifle.

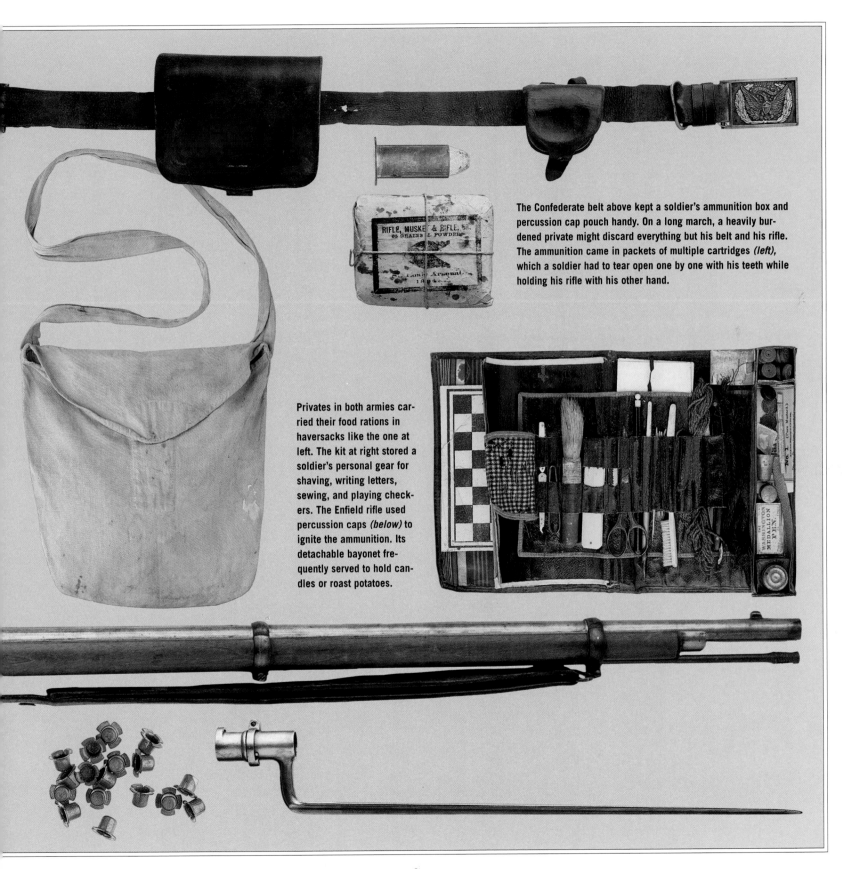

The Confederate belt above kept a soldier's ammunition box and percussion cap pouch handy. On a long march, a heavily burdened private might discard everything but his belt and his rifle. The ammunition came in packets of multiple cartridges *(left)*, which a soldier had to tear open one by one with his teeth while holding his rifle with his other hand.

Privates in both armies carried their food rations in haversacks like the one at left. The kit at right stored a soldier's personal gear for shaving, writing letters, sewing, and playing checkers. The Enfield rifle used percussion caps *(below)* to ignite the ammunition. Its detachable bayonet frequently served to hold candles or roast potatoes.

85

DRESSED FOR WAR

The Union private at left probably received his uniform as described by a recruit: "Coats, trousers, and the other clothes were piled up in separate heaps, and each man was just thrown the first garment on the top. . . . If it was an outrageous fit, he would swap with someone if possible, otherwise he got along as best he could." Soldiers greatly preferred socks knitted at home *(right)* to the coarse military issue.

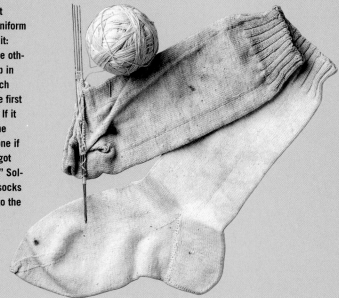

"I have seen men literally wear out their underclothes without a change and when they threw them off they would swarm with Vermin like a live Ant hill when disturbed."

CYRUS F. BOYD, 15TH IOWA INFANTRY, USA

Felt slouch hats were popular among Rebels. Claimed one Virginian, "A man who has never been a soldier does not know the amount of comfort there is in a good soft hat."

Privates in both armies wore short coats known as fatigue blouses *(above)*. The long underwear at right could be tied at the ankle to keep out drafts. Standard army shoes wore out in 20 to 30 days.

What Kept Them Going

Yankee soldiers could depend on the U.S. Mail Service *(above)*, but the Confederate Postal Department was unreliable. One anxious Alabaman wrote his wife, "I haint got nary letter from you for somtime when you fail to Rite . . . it ceeps mee uneasy all the time."

"Boys who will lie on their backs with hardly energy
enough to turn over, will jump up
and hurry to captain's tent to get it [mail]."

J. WILLIAM JONES, CHAPLAIN, CSA

Soldiers everywhere played cards *(right)*, often for money. Wrote Ruffin Thomson of Mississippi to his mother in 1862: "Open gambling has been prohibited, but that amounts to nothing." Gamblers often repented on the way to battle; one Georgian noted: "Have been in many battles where you could have traced the different lines going in by the decks of cards being thrown away."

A tent serves as a church for Father Thomas H. Mooney *(left)*, who christened a cannon for the Irish 69th New York before the First Battle of Bull Run, to the chagrin of his bishop. Religious literature was distributed among Yankee and Confederate troops; on both sides the Bible was the most widely read of all books.

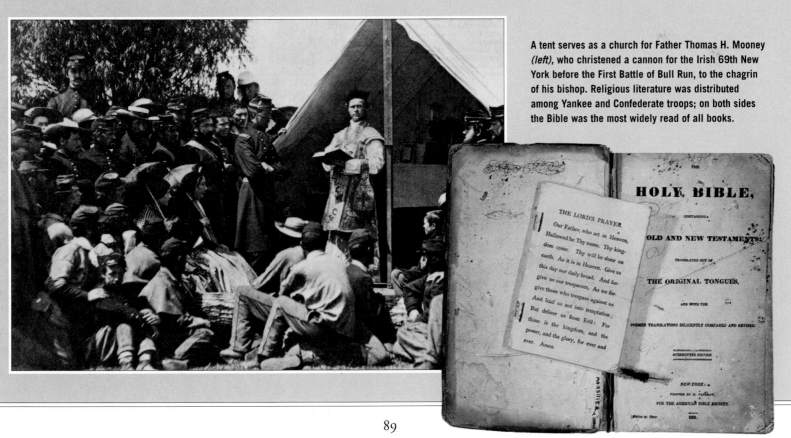

CHAPTER 3

HIGH-WATER MARK OF THE CONFEDERACY

"He has lost his left arm, but I have lost my right."

ROBERT E. LEE, UPON HEARING OF STONEWALL JACKSON'S WOUNDING AT CHANCELLORSVILLE

Glistening in a steady spring rain, the mail train from Richmond squealed to a stop at Guiney's Station, 15 miles south of Fredericksburg, Virginia, at noon on April 20, 1863. On board the passenger car a young woman, plain in her appearance and dress but animated by joyous anticipation, prepared her five-month-old daughter for the infant's first meeting with her soldier father.

He was easy enough to spot, even through the rain-streaked windows of the coach. The off-duty Confederate soldiers idling around the station platform, hoping for letters from home, hung back in deference to the lean, brown-bearded figure in the visored forage cap and rubber overcoat who had watched for the appearance of the train with a special intensity. In a moment the man was on board the car, striding down its length with his awkward yet purposeful gait toward Anna, the wife he had not seen for nearly a year, and Julia, the daughter he had never seen at all.

"His face was all sunshine and gladness," Anna recalled. "It was a picture, indeed, to see his look of perfect delight and admiration as his eyes fell upon that baby." With a great deal of tenderness, he sheltered mother and child from the rain as he escorted them to the carriage that was waiting to take the young family to a plantation 10 miles from Fredericksburg belonging to his friends, the Yerby family. "Upon our arrival at the house," she wrote later of the occasion, "he speedily divested himself of his overcoat, and, taking his baby in his arms, he caressed her with the tenderest affection, and held her long and lovingly."

To such a state was reduced, for the next nine days, the legendary "Stonewall" Jackson. Admired by his peers as the strong right arm of his commander, Robert E. Lee, revered by his men as a stern taskmaster and disciplinarian, and feared by his enemy as an unpredictable and merciless warrior, General Thomas Jackson was for the moment simply a loving husband, a doting father.

Four months previously, the Confederate Army of Northern Virginia and the Federal Army of the Potomac had gone into winter quarters. The two

Stonewall Jackson sat for this portrait only after much cajoling by his wife, Anna *(right)*. One week later he was felled in battle at the moment of his greatest triumph. Returning to Confederate lines from a scouting foray following his corps's stunning flank attack at Chancellorsville, Jackson and his aides were mistaken for enemy cavalry. The general was mortally wounded by his own men.

armies faced each other across the Rappahannock River, which flowed southeastward past the opposing encampments and toward the town of Fredericksburg, on the river's south bank. Now, as the roads and fields recovered from February's ice and the subsequent mud of March, fighting was again imminent. "On to Richmond!" was still the North's battle cry, and Jackson had begun his preparations to meet the renewed Union threat. Only days before Anna's arrival he had declared, with sudden fire, "I wish they would come!"

The Yankees would come soon enough. But for the moment the two armies simply watched each other, and while they did, Jackson played with his baby daughter. "He rarely had her out of his arms," Anna recalled, "walking her, and amusing her in every way that he could think of—sometimes holding her up in front of a mirror and saying playfully, 'Now, Miss Jackson, look at yourself.' " When she napped, he would lean over her, gazing at her little face in admiration.

Others gained glimpses of the fearsome Stonewall's softer alter ego. One day General Lee himself came to call on the Jacksons and managed to put the thoroughly intimidated Anna immediately at ease with his dignified, fatherly charm. On April 23,

A Federal signal party uses a telescope and field glasses to keep watch on Confederate positions near Fredericksburg in the spring of 1863. The men's casual demeanor reflects the informal truce between the two armies that preceded the Chancellorsville campaign.

Jackson's staff officers got a chance to see the domestic side of their leader when they filed into the Yerby house and watched him dote on his baby during her christening.

For five more days the idyll continued. During this time a photographer appeared at the Yerbys' asking permission to make a portrait of the general. Jackson at first would have none of it, but Anna changed his mind. She had been wishing fervently that the picture of "that father kneeling over the cradle of that lovely infant could have been put upon canvas." Here was the next best thing. She posed him on a chair in the hall of the house and carefully arranged his hair, which was unusually long, into large ringlets. As the camera lens was opened a strong breeze blew in through the hall door and made the general frown, "giving a sternness to his countenance that was," Anna insisted, "not natural." Perhaps not. Stonewall's soldiers, however, thought the resulting image had caught him just about right.

Then, at dawn on April 29, came the heavy tread on the stair, the sharp knock at the bedroom door, and a messenger from the front. Anna watched from the bed as Jackson sprang up, dressed hurriedly, and went downstairs. She listened to the murmurs, then heard his returning footsteps. It was as she had feared. The Federals were crossing the Rappahannock. It was time again for battle, and she must take the baby and catch the morning train for Richmond and safety.

Now there was time only for one last kiss for Anna, one long last look at the sleeping Julia. Then Stonewall Jackson was out the door and on his way to his command of one of the three corps that made up the Army of Northern Virginia. As Anna and the baby climbed into a wagon to be rushed to Guiney's Station, she could hear firing off in the distance. The third year of the war had begun.

May 1 was a mild and clear spring day that ended in a soft dusk. As the day's hard fighting sputtered to a halt, Generals Lee and Jackson, on horseback and flanked by their staff officers, met each other at the intersection of two roads about 10 miles west of Fredericksburg. The two men dismounted and strolled a little way into the pine forest that crowded in on the crossroads; there they sat down on a log to talk about the last three days.

They had been eventful days, and it would take the two men much of the night to sort it all out. On April 29 Federal troops had lunged across the Rappahannock near Fredericksburg, formed a line of battle, indulged in some preliminary skirmishing—and then done nothing more. This pause in the action had proved to be a ruse designed to lull the Confederates into letting down their guard while the main Union force crossed the river 20 miles upstream and advanced down the south bank of the river toward the town. The Yankees already on the outskirts of Fredericksburg nearly equaled the strength of Lee's 60,000-man army; the force marching in from the west exceeded it. Another commander might have been paralyzed by the danger, but Lee had reacted with breathtaking audacity. On April 30, he had left a small holding force to watch the Yankees around Fredericksburg and sent the bulk of his army—40,000 men—westward to confront the 75,000 Federals advancing from that direction. And he had moved just in time; early the next day the Confederates marching west clashed with the enemy.

The encounter began at the edge of a 10-mile-square area of young pines and scrub oak that had grown up since the original forest had been cut in order to provide fuel for the iron furnaces that once operated there. A few patches had been cleared for farming, but most of the expanse was a dense thicket of young trees and brush that were penetrated by only a few roads. To one Yankee private it was a mournful-looking country, "a good place to die in." It was known as the Wilderness.

The Federal force had deployed for battle just east of this wooded area, taking strong positions on high ground and massing its men for battle. But before serious fighting could be joined, the troops had been ordered to break off the engagement and fall back several miles, into the Wilderness. The order to withdraw had come from General Joseph

Hooker, who had recently been appointed commander of the Army of the Potomac. Forty-eight-year-old Hooker was an imposing looking soldier six feet tall with wavy blond hair, a perpetually flushed complexion, and sparkling gray blue eyes. He also had a name as a fighter.

Hooker's reputation had begun to outrun his performance, however, when press reporters had filed several stories that were slugged "Fighting—Joe Hooker." Some newspapers had run the headline without the dash, and as a result Hooker had become widely known as "Fighting Joe." He also gained a name for drinking and talking too much, and for an exaggerated sense of his own abilities. "May God have mercy on General Lee," he had said as he began his spring campaign, "for I will have none."

But Hooker's sudden abandonment, on May 1, of an attack that had every prospect of success—numerical superiority, high ground, open fields of fire, and plenty of room to maneuver—betrayed an astonishing loss of nerve and left his subordinates appalled. "My God!" one of them raged. "If we can't hold the top of a hill, we certainly cannot hold the bottom of it." In an attempt to reassure another of his officers, Hooker told the man, "I have got Lee just where I want him. He must fight me on my own ground." But no trained soldier could miss the fact that Fighting Joe had squandered a great opportunity and had given the initiative over to his enemy. The officer left in disgust, convinced his commanding general was "a whipped man."

On Hooker's instructions, the Federals had established a six-mile-long defensive line around a cleared farm in the middle of the Wilderness. The line faced south and bulged out in the shape

LIFE IN THE SADDLE

Many Confederate cavalrymen adopted the jaunty style of their leader, Jeb Stuart, shown above with his ostrich-plumed hat. In defense of his rakish elegance, Stuart once declared, "We must substitute *esprit* for numbers."

Infantrymen grumbled that the cavalry led a pampered existence removed from the carnage of battle. A common taunt aimed at mounted troopers was, "Who's ever seen a dead cavalryman?" In fact, horse soldiers had to master skills that were unknown to riflemen and also suffered their share of casualties.

The primary task of mounted units was to keep track of enemy troop movements while preventing the other side's cavalry from doing the same. In addition, horse soldiers carried dispatches, guarded prisoners, escorted supply trains, and acted as military police. "There is no rest for the cavalryman," lamented a Confederate horse soldier.

of a horseshoe. At a crossroads in the center of the clearing stood a single red-brick, white-columned house where a woman named Frances Chancellor had operated a hotel. Hooker set up his headquarters there, in the building that gave the area its name: Chancellorsville.

So it was that on the evening of May 1 Lee and Jackson came to sit in the woods two miles from the Chancellor House considering their next moves. It would be a long night. While aides set up camp and built a fire, the two generals huddled over maps, consulted with messengers, and discussed what to do next. The flickering flames threw eerie shadows in the dark woods, and the white upturned face of a dead Confederate soldier gleamed grotesquely in the brilliant moonlight nearby.

Aggressive as they were, both Lee and Jackson knew that a frontal attack on an entrenched enemy that outnumbered them by nearly two to one would be madness. They needed to find a weakness that could be exploited. As they discussed these matters, Lee's cavalry commander, Jeb Stuart, rode up. Just returned from a scouting expedition, he reported that the right of the Union line was vulnerable to attack. Whenever possible, commanders tried to anchor their defensive positions on some natural feature—a river or a ridge, for example—that made getting around the end of their line difficult. But the Yankees had taken no such precautions on their right flank, which was, as Stuart put it, "in the air."

Lee gazed at a crude map of the area and then at Jackson. "How can we get at those people?" he asked, employing the term he used most often when speaking of the Federals. As if answering his own question, Lee traced on the map a way around the Union right. Jackson understood that the job was to be his. He stood up, saluted, and said that his troops would be ready to go early the following morning. It was almost midnight by now, and the two men retired in order to get some rest. Jackson walked off a little way into the woods, unbuckled his sword, and leaned it against a tree. The night was chilly and the ground was hard. He lay down on his saddle blanket, with only a cape to cover him, and fell asleep.

Just before dawn Jackson awoke, stiff and cold, and sought to warm himself at the dying embers of the campfire. He dispatched his topographical engineer to consult with residents of the area about routes leading through the Wilderness toward the Federal right wing. Then he waited, shivering by the fire, clutching a cup of coffee. The sword that he

Jackson gestured toward the map and the route that led to the Federal right. "Go around here."

"What do you propose to make this movement with?" queried Lee.

"With my whole corps," Jackson replied.

Jackson was suggesting one of the most daring gambles of the war. The army had already been divided once between the Wilderness and Fredericksburg. Now Jackson wanted to divide it again. He proposed taking 26,000 men on a perilous march around the Federal right while a mere 14,000 remained with Lee to confront 75,000 Yankees. If Hooker recovered his nerve and came out of his entrenchments, he could easily overwhelm Lee's small force—or destroy Jackson's. Lee knew his opponent, however. He also knew his corps commander. His answer was as immediate as it was concise. "Well, go on," he said.

"His expression was one of intense interest, his face was colored slightly with the paint of approaching battle."

CONFEDERATE GENERAL FITZHUGH LEE, ABOUT STONEWALL JACKSON ON THE EVE OF THE FLANK ATTACK

had propped against the tree suddenly clattered to the ground. With a shiver, a staff officer wondered if it was a bad sign.

As the light of dawn spread over the tangled Wilderness, Lee appeared, looking fresh, well groomed, and confident as usual, and took a seat next to his lieutenant. Before long Jackson's engineer returned with a map showing a series of connecting trails leading to and around the end of the Union line. Together the trails formed a 12-mile route through the woods, and any force that took it would be in extreme danger the whole way, for it would be marching all day across the face of the enemy.

But at least Lee and Jackson now had the information they needed. It was time to decide. The two generals, veterans of a year of high command, at the height of their powers, and at a climactic moment in the struggle between North and South, conducted one of its shortest councils of war. "General Jackson, what do you propose to do?" asked Lee.

This was quintessential Lee: the calm wait for information, the steady piecing together of a vision of the battlefield, then a willingness to move boldly, to gamble everything on the correctness of that vision. The decisions made around the campfire in those early hours of May 2 set the stage for a battle that would be the masterpiece of Lee's career. These same decisions would set in motion another contest, far to the north two months later, that would take place on the darkest day of his life.

After the Confederate victory at the Battle of Bull Run in 1861, the war in the East had subsided until the spring of 1862, when an enormous Union army had sailed down the Chesapeake Bay to the Virginia Peninsula and moved ponderously toward Richmond *(pages 42-51)*. Lee was put in command of the Confederate Army of Northern Virginia and charged with defending the capital. In the year since, he had won victory after victory, frus-

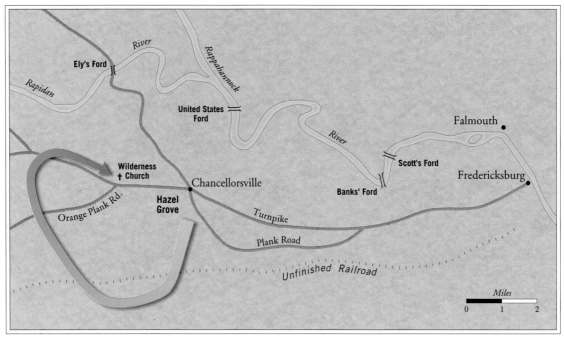

In a great scything stroke, Stonewall Jackson's 26,000-man force *(red arrow)* hooks around a Union line that extended from the Wilderness Church to the crossroads at Chancellorsville and back to a ford on the Rappahannock River. Around 5:00 p.m. on May 2, the Confederates fell upon the unsuspecting Federals, driving them back toward Chancellorsville.

trating the Federals on the Peninsula, then defeating another Union army in a second battle at Bull Run. Lee had invaded the North and fought the Yankees to what was in effect a bloody draw at Maryland's Antietam Creek, then returned to Fredericksburg, where he stopped the Army of the Potomac cold before winter brought an end to the campaign.

In defeating his enemies, Lee not only had demonstrated his own prowess but also had developed the skills of brilliant subordinates. One of these men was Stonewall Jackson, whose Shenandoah Valley campaign of 1862 had bled Federal strength away from the Peninsula. Another of them was James Longstreet, called Pete by his friends and "my old war horse" by Lee. Longstreet had gained a reputation for being, said one aide, "a rock in steadiness" and a master of defensive tactics. And there was Jeb Stuart, Lee's flamboyant chief of cavalry, a striking figure in his red-lined cape and hat decorated with a black ostrich plume. The jaunty Stuart seemed to think of war as an exciting game and had a banjo player on horseback follow him on the field of battle. But in spite of his air of bravado, he and his capable horsemen were the sharp and dependable "eyes and ears" of the Southern army.

In the weeks and months ahead, Lee would need the services of these commanders as never before. For now he was thinking about invading Union territory again—about how that would demoralize the North and perhaps even bring England into the war on the side of the Confederacy. But first he would have to deal with Fighting Joe—or, as Lee referred to him, Mr. F. J. Hooker.

The morning turned warm and fragrant, a typical spring day in Virginia. Jackson's men inhaled the moist May air, felt their spirits rise, and stepped out with a vigor for which they had become famous. For it was said that Stonewall could move soldiers on foot about as fast as other officers could maneuver mounted men. In the Confederate army they were known as "Jackson's foot cavalry."

Their dour commander rode alongside them that May 2 morning astride his favorite horse, Little Sorrel, whose gait he found "as easy as the rocking of a cradle." In spite of the fine weather, Jackson wore an oilcloth raincoat, and his forage cap was jammed down over his glittering blue eyes. His beard jutted forward pugnaciously. He and Little Sorrel ambled past his patrician commanding general a few minutes after 8:00 a.m., as if passing in review. Their eyes met, these men who understood each other so well, and as always words were superfluous. Jackson rose in his stirrups and pointed down the road. Lee nodded. The thing was in motion.

"Press forward! See that the column is kept closed!" chanted Jackson, riding up and down the line. Hour after hour the men marched, tramping steadily for 50 minutes, resting for 10, then moving on again, all the time their leader encouraging them: "Press on, press on!"

Thomas Jonathan Jackson was born into a Scotch-Irish family in the mountain hamlet of Clarksburg, western Virginia, in 1824. His lawyer father died of typhoid two years later, and his mother five years after that, leaving the seven-year-old to be brought up by various relatives. It was during this time that he began to complain of the mysterious digestive ailments that were to preoccupy him for his entire life—miseries that no physician could ever diagnose but for which Jackson developed a bewildering variety of defenses. For example, he refused to let his spine touch the back of a chair for fear that slouching would compress some internal organ and cause a malfunction. And he noted so many adverse reactions to foods that by the time of the Civil War his diet was reduced to little more than bread, raspberries, and milk.

In 1842 the impoverished, ill-educated 18-year-old reported to West Point, thanks to the efforts of a congressman who owed Jackson's family a favor. The young man was utterly unprepared for the academic rigors of the academy, however, and very nearly washed out in his first semester. He hung on by dint of the characteristic that would make him one of the world's foremost generals—a force of will that would not admit even the possibility of defeat. When other cadets were socializing, Jackson was studying; long after his roommates were asleep, he was stretched out on the floor of his room in front of a coal fire, reading by its dim red glow. In this way he slowly, agonizingly progressed, and by graduation day he had achieved

A middle-aged Robert E. Lee poses with his eight-year-old son Rooney around 1845. A devoted father, Lee greatly missed his seven children during his frequent absences from their Virginia home and wrote them many affectionate letters.

THE FORGING OF A SOUTHERN CHAMPION

Though related to the first families of Virginia, Robert E. Lee grew up in genteel poverty. His father, Revolutionary War hero Henry "Light-Horse Harry" Lee, had squandered the family fortune before abandoning his wife and children. Robert's mother, Ann, managed to raise him and his four siblings with the income from a small trust fund. He later claimed he owed everything, including his deep sense of honor, to her.

Entering West Point in 1825, Lee embarked on a distinguished military career. After graduating second in his class, he won a spot in the elite Corps of Engineers. The demands of military life, however, often meant lonely separations from his wife, Mary Custis, whom he married in 1831, and their children. During the Mexican War, which began in 1846, he was away for nearly two years. But in that time Lee learned the skills most vital to his future career as a tactician and leader of men.

At the onset of the Civil War, Lee was offered command of the Union forces. A Virginian first and foremost, he tendered his resignation from the U.S. Army. "Save in defence of my native State," Lee wrote, "I never desire again to draw my sword."

the respectable rank of 17th in his class of 59. His fellow cadets firmly believed that had the course lasted another year, he would have graduated first.

Commissioned a second lieutenant of artillery just as war broke out between the United States and Mexico in 1846, Jackson applied himself to military advancement with the same intensity with which he had mastered his studies. For "gallant and meritorious conduct" during the war he was promoted to first lieutenant and later won brevet, or honorary, promotion all the way to major.

After hostilities with Mexico ended, Jackson discovered that a drive that had served him so well in war did not suit him to the peacetime army. Following a series of largely pointless quibbles with superiors and a lengthy period of ill health that had him fearing for his life, he resigned his commission and in 1851 joined the faculty of the Virginia Military Institute in the little Shenandoah Valley town of Lexington, Virginia.

While at VMI, Jackson observed the dietary regimen he believed essential to his digestive well-being, practiced the Presbyterian faith to which he had been drawn during his illness, and enforced the regulations of the institute—all with the single-mindedness that marked his every pursuit. He also followed the advice of a doctor who thought that in addition to regular doses of buttermilk, marriage might be conducive to a more settled stomach. Within two years Jackson had conquered this objective as well. In 1853 he married Elinor Junkin, but a year later his wife died, taking with her to the grave their stillborn child.

Reconciled to the routines and comforts of religion, diet, and work, Jackson plodded on, eventually rekindling his interest in the opposite sex. Around Christmastime in 1856 he arrived unannounced at the home of Mary Anna Morrison, whom he had met once and with whom he had corresponded briefly. There he asked her minister father for her hand in marriage. They were wed the following summer.

For the next four years, Jackson's life was about as spontaneous and free flowing as the workings of a clock. He arose every morning at 6:00, spent time alone in prayer, took a walk, led his wife and servants in prayer promptly at 7:00 a.m., ate his breakfast, taught classes from 8:00 a.m. to 11:00 a.m., studied his Bible and his next day's lessons, took lunch at 1:00 p.m., held a 30-minute conversation with his wife, spent the afternoon working in the garden and the evening reviewing his lessons, and then to bed. Every day. His students, who found his lectures boring and his habits bizarre, dubbed him Old Tom Fool.

When hostilities between North and South began, Jackson was dispatched to Richmond with his VMI cadets to help train the thousands of recruits who were pouring into the Confederate armies. At the war's first battle, Bull Run, he commanded a brigade of Virginia infantry and earned for himself and his troops the immortal nickname Stonewall. But the name actually belied the tactics that made Jackson's later campaign in the Shenandoah Valley one of the most studied in military history. "Always mystify, mislead, and surprise the enemy, if possible," he said in one of the few times he tried to explain what he did. "Never fight against heavy odds if by any possible maneuvering you can hurl your own force on only a part, and that the weakest part, of your enemy and crush it."

Jackson was all about rapid, astonishing movement and—except in his determination—nothing at all like a stone wall. And now, on May 2, 1863, he was engaged in his favorite maneuver, a flanking march. Leaning forward over the neck of Little Sorrel as if this could spur his men on, he was again repeating his most characteristic orders: "See that the column is kept closed! Press on, press on!"

Reports of a large Confederate force on the move had been trickling into Hooker's headquarters at the Chancellor House all afternoon. But the Union commander had come to believe that the Rebels were in no position to threaten him. By marching north along the Rappahannock from Fredericksburg and getting his large army across the river unopposed, Hooker felt confident that he had successfully outmaneuvered Lee. If an enemy column *was* moving, he concluded, it must be retreating.

The general's complacency was shared by the troops on the right of the Union line, most of whom were German immigrants, dubbed Dutchmen by their native-born comrades. They were preparing supper, or playing cards, or just relaxing in the sun—stretched out with their heads pillowed on their knapsacks, laughing, talking, smoking. Their arms were stacked, like so many shocks of corn, at regular intervals throughout their camp. And Stonewall Jackson was almost upon them.

By late afternoon the Confederates were only a few hundred yards away from the Union positions. Shoulders hunched, Jackson sat Little Sorrel, pocket watch in hand. The dial read 5:15. When one of his field commanders rode up to say his men were ready, Jackson was satisfied: "You can go forward, sir." A few moments later, the woods erupted with the thrashing forward rush of thousands of soldiers, bugle calls, the bloodcurdling Rebel yell, and the crackle of musket fire.

Driving a wave of terrified rabbits, foxes, and deer before them, the attackers dashed forward, ignoring the dense underbrush that ripped their clothes and flesh and tore at their weapons. Under the fury of the onslaught, the astonished Yankees grabbed muskets, fired into the onrushing Rebels, then fled, Jackson in full pursuit. "They are running too fast for us!" one officer attempted a joke with the general. "We can't keep up with them."

"They never run too fast for me, sir," Jackson retorted. "Press them, press them!"

Only when he came across the corpse of an old veteran would Stonewall check his horse and raise his hand, as if in blessing, before moving on.

"It was a perfect whirlwind of men," one of the Federals said later. "The enemy seemed to come from every direction." One Union general who had lost a limb during the course of the Peninsular campaign clutched a flag under the stump of his right arm and rode into the tide of panicked men. But it was too late. In another attempt to steady the foot soldiers, a

> *"Always mystify, mislead, and surprise the enemy....Never fight against heavy odds if by any possible maneuvering you can hurl your own force on only a part, and that the weakest part, of your enemy and crush it."*
>
> STONEWALL JACKSON

Pennsylvania cavalry regiment moved forward along a narrow lane through the woods—and straight into the midst of the Rebel attack. "We struck it as a wave strikes a stately ship," one of the horsemen remembered. "The ship is staggered, but the wave is dashed into spray." In the blink of an eye, more than 30 riders and 80 horses were down. The body of one dead cavalry officer was later found to contain 13 bullets.

While the right of the Union line was disintegrating, Joe Hooker and his aides were relaxing on the porch of the Chancellor House, enjoying the balmy late-afternoon sun. The normally heavy-drinking general had forsworn alcohol for the duration of the campaign and was confining himself to the pleasures of tobacco. Hearing the roar of muskets off to the west, he concluded that his men were giving pursuit to the retreating Rebels. One officer stepped down from the porch, intending to stretch his legs. Suddenly he cried out, "My God! Here they come." Panic-stricken soldiers burst into view.

Hooker sprang to life. Jumping onto his horse, he galloped straight into the mob in an effort to stop the fleeing soldiers. Union officers hurriedly formed a new defensive line and faced west with their guns on Hazel Grove, a low hill that lay a mile to the south of the Chancellor House. The cannon fire, the stiffening resistance of the Union troops, and the deepening darkness—which was complete by about 7:00 p.m.—finally brought the Confederate advance to a halt.

But Jackson was not yet finished. Encouraged by the brightness of the rising moon in a clear sky, he decided upon that rarest of Civil War maneuvers—a night attack. Jackson was intent not merely on victory, however: He wanted to destroy the Army of the Potomac, and that required blocking its escape routes to the Rappahannock. "Cut them off from United States Ford!" he hissed at one of his senior officers. "Press them."

While his troops were picking their way through the thickets, Jackson sought a path between the Federals and their way back across the river. Riding slowly over unfamiliar ground in the moonlight, Jackson led his staff forward. Only when he heard the voices

of enemy soldiers did he turn about and head back toward his own men.

On the Confederate front line, jittery troops were watching the dark woods for signs of a Yankee counterattack, possibly by cavalry. Seeing horsemen coming at them, a few snapped off shots that grew into a volley, raking the approaching figures. No one knew what he was shooting at. Two in Jackson's party were killed outright, and Little Sorrel plunged into the woods, knocking Jackson's hat off and badly scraping his face. When aides caught up with the trembling animal and grabbed her reins, they saw that the general had been hit: A bullet had struck the palm of his right hand, another had pierced his left forearm, and a third had shattered his upper left arm.

Jackson's officers bore him away to a field hospital four miles to the rear. He was suffering from pain, shock, and loss of blood. But Jackson bore it all stoically, his thin lips compressed so tightly, one witness noticed, that the impression of his teeth showed through them. At 2:00 a.m. Stonewall's left arm was amputated just below the shoulder. Lee was shaken when he heard the news: "He has lost his left arm," he grieved, "but I have lost my right."

The Confederate commander knew that despite the success of Jackson's flank attack, the army was in mortal danger. His men had advanced to within a mile of Lee's troops, but as long as the two wings of the army remained separated by the tangle of the Wilderness, they risked destruction by the vastly superior Federal force. At 3:00 a.m. Lee sent orders to Jeb Stuart, who had taken over Jackson's command after the general was wounded: Stuart was to attack at first light, pushing forward in an all-out effort to link up with Lee's smaller wing of the army.

An aggressive commander, such as Joe Hooker was reputed to be, might have seized the chance and

Federal infantry and artillery defend General Hooker's headquarters at the red-brick Chancellor House, while cavalry charge down the road *(center)* toward onrushing Confederates in this fanciful representation of the situation at sunset on May 2. In the foreground at right, Lee's infantry moves in from the southeast, an attack that actually occurred the next day.

counterattacked, forcing his way through the gap between the Rebel detachments and eliminating them one at a time. But Hooker was looking in another direction. In case of a renewed Confederate offensive, he had his engineers work all night in order to strengthen his defenses around the Chancellor House and protect his escape routes across the fords of the Rappahannock. The key to the new Union position was Hazel Grove and its cannon, which acted as an immense wedge between Lee and Stuart. But fearing that his troops might be cut off, Hooker ordered them to abandon the hill during the night and fall back on his lines of defense around the house.

As the first gray streaks of dawn arrived, then, Lee and Stuart launched their attacks against the 75,000-man Federal army, Stuart driving to his right while Lee extended his left, attempting to close the gap between them. As Stuart's men swept forward, they could see floating before them the ostrich feather on their commander's hat and hear him singing out, "Old Joe Hooker, won't you come out of the Wilderness?" Stuart soon had 30 cannon atop the vacated Hazel Grove, and the two wings of Lee's army were joined. The Confederate guns were turned on the enemy's new defensive positions and began to play with devastating effect.

While the battle raged around Chancellorsville, the Wilderness began to catch fire. In one area the flames raced through a thick covering of dry leaves, roasting the wounded where they lay. A South Carolina officer never forgot the sight of "charred bodies hugging the trees, with hands outstretched as if to ward off the flames." The officer noticed that around the bodies were "little cleared circles" where the dying had tried to brush away the leaves and twigs in a vain effort to stop the progress of the fire.

A Union soldier who was wounded in battle and then nearly burned to death in the flames remembered trying desperately to help some Confederates

"Fighting Joe" Hooker could certainly talk a good game. "The enemy must either ingloriously fly or come out from behind his defences and give us battle upon our own ground, where certain destruction awaits him," he said in late April. Indeed, his opening move in the Chancellorsville campaign—a march around Lee's left flank—was shrewdly conceived and skillfully executed. Then, inexplicably, the general lost his nerve: He withdrew his advancing forces into defensive positions, handing the initiative to Lee and Jackson. "To tell the truth," he later admitted, "I just lost confidence in Joe Hooker."

rescue one of their injured comrades. "The last I saw of that fellow was his face," he recalled. "His eyes were big and blue, and his hair like raw silk surrounded by a wreath of fire. I heard him scream 'O, Mother! O, God!' It left me trembling all over, like a leaf. After it was over my hands were blistered and burned so I could not open or shut them; but me and them rebs tried to shake hands."

After three hours of intense fighting, the Confederates closed to within 500 yards of the Chancellor House and began directing their fire on the building. At about 9:30 a.m., General Hooker was standing on the south porch of the house, leaning against a pillar with his right hand and receiving a dispatch from a courier with his left, when a Confederate artillery round smashed into the pillar against which he was resting and split it from end to end. Shock waves ran up the column and down Hooker's arm to his body, throwing him to the ground. Then, as the general lay dazed by the impact, part of the pillar fell on his head, knocking him senseless for a few moments.

Word quickly spread that Hooker was dead, and to show that he was alive and well, Fighting Joe clambered onto his horse and insisted on riding around. Alive he may have been, but he was far from well. After he had ridden about half a mile to the north, away from the now-burning Chancellor House, his pain was so great that he had to be laid on a blanket and given some brandy. He then struggled back onto his horse—and just as he did, another Confederate shell thumped into the middle of the blanket. Any fight left in him was gone. Hooker gave orders to fall back to prepared defenses anchored on the river fords.

The next day Hooker convened a council of war. He told his disgruntled officers that his main responsibility was to protect Washington, then asked his officers to vote on their course of action. Most opted to stay and fight. Nevertheless, Hooker ordered a

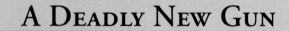

retreat. "Thus ended," recalled a disgusted soldier, "the campaign which Hooker opened as with a thunderbolt from the hand of Mars and ended as impotently as an infant who has not learned to grasp its rattle." On May 6 the Army of the Potomac abandoned the field and trudged back to the north side of the Rappahannock.

But it was Hooker, and not his army, that had been defeated, outgeneraled and demoralized by the tactical boldness shown by his enemy. A few people speculated that alcohol may have been to blame for his loss of nerve. But those around him at the time disagreed. In fact, some expressed the opinion that a drink or two might have improved Hooker's performance.

No failure of nerve had been evident in the actions of Robert E. Lee, who had just fought the best battle of his career. The Chancellorsville victory had come at a great price, however. Lee's 13,000 casualties, although a quarter less than those of the Federals, represented 22 percent of his army. In the hard-pressed South it would be difficult to replace these men. And one man in particular could never be replaced.

May 7 Anna Jackson and the infant Julia once again arrived by train at Guiney's Station and were driven by carriage to a small farmhouse where General Jackson was being treated. There she was told that her husband was doing "pretty well." But Anna could tell that something was wrong—and her heart "sank like lead."

In fact, something *was* wrong. Early that morning, Jackson had complained of nausea and a pain in his stomach. His doctor diagnosed pneumonia; there was nothing the physician could do now but make the patient comfortable, and wait. When Anna was admitted to the sickroom, the sight of her husband appalled her. "Oh, the fearful change since last I had seen him!" she wrote. "It required the strongest

A DEADLY NEW GUN

In the early days of the war, most soldiers faced the enemy with smoothbore muskets. Ulysses Grant wryly commented on the efficacy of this particular weapon when writing of his previous battle experiences in Mexico: "At the distance of a few hundred yards a man might fire at you all day without your finding it out." As Grant could attest, the smoothbore was accurate against an individual target only up to about 100 yards. If an infantryman hit something much farther away, it was likely that luck rather than skill had guided the bullet. But as the Civil War progressed, the North and the South began arming their troops with a newer, deadlier gun called the rifle musket. Unlike its predecessor, the rifle could bring a man down at 400 yards.

For centuries, gun manufacturers had known that a weapon's range and accuracy could be increased by rifling—cutting spiral grooves into—the bore to propel the shot outward with a spin. Prior to the mid-19th century, however, rifled guns had proved impractical on the battlefield. For the rifling to be effective, the ball had to fit firmly against the groove. Ramming snugly fitting ammunition down the muzzle was easy while the gun's bore remained clean but became increasingly difficult after repeated firings dirtied it. To compensate, shooters used smaller-caliber balls but had to wrap each one in a greased cloth patch during early firings so the ball could make close contact with the groove. In the midst of battle, the average infantryman could not afford such a time-consuming reloading process, so only specialized regiments, such as snipers, used rifled guns.

In the 1840s French army captain Claude-Étienne Minié advanced rifle technology by improving the ammunition. He developed an elongated bullet with an iron or wood plug inserted in a hollow in the base. When a gun's powder exploded, the plug expanded and forced the soft lead of a small-caliber bullet into the weapon's spiral grooves. Unfortunately Minié's composite bullet was expensive to manufacture. Then, early in the 1850s, American James H. Burton discovered that the cavity in the bullet's base could cause expansion by itself, without a plug. American and European manufacturers began producing a

In a battle at Cedar Mountain in August 1862, the two sides fired at close range without defense works, a tactic that the new rifle musket would make obsolete.

variety of rifled weapons, including the Springfield 1861 model above.

The new guns immediately impressed the soldiers. After a New Hampshire regiment received a shipment of Springfields in October 1861, a private wrote to his parents: "We went out the other day to try them. We fired 600 yards and we put 360 balls into a mark the size of old Jeff." However, gun manufacturers could not meet the demands of two American armies right away, so rifled weapons did not predominate until 1863.

The increase in range and accuracy of the infantryman's gun required an equivalent change in tactics. But the generals, many Mexican War veterans, adapted slowly, con-

"General, if you put every man on the other side of the Potomac on that field to approach me over the same line, and give me plenty of ammunition, I will kill them all before they reach my line."

JAMES LONGSTREET, MARYE'S HEIGHTS

tinuing to order the frontal attack and bayonet charge previously so successful. Now, however, such infantry charges, and cavalry charges, were often costly, fruitless maneuvers that left the field littered with the dead and dying, since a man in a well-sheltered position could cut down an exposed enemy at several hundred yards. In one particularly lopsided battle in December 1862, 35,000 Union troops charged 9,000 Confederates posted behind the stone wall on Marye's Heights outside Fredericksburg. The Confederates lost 1,200 men, the Federals 7,000, not one of whom ever reached the wall. A horrified Rebel infantryman later wrote, "It is no longer a battle, it is a butchery!"

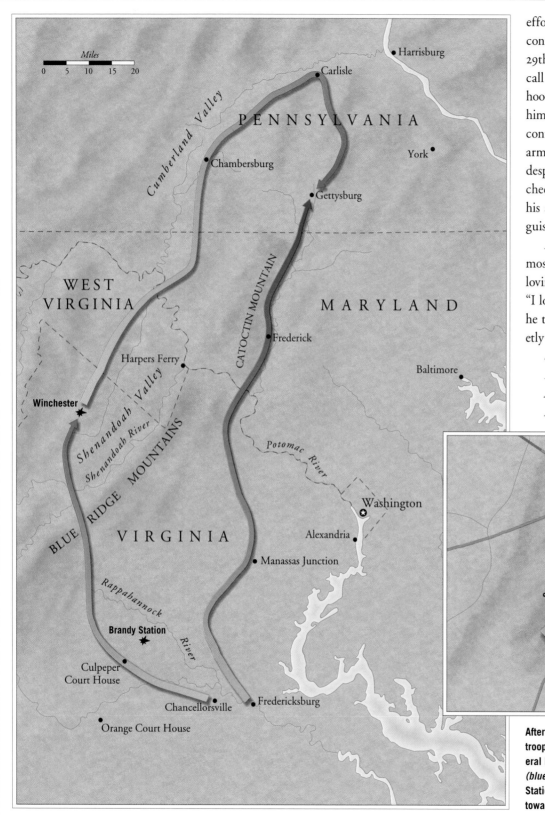

effort of which I was capable to maintain my self-control. When he left me on the morning of the 29th, going forth so cheerfully and bravely to the call of duty, he was in the full flush of vigorous manhood, and during that last, blessed visit, I never saw him look so handsome, so happy, and so noble." She continued, "Now, his fearful wounds, his mutilated arm, the scratches upon his face, and, above all, the desperate pneumonia, which was flushing his cheeks, oppressing his breathing, and benumbing his senses, wrung my soul with such grief and anguish as it had never before experienced."

Although Jackson was in a semiconscious state most of the time, during his lucid moments he spoke lovingly to Anna, asking her not to feel sad for him. "I love cheerfulness and brightness in a sick room," he told her, and asked her to sing for him. She quietly sang a hymn based on the 51st Psalm:

> *Show pity, Lord; O Lord forgive;*
> *Let a repenting rebel live;*
> *Are not Thy mercies large and free?*
> *May not a sinner trust in Thee?*

After General Lee's victory at Chancellorsville, Confederate troops headed north toward Pennsylvania *(red line)*, while General Hooker's Union army followed a parallel route to the east *(blue line)*. There were brief but fierce encounters at Brandy Station and Winchester, Virginia, as the two armies pushed on toward Gettysburg *(inset)*.

Confederate forces marching toward Gettysburg on the Chambersburg pike around dawn on July 1 scavenged rails from roadside fences to feed their campfires. The first clash of the Battle of Gettysburg took place later that morning at McPherson's Ridge a little to the west of the town.

The words brought Jackson comfort. But every time Anna offered to bring Julia in, he said, "Not yet, wait till I feel better."

General Lee had been convinced that Jackson would recover. "God will not take him from us now that we need him so much," he had said. But on Sunday morning, May 10, Anna was given the news that all hope was gone, that death was only hours away, and she determined to tell her husband the truth. She recalled, "I had heard him say that, although he was ready to die at any moment that God might call him, still he would prefer to have a few hours' preparation." When Anna informed him that the end was near, Jackson pronounced himself satisfied. "Very good, very good," he whispered to her. "It is all right, it is the Lord's day, my wish is fulfilled. I have always desired to die on Sunday."

That morning little Julia was finally brought to her father's sickroom and placed on the bed beside him. "Although he had almost ceased to notice anything," Anna remembered, "he looked up, his countenance brightened with delight, and he never smiled more sweetly as he exclaimed, 'Little darling! Sweet one!'" But by early afternoon Jackson's breathing had become more labored, his times of consciousness shorter. A little after 3:00 p.m. he suddenly started up and shouted orders to subordinates to prepare for battle. Then his pale features broke into a smile, and he closed his eyes. "Let us cross over the river," he said in a firm but quiet voice, "and rest under the shade of the trees." In a few moments Stonewall Jackson was no more.

The Battle of Chancellorsville cemented the opinion that Lee's men had been forming of him, and, more important, confirmed his faith in them. They began to think of each other as invincible. "Nothing gave me much concern as long as I knew that General Lee was in command," one Confederate remembered. "We looked forward to victory under him as confidently as to successive sunrises." For his part, Lee considered his soldiers "the finest body of men that ever tramped the earth."

By the summer of 1863 Robert E. Lee seemed at the height of his power. Lieutenant Colonel Arthur Fremantle of the British army, who was observing Confederate military operations for his government, met the Rebel leader in June and thought him "the handsomest man of his age I ever saw. He is 56 years old, tall, broad-shouldered, very well made, well set up—a thorough soldier in appearance; and his manners are most courteous and full of dignity. He has none of the small vices, such as smoking, drinking, chewing or swearing, and his bitterest enemy never accused him of any of the greater ones."

But on the field of battle Lee's manner changed. "No man who ever saw his flashing eyes and sternly set lips," said one observer, "is ever likely to forget them." At Chancellorsville his willingness to take risks, to do the unexpected, to risk defeat in order to snatch victory, had routed and demoralized his opponent. Now he was planning a campaign that would confound friend and foe alike.

Most military and political leaders of the Civil War had a simplistic view of strategy, one that involved advancing a line of men northward or southward until the rival capital could be taken. Politicians were especially insistent that a large army always be situated between their capital and the enemy. On June 3, however, Lee marched his troops away from their positions in front of Richmond, pushed west into the Shenandoah Valley, then drove north behind the ramparts of the Blue Ridge Mountains and into Pennsylvania, considerably above Washington, D.C. As Lee knew it would, the Union army gave pursuit.

Lee's mere crossing of his country's northern border, as he called the Potomac River, was a great symbolic move; a victory in Federal territory would strengthen the growing peace movement in the North and encourage England and France to recognize and support the Confederacy. But at a small Pennsylvania town called Gettysburg Lee realized that the Yankees were not going to roll over as they had at Chancellorsville. The Army of the Potomac was going to fight.

The morning of July 3, 1863, Robert E. Lee sat astride his big gray horse, Traveller, his eyes fixed on the Federal lines three-quarters of a mile distant. Just five days earlier Abraham Lincoln had replaced Hooker—now known as Fallen Joe—with the steady if unimaginative George Meade. The new commander of the Union army was a Pennsylvanian who, said Lincoln, "will fight well on his own dunghill." Meade's men were entrenched along a ridge extending two miles south of Gettysburg, and they showed no sign of budging. Secure behind breastworks, fences, and a low stone wall, they awaited Lee's next move. The high ground the Federals occupied had the ominous name of Cemetery Ridge; the Confederates were drawn up along a second, roughly parallel ridge to the west known as Seminary Ridge. Between the two stretched the green and yellow of rich pastureland and fields of ripened wheat.

For two days now Lee had thrown his troops against the Yankees on the ridge, once on their right flank and once on their left. Both times his men had been repulsed. If only his commanders had moved with more decisiveness. If only his cavalry chief, Jeb Stuart, had kept him better informed on enemy dispositions. If only he had Stonewall by his side.

Having failed on both Union flanks, Lee determined that his next effort would be against the center. But his plan to punch a hole through the middle of the Federal line was bitterly opposed by his most senior general, James Longstreet. Standing a husky six foot two, with a bushy brown beard and beetle brows, Lee's "Old Warhorse" was an imposing man who thought deeply about the business of war. He was the army's leading advocate of entrenchments, and he had a view that was contrary to Lee's of how the Army of Northern Virginia should be conducting its business in Pennsylvania.

A Bloody Standoff

As daylight began to wane on July 2, Lee's army had yet to gain Cemetery Hill, the most heavily defended Yankee position. Just after sunset, a brigade led by Colonel Isaac E. Avery *(right)* charged partway up the slope. As the Rebels moved over a rise that had shielded them, Federal cannon opened at point-blank range. Long streaks of orange flame from their muzzles pierced the summer twilight. "It was one solid crash," wrote a Union gunner, "like a million trees falling at once." Among the many casualties was Avery, who managed to scrawl a last message *(far right)* to his subordinate—"Major: Tell my father I died with my face to the enemy."

Avery's sacrifice was in vain; the Federals rallied, sending in a fresh brigade to seal the breach. The Confederates withdrew under cover of darkness, and the fighting subsided for the night.

Six smoothbore Napoleons of a Union artillery battery pour canister into the flank of swarming Confederates on Cemetery Hill on the evening of July 2. Disorganized by darkness and suffering heavy casualties, the Rebels were finally driven from the hilltop.

Like all military men, Longstreet knew that a defending army always had an advantage over its attackers, especially when it possessed the high ground, as the Yankees now did at Gettysburg. Instead of playing to the enemy's strengths, then, Longstreet had argued that the thing to do was to maneuver around the Union right, get between the army and Washington, find and fortify some good, high ground—and wait. The Federals would be forced to attack, and the Confederates would then enjoy all the advantages they now lacked.

But Lee had been worried about the logistical difficulties that accompanied such a course of action. For days Jeb Stuart had been out of contact with the rest of the Confederate army, and Lee felt constrained by his lack of intelligence regarding Union strength and deployments. Moreover, maneuvering as Longstreet had suggested would expose the army's line of communications back to Virginia and would restrict the area in which it was able to forage for food. Besides, Lee was in the mood for a move that showed more decisiveness.

Ever since the Battle of Bull Run, the Confederates had defeated Northern armies that had simply walked back to Washington, reorganized, then marched back out to give battle again. The same thing had happened after Chancellorsville. In the long run, the South—with its smaller armies and population—could not hope to prevail in such a war. And to Lee's mind, Longstreet's defensive approach could only lead to more bloody and indecisive combat. Here in Pennsylvania Lee needed to win—and to win big. He could not retreat to battle-ravaged Virginia with nothing gained and await the Union army there. Neither could he remain where he was indefinitely, for his limited supplies would not permit it. But he could attack. "The enemy is there," he told Longstreet bluntly, "and I am going to strike him there." It was a rare occasion indeed when Robert E. Lee called his adversary "the enemy."

Longstreet saw there was no way to change his commander's mind. But if an infantry charge had to be carried out, then "Old Pete" Longstreet insisted

that the Army of Northern Virginia should rely on one of his divisions, which was just now arriving on the battlefield. These troops had not taken part in the first two days of fighting at Gettysburg and were the freshest of the Confederate units. Besides, James Longstreet had faith in the division's general, overlooking the man's flamboyant ways—his devotion to ruffled shirts, flowing locks, and strong cologne. The officer had won Old Pete's favor ever since the occasion on which he grabbed the regimental colors from a wounded Longstreet and scaled the ramparts of an enemy fortress during the Mexican War. And for less than an hour of combat

The painting below depicts the moment when Federal defenders, seen at left, repulsed the furious onslaught of General George Pickett's infantry. "Men fire into each other's faces," a participant wrote, "not five feet apart. There are bayonet thrusts, sabre strokes, pistol shots . . . men going down on their hands and knees, spinning round like tops." Watching in horror was General James Longstreet *(opposite, left)*, who had tried to persuade General Lee that such an assault had no hope of success. Pickett *(opposite, right)* never forgave Lee. "That old man," he later observed, "had my division slaughtered at Gettysburg."

on the afternoon of July 3, 1863, the name of George Pickett would be remembered forever.

When Longstreet chose Pickett to lead the attack, the 38-year-old general, who had not yet snatched the glory he so desired from the war, was ready and eager for such a challenge. His aristocratic Virginia family, the "Fighting Picketts of Fauquier County," had served in every major American conflict since the French and Indian War. He was determined to maintain the family's martial tradition.

Pickett was appointed to West Point by Abraham Lincoln when the future president was a young congressman from Illinois. The cadet found difficult the academy's rigid program of drill and study, however, and graduated at the very bottom of his class. But in addition to the heroics that had so impressed Longstreet, Pickett did see a considerable amount of fighting in Mexico, and he had achieved gradual promotion during the first two years of the Civil War. Now, at Gettysburg, he saw his chance. In the words of a fellow officer, he appeared "entirely sanguine of success in the charge and was congratulating himself on the opportunity." In fact, Pickett would not come to understand the gravity of what was being asked of him until he rode over to Longstreet's camp to receive his final orders. He found his old friend in an agony of distress.

As Longstreet learned more about Lee's plans for the day, his fears had grown. Earlier that morning Lee had indicated to him a copse of oak trees that rose above the center of the Federal line. The umbrella-shaped clump that stood out against the sky on the otherwise bare crest of Cemetery Ridge was to be the target of the attack. He informed Longstreet he would have 15,000 men with which to overrun it, an estimate that would turn out to be more than 20 percent too high. It was not to be the only miscalculation of the day.

One more time Longstreet faced his commander and spoke his mind. "General, I have been a soldier all my life," he said, "and should know as well as anyone what soldiers can do. It is my opinion that no 15,000 men ever arrayed for battle can take that

BATTLING DEATH AT GETTYSBURG

When the Confederate army retreated on July 4, some 20,000 wounded, 6,000 of whom were Rebels, remained in Gettysburg. Houses, barns, and churches were appropriated to serve as field hospitals, but providing shelter for all the casualties proved to be impossible. Many of the injured lay on the bare ground, tormented by rain, insects, and stifling heat, and forced to listen to the groans and cries of their comrades. Those who could be stabilized were evacuated to general hospitals in the North. To care for those who were too weak to be moved immediately, the Union army set up more than 400 tents to function as a temporary hospital at Gettysburg. It was woefully understaffed; there were only 106 Federal doctors who could be spared from battlefield duty to care for the wounded.

During the first week, surgeons labored unceasingly, extracting bullets and shell fragments and performing amputations. One remembered operating for the better part of four days, "my legs swollen and painful, my arms and hands immersed in blood and water so long that it became difficult to hold the knife."

The greatest danger to a patient's welfare was not physician exhaustion, however, but infection. Medical science had not yet grasped the importance of operating room sanitation. At Gettysburg as elsewhere, neither the doctor's hands nor his instruments were routinely disinfected. Observers reported seeing physicians simply

Union hospital tents dot Gettysburg following the war's bloodiest clash. The Union army did not strike the last of the tents until mid-November, four and a half months after the battle.

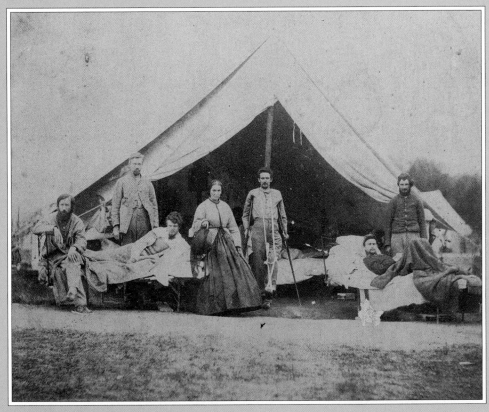

A nurse poses with recuperating patients outside their tent. Hundreds of civilian volunteers were recruited by relief agencies. Though many lacked formal training, they helped bathe, bandage, and comfort the wounded.

wipe their surgical saws across their already blood-encrusted aprons before calling for the next patient.

As news of the battle spread throughout the North, nursing volunteers began arriving. The newcomers were horrified by Gettysburg's grisly scenes, including putrefied, unburied corpses and heaps of severed limbs. But all of their attention was soon claimed by the demanding, and often heartbreaking, task of tending the injured. "To many mothers, sisters, and wives," 23-year-old attendant Cornelia Hancock sadly recalled, "I penned the last message of those who were soon to become the 'beloved dead.'"

A Civil War surgeon's kit included scalpels, forceps, and amputation saws.

position." Lee was unmoved. Longstreet said no more. Riding away to execute the orders, Old Pete experienced a sense of depression he had never felt before. He thought for certain his men were about to make a vain sacrifice—and that he would have to order them to do it.

Around 9:00 a.m., Longstreet began forming his line of battle in woods on the western slope of Seminary Ridge, where his troops would be concealed from the enemy. Still his mind wrestled with what he had to do. As his men took their positions, Longstreet began to see that he had one—albeit slim—hope, and that lay with the artillery. If his cannon could blast a path for Pickett's infantrymen, then perhaps the attack would be successful. In order to carry out this bombardment, Longstreet would have to rely on his 27-year-old colonel of artillery, Porter Alexander.

Longstreet considered young Alexander to be a soldier of "unusual promptness, sagacity, and intelligence." That morning the artilleryman had deployed more than 150 Confederate guns in front of the woods where the attack force was forming. He had notified all of the Rebel batteries that the signal to commence the bombardment would be two gunshots that were fired in quick succession.

But while he was making his final preparations for battle he received a message from Longstreet. The note explained the importance Alexander would have in the hours to come; in short, Longstreet told him that if his guns should fail to "drive off the enemy or greatly demoralize him so as to make our efforts pretty certain, I would prefer that you should not advise General Pickett to make the charge."

Alexander was startled. Longstreet seemed to be assigning to him, a mere colonel, the decision of whether the infantry charge should be made at all. The young gunner was not about to accept such responsibility. Quickly, he sent off a message of reply to the general. "When our fire is at its best," he wrote to Longstreet, "I will advise General Pickett to advance."

Meanwhile, the foot soldiers who would have to make the attack readied themselves as best they could. Each prepared for battle in his own way. Some joined with chaplains in prayer; others listened to patriotic speeches delivered by officers; some sought to relieve the tension by pelting each other with green apples. When a hare that had been hiding in the bushes sprang out and bounded toward the rear, a gaunt Virginian yelled after it, "Run, old hare! If I was an old hare I'd run too!"

At 1:00 p.m. two cannon fired off the signal. All of the guns responded, roaring into action, said Porter Alexander, "as suddenly as the full notes of an organ would fill a church." Firing as quickly as they could reload, the Southern gunners unleashed the most colossal artillery barrage that was ever seen on American soil and one that dwarfed even the Confederate pounding of the Hornet's Nest at the Battle of Shiloh the year before. The air was darkened with sulfurous clouds that obscured the sun, and the earth itself seemed to tremble. Some of those who were manning the guns bled at both ears from the concussive action of the guns.

On the receiving end of the bombardment, a number of witnesses recorded the savage scene. "Streams of screaming projectiles poured through the hot air falling and bursting everywhere," recalled an officer on Cemetery Ridge. "Men and horses were torn limb from limb; caissons exploded one after another in rapid succession, blowing the gunners to pieces. No spot within our lines was free from this frightful iron rain." A New York newspaper correspondent who was watching from the north end of the Union line wrote of the battle: "The storm broke upon us so suddenly that soldiers and officers—who leaped as it began from their tents, and from lazy siestas on the grass—were stricken in their rising with mortal wounds, and died, some with cigars between their teeth, some

A keepsake picture carried by a Confederate soldier was one of thousands of mementos that were found on the battlefield at Gettysburg. This poignant remembrance was among the items collected by a young Pennsylvania schoolteacher who was fascinated by what he called "the thickly littered debris of battle."

with pieces of food in their fingers, and one at least—a pale young German from Pennsylvania—with a miniature of his sister in his hands."

And a Union captain remembered the effect of the fierce firing on some of the wildlife of the area: "It was touching to see the little birds, all out of their wits with fright, flying wildly about amidst the tornado of terrible missiles and uttering strange notes of distress. It was touching to see the innocent cows and calves, feeding in the fields, torn in pieces by the shells."

But in spite of the casualties that they were inflicting, many of the Confederate rounds were high—"quartermaster hunters," the front-line troops called them, as if the enemy artillery were deliberately aimed at rear-echelon units. "All we had to do," recalled one man, "was flatten out a little thinner, and our empty stomachs did not prevent that."

The Federal troops had been issued three days' worth of rations on July 1—hardtack, salt pork, coffee, and sugar—and as was usually the case, most consumed them immediately. Veterans defended the practice by saying that it was easier to carry the food in your belly than in your pack. Water was also in short supply for the men who lay hugging the ground, and the heat was oppressive. As the temperature climbed to 90 degrees, one parched soldier recalled the sweat running off his face and forming a muddy spot on the ground underneath him.

When Union gunners began to answer the Confederate barrage with more than 70 of their own cannon—a third of them from central positions near the landmark copse—they tended to shoot high as well. But although the Confederate rounds were doing comparatively little damage in the enemy's rear area, the Federal shells often burst among the massed Rebel soldiers who were held back in the woods; 500 men in Pickett's division alone were killed before the attack even started.

Working among the wounded west of Seminary Ridge was Dr. John Holt, a surgeon from Mississippi. Soon after the Union bombardment began, litter bearers carried into Holt's aid station a young private called Jeremiah Gage—a "princely fellow," in the words of the doctor, and one whose ruddy face, mane of red gold hair, athletic build, and deferential manner he found "singularly attractive." Gage was a member of the Mississippi Greys, a unit made up entirely of students from the University of Mississippi. A cannonball between the shoulder and elbow had nearly torn off his left arm. When the surgeon murmured some words of encouragement, Gage smiled. "Why, doctor, that is nothing," he said, folding back a blanket that covered his belly. "Here is where I am really hurt."

Another cannonball had smashed into the young man's lower abdomen, tearing away much of his intestines and part of his pelvis. In a strong voice, Gage asked, "Doctor, how long have I to live?"

"A very few hours," Holt replied.

Seemingly calm, the private asked for help to write a message to his mother. The doctor found pencil and paper, then steadied Gage's hand as he wrote hurriedly: "My dear Mother, this is the last you may ever hear from me. I have time to tell you that I died like a man. Bear my loss as best you can. Remember that I am true to my country and my greatest regret at dying is that she is not free and that you and my sisters are robbed of my worth, whatever that may be. I hope this will reach you, and you must not regret that my body cannot be obtained. It is a mere matter of form anyhow."

With a final word of farewell to his sisters—and to a certain "Miss Mary"—he signed it. "I dip this letter in my dying blood," he said quietly to himself, pressed the page to his wounds, and handed it to the doctor, who promised to see it delivered. Holt then offered Gage a tin cup containing a dose of concentrated opium. But Jeremiah Gage was not yet finished. Calling to the litter bearers who had carried him to the aid station, he raised his cup in salute. "Come around boys," he called out, "and let us have

The War Moves North

"I had just put my bread in the pans when the cannons began to fire, and true enough the battle had begun in earnest, about two miles out on the Chambersburg pike....No one knew where to go and what to do."

SALLY BROADHEAD, RESIDENT OF GETTYSBURG

The battle at Gettysburg, and the skirmishes preceding it, touched the lives of many civilians. Among them was Mrs. L. L. Rewalt of Wrightsville, Pennsylvania. On June 28, 1863, while en route to Gettysburg, Confederate general John B. Gordon and his men saved her town from a fire accidentally set by retreating Union soldiers. To show her gratitude, Rewalt invited the Rebels to her home. The general later recalled her admiringly:

At a bountifully supplied table in the early morning sat this modest, cultured woman, surrounded by soldiers in their worn, gray uniforms. The welcome she gave us was so gracious, she was so self-possessed, so calm and kind, that I found myself in an inquiring state of mind as to whether her sympathies were with the Northern or Southern side in the pending war. . . . With no one present except Confederate soldiers who were her guests, she replied, . . . "I am a Union woman. I cannot afford to be misunderstood, nor to have you misinterpret this simple courtesy. You and your soldiers last night saved my home from burning, and I was unwilling that you should go away without receiving some token of my appreciation. I must tell you, however, that, with my assent and approval, my husband is a soldier in the Union army, and my constant prayer to Heaven is that our cause may triumph and the Union be saved."

No Confederate left that room without a feeling of profound respect, of unqualified admiration, for that brave and worthy woman.

During the battle, 15-year-old Gettysburg resident Tillie Pierce was sent from one farmhouse to another in an attempt to ensure her safety.

Euphemia Goldsborough *(above, left)* of Baltimore went to Gettysburg to care for wounded Confederates. On September 22, 1863, she wrote to one patient's mother.

Resident Elizabeth Salome Myers began nursing wounded soldiers at the Roman Catholic church at Gettysburg on July 2.

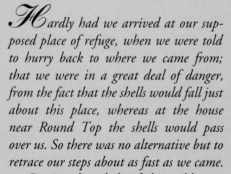

Hardly had we arrived at our supposed place of refuge, when we were told to hurry back to where we came from; that we were in a great deal of danger, from the fact that the shells would fall just about this place, whereas at the house near Round Top the shells would pass over us. So there was no alternative but to retrace our steps about as fast as we came.

During the whole of this wild goose chase, the cannonading had become terrible! . . . Occasionally a shell would come flying over Round Top and explode high in the air over head. It seemed as though the heavens were sending forth peal upon peal of terrible thunder directly over our heads; while at the same time, the very earth beneath our feet trembled.

He died in my arms, Sunday evening, Sept. 13, **just at sunset** *his precious brown eyes fixed in mine, without a struggle, and his last fleeting breath I caught upon his lips. . . . You* **must not** *feel that your son died in an enemy's country with* **none** *to* **love** *or care for him. His whole Brigade loved him as did all who came in contact with him,* **even those** *who were opposed to the glorious cause for which so many brave and noble have already been sacrificed, and many were the bitter tears shed over his untimely grave. If this should ever reach you, may I ask that you will answer it. I hope that we may meet after this unhappy war is ended and that I may be able to give you back your* **darling son's** *dying kiss.*

I went to the church, where men were lying [on] the pews and on the floors. I knelt by the first one inside the door and said: "What can I do for you?" He replied: "Nothing, I am going to die." . . . To be thus met by the first one addressed was more than my nerves could stand and I went hastily out, sat down on the church steps and cried.

In a little while I re-entered the church hospital and spoke again to the dying man. He was Sergeant Alexander Stewart of the 149th Pennsylvania Infantry Regiment.

He lingered until Monday, July 6. . . . I held him in my arms until nearly 11 when his head sank on the pillow and he died with only a slight struggle.

As caretaker of the local cemetery in her husband's absence, Elizabeth Thorn was obliged to dig graves despite being six months pregnant.

Two [friends] came [to help], but one only stayed two days, then got deathly sick and left. The other stayed five days, then he went away very sick, and I had to pay their fare here and very good wages for their work. . . . And then father and I had to dig on harder again. They kept on burying the soldiers until they had the National Cemetery ready, and in that time we buried one hundred five soldiers. In front of this house there were fifteen dead horses and beside the Cemetery there were nineteen in that field. So you may know it was only excitement that helped me to do all the work, with all that stench.

a toast. I do not invite you to drink with me, but I drink the toast to you, and to the Southern Confederacy, and to victory!" Then he gulped the liquid down and sank into a drugged sleep. Holt covered him up with a blanket and moved on to help other wounded. For Jeremiah Gage the battle was over; for most, it was about to begin.

For almost two hours Colonel Porter Alexander had been pounding away at Cemetery Ridge. His original plan had been to send word to Pickett to advance 15 minutes after the cannonade began. But the Yankees were so well entrenched behind the stone wall running along the crest of the ridge that 15 minutes of bombardment hadn't had the effect the Rebel colonel had planned on. Twenty minutes passed, then 25, then 30, with Alexander all the while "hoping vainly for something to turn up." Meanwhile, Pickett was waiting for instructions to begin his advance. Then, shortly before 3:00 p.m., Alexander saw some of the Union cannon retreating from their position near the copse and sensed that the enemy gunners were slackening their return fire. "We Confederates often did such things as that to save our ammunition for use against infantry," he recalled. "But I had never before seen the Federals withdraw their guns simply to save them up for the infantry fight." Aware that he was running low on ammunition, Alexander realized this might be his best chance of the day. He dispatched a note to Pickett: "For God's sake, come quick."

Alexander's messenger found Pickett conferring with Longstreet in the woods west of Seminary Ridge. When he read the artilleryman's note, Pickett asked, "General, shall I advance?" He would always remember the look on his commander's face. In obvious distress, Longstreet merely lowered his head. It was enough for Pickett. "I shall lead my division forward, sir."

Pickett had ridden off a few paces when he remembered that he was still carrying a letter he had written to his 16-year-old fiancée, LaSalle Corbell. He pulled it out and on a corner of the envelope scribbled

a last message to his "Sally of the sunset eyes": "If Old Peter's nod means death, then goodbye and God bless you, little one." Then he rode to Longstreet to leave the letter with him for mailing. "The stern old war horse," recalled Pickett, "was weeping for his men."

When Pickett reached his division, his troops were eager to go. In fact, after the Union cannonade, most were relieved that they were about to advance. Once, in the midst of the barrage, they had looked up from their positions crouching on the ground to see a mounted officer pass by. It was General Lee on Traveller. The men were horrified to see "Marse Robert" in a position of such danger, and they called on him to move quickly on. In acknowledgment of their concern, Lee tipped his hat to them, then spurred his gray charger on.

Pickett's three field commanders would lead the division forward: General James Kemper, who had left his seat in the Virginia General Assembly to serve at the Battle of Bull Run and had stayed to fight ever since; General Richard Garnett, who would ride because a horse's kick had left him unable to walk; and gray-bearded Lewis Armistead, whose best friend in the United States Army before the war was the man commanding the line they were about to assault. Astride a great black horse and wearing a fancy new uniform, Pickett galloped to the center of his line and shouted to his troops: "Up, men, and to your posts! Don't forget today that you are from old Virginia!"

Even though George Pickett would give his name to the charge, his were not the only troops to participate. His Virginia division would take the right of the line and a division of mostly North Carolinians the left. Behind them were four brigades cobbled together from troops from Mississippi, Tennessee, Alabama, and other parts of the South. The whole Rebel force, including support troops and artillerymen, had units from every state of the Confederacy except Arkansas and Texas; together, they formed a front half a mile long.

Forbidden to fire or to give the Rebel yell until the moment for the final rush on Cemetery Ridge

Confederate dead are laid out in a shallow trench that was dug hastily in the July heat by the burial detail shown in the background. "The ground here is very hard, the dead are many," wrote a soldier from New Jersey. "The time is short, so they got but very shallow graves. . . . Most of them were buried as near where they fell as possible, so as not to have to carry them far. . . . The graves were filled by throwing earth right on the body, no coffins, not even wrapped up in anything."

arrived, 12,000 men emerged silently from the woods, 38 battle flags raised in the hot, still air—"as grand a sight as ever a man looked on," thought Porter Alexander. "Sergeant," shouted General Armistead to the flagbearer of a Virginia regiment, "are you going to put those colors on the enemy's works today?"

"I will try, sir," he called back, "and if mortal man can do it, it shall be done."

Farther up the line, another officer was calling to his Carolina troops, "For the honor of the good Old North State, forward!"

Waiting for the Rebels on Cemetery Ridge, around the copse, was a Federal force of about half the Confederate number. That morning the Yankees had watched as battery after battery appeared along Seminary Ridge. They had seen guns unlimbered and deployed and the horses taken to the rear. And then Alexander's two signal guns broke the afternoon's quiet. Within moments, reckoned one Union officer, every soldier in the line knew that an attack was imminent.

Placed in command of the Federal defenses by General Meade was Winfield Scott Hancock, Lewis Armistead's old friend. At age 39 one of the finest generals in the army, he had won the nickname Hancock the Superb during the Peninsular campaign in 1862 and had embellished it in every battle since. He was about to add further luster to his reputation.

Sitting ramrod straight on his prancing horse and seemingly oblivious of the Rebel cannonade, Hancock rode slowly along the crest of Cemetery Ridge, followed by a single orderly bearing a Union flag. Thousands of Yankee soldiers looked at him and, said one staff officer, "found courage longer to endure the pelting of the pitiless gale." It was, thought one of the inspired troops, "a deed of heroism such as we are apt to attribute only to the knights of the olden time."

At last, at about 3:00 p.m., the Federals saw the gray line move out of the woods three-quarters of a mile away, red Confederate flags flying over the right of the line, blue flags of Virginia over the left. "Here they come! Here they come!" shouted the Yankees. "Here comes their infantry!"

Seated atop a rail fence, James Longstreet looked on as his troops marched by. Pickett rode out past him, still jaunty, thought Longstreet, and took up his command position behind his line. Old Pete could also see General Armistead, striding across the field, his black slouch hat on the point of an uplifted sword to serve as a guide to his troops. To their grim amusement, the sword pierced the cloth, and Armistead had to keep repositioning the hat at the tip of the sword. Beyond Armistead the injured Garnett was visible too, one of just a handful of mounted figures among the ranks of infantry.

Their wool uniforms soaked with sweat under a broiling sun, the Rebels started out toward the crest of Cemetery Ridge. Except for the drums beating out a steady pace of 110 steps per minute, the troops moved forward in silence. The flawless line soon halted briefly in a little depression—and then it went steadfastly into the full fury of the enemy's fire. No longer targeting the positions on Seminary Ridge, Federal gunners now unleashed a punishing barrage on the oncoming foot soldiers. Cannon shot after cannon shot blasted 10-man gaps in the Confederate formations. "We could not help hitting them at every shot," a Northern artilleryman recalled. But still the gray-clad troops came on. "Home boys, home," shouted a lieutenant. "Remember, home is over beyond those hills!"

Filling the holes in the line from behind or by closing up on the colors, the Rebels pushed on, moving forward in a half-stoop, heads down as if they were advancing into a storm. Ahead of them they could see the long line of Yankees that awaited them.

Suddenly, the Confederates started to come under fire from another direction. The 8th Ohio Regiment had been posted as a skirmish line west of the main Union positions the previous afternoon—and

Unlike many soldiers whose Gettysburg graves bore the single word "Unknown," this Federal officer's temporary headstone gives his name, unit, and date of death. Since Civil War troops didn't wear dog tags, identifying the dead was often difficult.

F.C. Goodrich
1st Lieut 2d U.S. Infy
Killed July 2d 1863

had never received orders to withdraw. Had the Ohioans done nothing, they might have been bypassed on this day. But their pugnacious colonel had his 160 men change front to face south and deploy in a single rank to give the impression of greater numbers. As the left of the Confederate line moved past him, he ordered them to open fire. The effect was astonishing. Hundreds of Rebels broke and ran, and at least 200 others raised their hands in surrender before the rest of the Confederate line swept past the 8th Ohio and on toward Cemetery Ridge.

Using the copse as their guide, the Southerners pressed on, their pace quickening as they approached the long, gentle slope that ran up to the ridge. Looking at the enemy ahead of him, a Virginia private exclaimed, "What a sublime sight!" Then he drew a watch from his pocket and remarked, "We have been just 19 minutes coming." They were the last words he uttered. Soon after, he was killed by a Federal shell.

When they came within 200 yards of the crest of the hill, they were hit by the first full volley from Hancock's men behind the low stone wall. A storm of lead crashed into the attackers, and a collective moan went up from the field. The Rebels, a Federal officer recalled, "were at once enveloped in a dense cloud of dust. Arms, heads, blankets, guns and knapsacks were tossed into the clear air."

The attackers were calling out for permission to fire back, and finally Confederate muskets answered the Union fire with volley after volley. And above the roar of the battle rose, for the first time that afternoon, the high quaver of the Rebel yell. The men broke into a running charge. But the left of the Confederate line had been badly mauled by Federal artillery and by the 8th Ohio. And now Yankees north of the copse were moving forward to overlap the Rebel flank and direct into it a deadly fire.

After witnessing the success of this last maneuver, Hancock galloped southward along Cemetery Ridge to see if a similar move could be executed at the other end of the line. He found that such an envelopment was already in progress. Three Vermont regiments, seeing that the enemy assault was passing them by to the north, had changed front and opened fire on Pickett's right flank. The effect of this double envelopment—Yankees firing from both sides—was to herd the attackers into an increasingly jumbled mass in the middle, 15 to 30 men deep, as soldiers clustered about their officers and their flags.

Determined to keep up the momentum of the charge, General Kemper stood up in his stirrups, raised his sword, and urged his men on. "There are the guns, boys!" he cried. "Go for them!" Just then a bullet struck the inside of his left thigh and passed upward to lodge near the base of his spine. General Garnett, wrapped in a blue overcoat and riding his big horse up and down in front of his men, continued to wave his hat and encourage them. Then he disappeared in the smoke of cannon fire. Moments later a Virginia private saw Garnett's bloody horse

"Come on, boys! Give them the cold steel! Who will follow me?" Hundreds did. Again the Rebel yell shrilled across the field. The Federal line seemed ready to break.

Triumphant, Armistead stepped over the stone wall. He knew that the guns he had just won from his friend Winfield Hancock had to be turned on the fleeing Yankees. The general reached out and put his hand on one of the cannon. But just then Hancock himself ordered Union reinforcements to re-take the guns, and a large force of Federals slammed into the Confederates. "Forward, men! Forward! Now's your chance!" he shouted at them. His old comrade, Lewis Armistead, fell mortally wounded.

Hancock was equally exposed. A bullet hit his horse's saddle, driving a nail and pieces of leather and wood into the general's thigh. Helped from his horse

"I could now thoroughly appreciate the term bulldog, which I had heard applied to him by the soldiers. Difficulties seem to make no other impression upon him than to make him a little more savage."

BRITISH COLONEL ARTHUR FREMANTLE, OBSERVER AT PICKETT'S CHARGE, COMMENTING ON GENERAL JAMES LONGSTREET

galloping, riderless, away from the Yankee guns; no trace of the general's body was ever found.

By now the Confederates had closed to within 100 yards of the Union line, and some of the defenders at the stone wall began to fall back. Heartened, the Rebels poured a volley into them, then another, and surged forward. "The Federal gunners stood manfully to their guns," a Southern lieutenant remembered. "I never saw more gallant bearing in any men. They fired their last shots full in our faces and so close that I thought I felt distinctly the flame of the explosion." One young artillery officer, holding his guts in his hands, ran his gun right up to the wall and fired off a last round into the attacking ranks. Then a bullet slammed into his mouth and out the back of his head.

Lewis Armistead, the only one of Pickett's field commanders left standing, had made it to the stone wall in front of the copse. Still waving his black slouch hat on his sword for his men to see, he yelled,

by two other officers, he extracted the bent nail, which he mistakenly believed had been fired by a Confederate cannon. "They must be hard up for ammunition," Hancock gasped, "when they throw such shot as that." A tourniquet was applied to his wound, but he refused to leave the field. All around him on Cemetery Ridge a furious fight developed.

Not five feet apart, Rebel and Yankee fired into each other's faces. Men went at each other desperately, thrusting with bayonets, slashing with swords, bludgeoning with the butt end of muskets that they had no time to reload. A Massachusetts soldier recalled, "Foot to foot, body to body and man to man they struggled, pushed and strived and killed. The mass of wounded and heaps of dead entangled the feet of the contestants, and, underneath the trampling mass, wounded men who could no longer stand struggled, fought, shouted and killed—hatless, coatless, drowned in sweat, black with powder, red with blood, with fiendish yells and strange oaths they blindly plied the work of slaughter." The Rebel line began to waver. But some of the attackers pressed on, all the way to the copse of trees. They were few in number, however. Desperately they looked round for support—and found none.

From their positions back on Seminary Ridge, some Southern officers had watched the charge with mounting hope. "I can see with my glass our battle flag waving in the enemy's batteries," said one, "where but a moment since the Yankee colors floated in the breeze." British colonel Arthur Fremantle was standing next to Longstreet at the rail fence. Believing that the Confederates were about to carry the day, he exclaimed, "I wouldn't have missed this for anything!"

"The devil you wouldn't!" Longstreet laughed,

grimly. "I would like to have missed it very much. We've attacked and been repulsed. Look there!"

As the two officers watched, soldiers in twos and threes, then in the hundreds, began to ebb back down the slope of Cemetery Ridge. Barely two minutes after General Armistead went over the stone wall, every Confederate east of the wall had been killed, wounded, or captured. The tide had broken. The dead, a New Jersey soldier recalled, "lay in crevices of the rocks, behind fences, trees, and buildings; in thickets, where they had crept for safety, only to die in agony; by stream or wall or hedge, wherever the battle had raged or their weakening steps could carry them." The entire attack had lasted no more than an hour. It was the Confederacy's high-water mark—its northernmost penetration into Union territory.

Three among the 5,425 unwounded Confederates taken prisoner at Gettysburg stand beside a breastwork on Seminary Ridge awaiting transport to a prison camp. The Federals also seized 6,802 Confederates who had been wounded in the battle.

"Four score and seven years ago..."

Although Union commander George Meade had no stomach for a follow-up assault by his own men, Lee watched with concern as the Rebel troops streamed back to Seminary Ridge, and he prepared for a Federal counterattack. Lee rode over to Pickett, who had by now moved to the rear, and told him to prepare his division for defense. "General Lee," responded Pickett, distraught, "I have no division now."

"Come, General Pickett," Lee said calmly, "this has been my fight and upon my shoulders rests the blame. The men and officers of your command have written the name of Virginia as high today as it has ever been written before."

Despite his army's battering, Lee maintained the appearance of composure. Riding back and forth in front of the woods on Seminary Ridge, he encouraged the returning troops, speaking words of comfort to the wounded, praising their gallantry, asking their forgiveness, urging them to stand against a Union charge. One exhausted soldier, barely able to walk, saluted him. "Are you wounded?" Lee asked.

"No, general, only a little fatigued. But I'm afraid there are but few so lucky as myself."

"Ah, yes! I am very sorry. The task was too great for you, but we mustn't despond. Another time we shall succeed. Are you one of Pickett's men?"

"Yes, sir."

"Well, you had better go back and rest yourself."

Even the horses did not escape his attention. When he saw an officer beating an excitable animal with a stick, Lee called out to him: "Don't whip him, captain, don't whip him. I've got just such another foolish horse myself, and whipping does no good."

As he looked at Lee, Arthur Fremantle could detect no signs of anxiety. Turning to the Englishman, Lee said, "This has been a sad day for us, colonel, a sad day. But we can't expect always to gain victo-

At the dedication of the Gettysburg National Cemetery on November 19, 1863, President Lincoln—bareheaded and seated near the center facing the camera—prepares to deliver his stirring address. Orator Edward Everett, who spoke before Lincoln, later wrote, "I should be glad if I came as near to the central idea in two hours as you did in two minutes."

ries." Then, advising Fremantle to withdraw to a more sheltered position, he rode on.

But when Lee met up with Longstreet and other Southern officers, he seemed close to despair. "It's all my fault," he told them. "I thought my men were invincible." When an officer came up to him, almost crying, to explain the state of his unit, Lee shook his hand. "Never mind," he told the man. "All this has been *my* fault. It is I who have lost this fight, and you must help me out of it the best way you can."

The Battle of Gettysburg was over, and Pickett's Charge had passed into history. The Union army had suffered 23,000 casualties, a quarter of its strength, and the Confederates 28,000, or 40 percent. All of the Mississippi Greys had been killed or wounded. After the charge, Dr. John Holt went to check on Private Jeremiah Gage. The young man was dead.

The next day was July 4, the nation's anniversary. While Lee was planning his army's return to Virginia, 1,000 miles to the southwest Federal general Ulysses S. Grant was celebrating the surrender of Vicksburg, Mississippi. He had given the Union its most clear-cut victory of the war so far. Within nine months, Grant would leave the western theater, establish his headquarters with the Army of the Potomac, and train his sights on Robert E. Lee, a Northern soldier who might even take the measure of the great Rebel leader. The war was about to get personal.

Throughout Independence Day, the Confederate and Union armies at Gettysburg stood at bay, glaring at each other across the field of battle. They were, said one Yankee lieutenant, "like two wild beasts that had fought one another almost to death, watching for a stroke or a motion, and listening for a growl that might indicate a further continuance of the struggle."

That night Lee headed his men south, toward the Potomac River and the Shenandoah Valley beyond. He had lost the decisive battle he had sought. Yet he had expelled the invaders from Virginia for a time, and his army was far from vanquished. "We'll fight them, sir, till hell freezes over," a survivor of Pickett's Charge had shouted to his beloved commanding general, "and then we'll fight them on the ice!" ◆

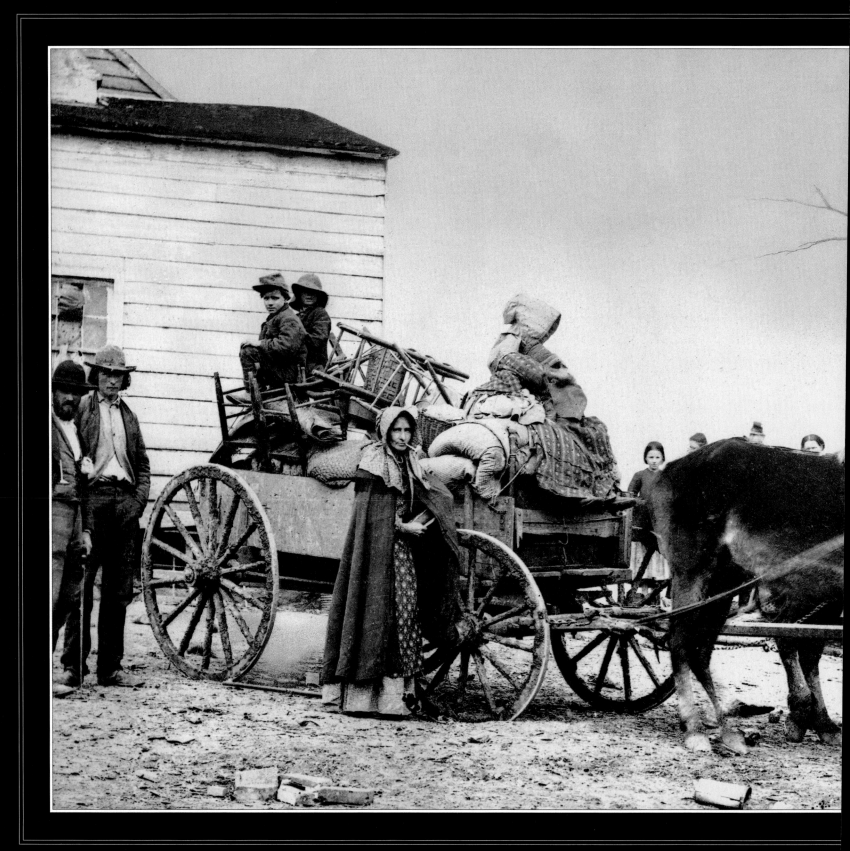

"The Yankees Are Coming!"

"All the roads as far as we could see were filled with vehicles of all sorts and descriptions, filled with women and children, and goods of all kinds…a continual stream."

ANNE FROBEL, ALEXANDRIA, VIRGINIA, MAY 1861

With most Southern men at war, their wives and children did not have many options when a Federal army approached: They could either leave their homes or stay and try to defend them. It was risky to flee, because an empty house was vulnerable to looting; worse, it might be burned to the ground. For women whose entire lives revolved around home and hearth, these were agonizing choices, typically made alone and under extreme stress.

Nor were Yankees the only soldiers that civilians had to worry about. Besides helping themselves to available foodstuffs and ani-mal fodder, the members of the Confederate army as well as those of the Union army routinely confiscated civilian horses, mules, and wagons wherever they found them, forcing many of the families in occupied territory to flee with only the belongings that they could carry. Some people escaped on foot, whereas others managed to board refugee trains, such as the one that a newspaper saw passing through eastern Tennessee whose "seats, aisles, platforms, baggage cars and tops of cars were covered with passengers, and thousands had been left at the depot begging to come."

Confederate States of America,

JACKSON, MISS. *March 17* 186*3*

Permission is granted *Mrs Wm W Patton & Child*

to visit *Charleston SC & return* upon honor not to communicate in writing or verbally, for publication, any fact ascertained, which, if known to the enemy, might be injurious to the Confederate States of America. (Subject to the discretion of the military authorities.)

J. J. Fitzpatrick
PROVOST MARSHAL.

The Virginia woman at left was lucky enough to have a team of mules to help her and her children flee to safety. To travel in Confederate war zones, civilians needed an official pass. (Above)

War on the Doorstep

"And thus I left my pleasant home, to see it never again. Heavy-hearted I was, for I knew nothing of what was before me, and I felt that I had let go the only hold I had on anything."

CORNELIA McDONALD, WINCHESTER, VIRGINIA, JULY 1863

"The orange blossoms and syringas were bursting out, and sweet violets were lurking in every nook and corner," Cornelia McDonald recalled of a spring morning in 1862. "It was the last look of beauty that scene ever wore, for as I stood by the window, the large gate opened and troop after troop of cavalry entered and wound along through the cedars that lined the drive. . . ."

Exiled from her home and grieving for a dead infant and her officer husband, Cornelia McDonald moved with her eight surviving children to Lexington, Virginia, where she gave art lessons. She wrote in December 1864: "I generally went all day with a cup of coffee and a roll. The children could eat the beans, and the sorghum molasses, but I could not. We seldom saw butter, but some idea can be formed of the difficulty of getting food when I say that I sent one hundred dollars (the proceeds of two weeks teaching) up town, and got for it a pound of fat bacon, three candles, and a pound of bad butter."

After the Battle of New Market, Eliza Clinedinst (*above, right*) nursed wounded VMI cadet Thomas G. Jefferson, 17

LIVING WITH THE ENEMY

"This is a dreadful war to make even the hearts of women so bitter!"

SARAH MORGAN IN BATON ROUGE, MAY 1862

To the widowed Sarah Hunt Fowler Morgan of Baton Rouge, Louisiana, and her daughters, May 28, 1862, began in a normal enough fashion—until a Union gunboat began shelling the town.

Twenty-year-old Sarah Morgan recalled, "Mother had just come in and was lying down, but sprang to her feet and added her screams to the general confusion. Miriam . . . ran up to quiet her, Lilly gathered her children crying hysterically all the time, and ran to the front door with them as they were; Lucy saved the baby, naked as she took her from her bath, only throwing a quilt over her. I bethought me of my 'running' bag . . . and in a moment my few precious articles were secured under my hoops, and with a sunbonnet on, I stood ready for anything."

Sarah's diary recorded the fear and confusion that swept the residents fleeing the town in order to escape the bombardment. "It was a heart-rending scene. Women searching for their babies along the road, where they had been lost, others sitting in the dust crying and wringing their hands, for by this time, we had not an idea but what Baton Rouge was either in ashes, or being plundered, and we had saved nothing."

The Morgan women found refuge with friends who were living outside the town, but after several days they decided to return home and safeguard the family property, in plain view of Union tents.

Sarah was dismayed when she examined her feelings toward the Yankee interlopers. "I hardly know myself these last few weeks, I, who have such a horror of bloodshed . . . whose only prayer is to have them sent back in peace to their own country, *I* talk of killing them! For what else do I wear a pistol and carving knife?"

In reality, the Morgans were able to live in relative peace until August. Then, when they were warned that Confederate troops were on their way to Baton Rouge in order to wrest it out of the hands of the occupiers, it became necessary for the family to aban-

Union regiments pitched tents just east of the Morgan family's Baton Rouge home (left). Sarah, 20 (above), kept a day-by-day record of life during the occupation.

"Let My People Go"

*"If I do nothing more while I live,
I shall give my children a chance to go to school."*

Charles Whiteside, FREEDMAN

Not all Southerners dreaded the arrival of the Yankees. To slaves it signaled freedom, even before Lincoln's Emancipation Proclamation of 1863. When the opportunity presented itself many slaves escaped into areas that were under Federal control and—while politicians debated this unanticipated situation—ended up in Federal refugee camps. One woman was heard to exclaim after her flight from bondage, "Bless the Lord, we'se on this side of the Jordan!"

On the Sea Islands of Georgia and South Carolina, by contrast, it was the slave owners who fled, abandoning thousands of slaves as well as large and valuable cotton crops. In the fall of 1861, the Union took control, hiring former slaves to harvest the cotton and load it on ships bound for the North. Northeastern benevolent societies sent teachers like Kate Foote of Connecticut, shown opposite with her students, to help feed and educate the destitute black islanders, who embraced education as a key to freedom. By the time the war was over approximately 9,000 former slaves along the South Carolina coast were attending classes.

A slave family fleeing north to the safety of a Federal camp fords the Rappahannock River in 1862 *(above).* Former

"ONLY DESOLATION REMAINS"

"Want and beggary are visible everywhere now. Hundreds of families in this parish are now without bread to eat, whilst but few, even of the wealthier classes, can boast of a pound of meat. The Federals on their retreat left the country a waste. The horses and mules are all gone; there is no labor left....Some neighborhoods are without men in them to bury the dead."

E. M. CULLAM, LOUISIANA, APRIL 1865

One Massachusetts officer remarked that it was "rather rough" on the civilians to have their homes looted and stripped of wood, ". . . but such is war, and war is what people wanted, especially the women, so I have not much pity for them."

For many women, such as the Frobel sisters of Alexandria, Virginia, the task of packing up their household goods and leaving a prosperous farm was simply too daunting: "There was no one to help us get ready," Anne Frobel wrote in September 1862, "and Lizzie and I could not do it alone and we well knew if such a thing was proposed to the negroes they would hoot at the idea." Anne remembered her farm "in beautiful order, luxuriant crops growing—every thing that heart could wish for. And now what a contrast, our beautiful home laid waste and destroyed, . . . all the out houses, barn, cattle sheds, fences, hedges, all our beautiful, valuable timber, every tree gone, all our orchards,

every thing—only desolation remains—and we almost in a state of starvation and beggary." The sisters sold cream from their two remaining cows to buy necessities and occasionally received food from neighbors. "Our resources are entirely exhausted . . . every thing is so high priced, and almost an impossibility to get anything from town that L. and I live almost entirely on tea and bread."

The Frobel sisters survived the entire war with Union regiments camped in their front yard: "Day after day it is the same thing. Threshing down the green fruit, robbing the beehives, tearing down the grape vines, and filling their hats with perfectly green grapes that no earthly use could be made of. Sometimes a whole squad will march by the windows and look in with the most insulting triumphant air, and call out some impudence, with their guns over their shoulders and their bayonets strung with fluttering chickens, and green melons."

On a hot day in August 1862, several slaves help a Baton Rouge family pick through the ruins of its house, which was burned by Federal forces decamping after their occupation of the city *(left)*.

CHAPTER 4

SHOWDOWN

"We cannot afford to underrate him and the army he now commands. That man will fight us every day and every hour till the end of the war."

GENERAL JAMES LONGSTREET FOLLOWING GRANT'S APPOINTMENT AS UNION GENERAL IN CHIEF

Nobody paid much heed as the army officer and the teenage boy with him made their way through the bustle of the hotel lobby. This was the Willard, the best hostelry in Washington, and through its doors passed the glittering elite of a nation at war—governors and senators, generals wearing sashes, swords, and gleaming boots, even the president of the United States himself. But this officer was ordinary looking, bearded, of less than average height, spare of build, and slightly stooped. As a matter of fact, in his shabby linen overcoat, high-crowned hat, wrinkled blue uniform, and scuffed boots he looked a bit seedy. He moved with a slouch rather than a commander's confident stride. Stepping up to the registration desk, he requested a room for himself and his son.

The clerk behind the polished oak desk eyed the man and said he had a small room on the top floor. That would be fine, the officer said, and signed the register. He and the boy, carrying a satchel, were just turning away when the clerk looked down at the register. Panic-stricken, he banged on the bell to summon a bellboy and then rushed after the man. Begging the guest's pardon, he announced that he had found something better. Not just a room but a suite, the best accommodation in the house: the

second-floor rooms where President Lincoln had stayed before his inauguration three years earlier.

What had spurred the hotel clerk into action was the simple, unassuming entry in the hotel register: "U. S. Grant and son, Galena, Illinois." The clerk, like the busy crowd in the lobby, had failed to recognize the arrival of the Union's most celebrated soldier, the fighting general with the initials that some insisted stood for "Unconditional Surrender"—the man Abraham Lincoln was counting on to win the war, Major General Ulysses S. Grant.

After his great victory at Vicksburg the previous July, Grant had been made commander of the Federal forces in the West. In November, he had won new laurels by defeating a Confederate army at Chattanooga, Tennessee. Three months later, with the clear intention of honoring Grant, Congress revived the old rank of lieutenant general. Only one other man—George Washington—had held that full three-star status. Now, on a raw March day in 1864, Grant was in Washington to receive his new commission and to take command of all the Union armies—and he accepted the clerk's offer of the Willard Hotel's best suite.

The hotel soon buzzed with the news of Grant's presence. He and 13-year-old Fred had scarcely sat

Two determined adversaries, Robert E. Lee *(far left)* and Ulysses S. Grant *(left)*, played out the war's final drama on battlefields in Virginia. By 1864 most of the incompetents in the Union high command had been weeded out, and the new leadership under Grant relentlessly pressed the Rebel Army of Northern Virginia.

At a White House reception on the evening before his formal promotion to lieutenant general, Grant stands with the president as he shakes the hand of an elegantly gowned guest. Artist Francis B. Carpenter took liberties with the facts by portraying several military men who were not actually present that evening, such as Winfield Scott, shown seated at far right.

down to begin eating their supper when other diners in the Willard's main dining room began to look over and whisper. Someone banged the table with a knife and called for quiet to announce that General Grant was among them. People leaped to their feet, cheering, shouting his name. Finally, Grant rose, nervously rubbed his mustache with his napkin, made an awkward bow, and then tried to finish his dinner. But all around him men and women pressed forward to shake his hand, and he had to abandon his meal and retire.

A little after 9:00 that evening, Grant left Fred at the hotel and walked two blocks up Pennsylvania Avenue in the direction of the White House. He intended merely to pay his respects to the president, whom he had never met; unschooled in the ways of

Washington, he did not have any idea this was the night on which Lincoln held a weekly reception. Attracted by reports that the general would be there, a larger crowd than usual jammed the public rooms of the executive mansion. Grant's entrance created a great stir. President Lincoln, greeting guests in the Blue Room, looked around to see what the excitement was about and recognized the general from his photographs. He stepped forward to grasp Grant's small hand in his own large, bony one and vigorously pumped it over and over again. "Why, here is General Grant," he exclaimed. "Well, this is a great pleasure, I assure you."

Those standing nearby were touched by the scene. Two heroes whose names would be indelibly etched in the story of the embattled republic, the

statesman and the soldier, stood face to face. Both men came from the heartland, from humble origins—and it showed. Lincoln, towering eight inches above the general, looked awkward in evening dress. His turned-down collar gaped a size too large on his long, scrawny neck, and his necktie was inexpertly tied. The president's face, beaming down at his guest, was creased with the worry of three years of civil war. Grant stood there before him, ill at ease, his head bent forward, eyes upturned, his right hand nervously tugging at the lapels of his coat.

Then Lincoln turned Grant loose to the crowd. The White House had rarely seen anything like it. "Grant! Grant! Grant!" the guests shouted, jostling one another to catch a glimpse of him. Elegantly attired women climbed up on chairs and tables to get a better view. Grant himself, egged on by the shouts of the crowd, stepped up onto a red plush sofa and stood there, blushing with embarrassment. Sweat streaked his face, and the veins on his forehead bulged. This, he thought as he looked out on the sea of rapt faces, was the hardest campaign he had ever fought.

The besieged general broke away after about an hour to meet privately with Lincoln and several aides. The meeting reinforced the president's conviction that he had found the man who would bring the Confederacy to its knees. His only concern had been political—the groundswell of support for Grant as a possible rival in the fall presidential election. But Grant expressed no interest in politics. His only inclination in that field, he said, had been to run for mayor in his hometown of Galena, so that he could pave the street that ran from the railroad station. Moreover, one of Grant's friends had shown

Grant received this commission certifying his promotion to the rank of lieutenant general on March 9, 1864. Only two years before, critics had called for Grant's removal from command in the West after heavy losses at Shiloh. Lincoln rebuffed them with a simple explanation. "I can't spare this man," said the president. "He *fights.*"

Lincoln a letter from the general disclaiming any political ambitions—"particularly so long as there is a possibility of having Mr. Lincoln reelected." The president had been relieved. He knew well the attraction of politics, the lure of high office. "When this presidential grub once gets to gnawing at a man," he told Grant's friend, "nobody can tell how far in it has got."

Lincoln briefed his general on the next day's official ceremony in which Grant would receive his third star. He gave him a copy of the short speech he planned to deliver and suggested that Grant, who was unaccustomed to public speaking, write out his own short acceptance speech ahead of time. The president recommended he say something to please the Army of the Potomac, which did not yet know him, and a few words to ease any jealousy other Union generals might feel.

Grant's speech the following afternoon in the Cabinet Room of the White House did not turn out quite as Lincoln had planned. Grant had penciled a few words of acceptance on a half sheet of notepaper. But he had a hard time reading his own writing, stumbling so badly that his embarrassment was plain for all to see. And though gracious enough—"it will be my earnest endeavor not to disappoint your expectations," he declared—Grant's words failed to mollify his fellow generals. And the Army of the Potomac was not even mentioned. The president seemed not to notice. But his secretary was quick to spot the omissions. He thought that Grant knew exactly what he was doing, that the new lieutenant general was demonstrating his independence of the White House from the outset. Given Grant's later independent prosecution of the war, the secretary may have been right.

The formalities of his promotion over, Grant prepared to leave Washington later that day in order to visit the Union forces in Virginia. But he had another appointment to keep before he boarded the train. Accompanied down Pennsylvania Avenue by Secretary of War Edwin Stanton, he stopped at the Seventh Street studio of photographer Mathew Brady. Grant had promised Brady that he would sit for a portrait, and he took a seat in what the photographer called his "operating room," in front of four big cameras.

But it was now late afternoon, the light fading, and Brady sent one of his assistants up on the roof to pull back the shades on a skylight located above Grant's head. The assistant stumbled into the skylight—and shards of glass two inches thick showered down around the nation's new general in chief. "Grant casually glanced up to see the cause of the crash," said Brady, "and there was a barely perceptible quiver of the nostrils, but that was all! It was the most remarkable display of nerve I ever witnessed."

General George G. Meade *(fourth from right)* visits an artillery staff in the vast Brandy Station encampment of the Army of the Potomac in the winter of 1863–1864. "I was much pleased with Grant," Meade remarked in a letter to his wife after meeting with his new commander. "You can rest assured that he is no ordinary man."

Stanton, however, came unhinged. He grabbed the photographer's arm and stammered, "Not a word about this, Brady, not a word! It would be impossible to convince the people that this was not an attempt at assassination."

Later that day Grant left Washington for the 60-mile trip to Brandy Station, Virginia, which was the winter headquarters of the Army of the Potomac. His special train was greeted by a driving rain and a small formal reception. A regiment of Pennsylvania Zouaves, looking snappy in their fezzes and baggy red trousers, stood smartly at attention, and a headquarters band blared forth "Hail to the Chief." Unlike other generals who gloried in such formalities, Grant felt uncomfortable. He could not for the life of him stay in step with a band, and he once remarked that he was so tone-deaf he could recognize only two tunes: "One was 'Yankee Doodle,' the other wasn't."

But Grant was pleased by the warm personal reception that was accorded him by the commander of the army, General George Meade. He might have expected Meade—one of those jealous generals whom Lincoln had wanted him to placate, and something of a snob as well—to look down on him because he was seven years Meade's junior and a midwesterner of obscure birth. For his part, Grant knew that the man lacked the killer instinct. On the same day that Grant had captured Vicksburg, Meade had hesitated to follow up the repulse of Pickett's Charge at Gettysburg and had let Robert E. Lee's beaten Army of Northern Virginia retreat back into Virginia. Now that Rebel force faced the Army of the Potomac across the Rapidan River, a tributary of the Rappahannock River, west of Fredericksburg.

In this meeting, however, both generals found something to like. Meade admired what he called Grant's "indomitable energy and great tenacity of purpose." And now he surprised Grant by putting the war effort ahead of his own career: Meade offered to step down from command if the new general in chief wanted to install someone of his own choosing. Impressed by the act of selflessness, Grant thanked Meade but asked him to stay.

Brief though it had been, Grant's time in Washington made him realize that he could not direct the war from the West as he and his old friend William Tecumseh Sherman had desired. Grant knew that he would have to stay in the East and take on the general whom many Union officers considered to be unbeatable, the one they referred to as Bobby Lee. Also, Grant needed to be near enough to Washington to maintain close relations with Lincoln, though not so close that he had to discuss every move.

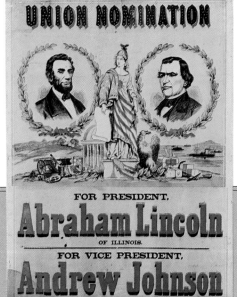

THE ELECTION OF 1864

In the summer of 1864 President Lincoln was pessimistic about his prospects for reelection in the fall. He told a friend, "I am going to be beaten. And unless some great change takes place, *badly* beaten."

The president's pessimism stemmed from the Union's continuing military failure. He had staked his presidency on the defeat of the Rebels, but his generals so far had disappointed him. Earlier he had appointed a new general in chief, Ulysses Grant, but the war was still dragging on.

The staggering death toll fueled the demands of war-weary Northerners to stop the fighting. Horace Greeley, the influential editor of the *New York Tribune*, wrote in midsummer: "Our bleeding, bankrupt, almost dying country longs for peace." The Democrats were campaigning on a peace platform, and some Republicans were agitating for Lincoln's replacement.

On September 2 a dispatch from General William Tecumseh Sherman dispelled Lincoln's gloom: "Atlanta is ours, and fairly won." The news electrified the North: Here was a decisive success that deprived Lee of an essential supply hub and revived the North's hopes. On November 8 President Lincoln was swept into office for a second term.

So in late March, after turning over the command of the western armies to Sherman, he joined the Army of the Potomac. Meade would continue to lead the army while Grant concentrated on directing overall strategy. The lieutenant general established his headquarters at Culpeper, Virginia, six miles south of the main Union camp at Brandy Station. To some people in the victory-hungry North even this was a good sign. Newspaper reporters were quick to point out that Grant was already closer to the Rebel army than was Meade.

The strategy that Grant developed in an effort to crush the Confederacy was as novel as it was simple. Up until that time, he pointed out, the various Union armies had operated independently of one another and without any coordination, "like a balky team," as he described it, "no two ever pulling together." This lack of coordination allowed the enemy to shift troops back and forth, from a quiet sector to a threatened area.

The new strategy called for all Federal forces to go on the offensive at the same time. The main thrusts were to be carried out by Grant and Meade driving south toward Richmond against Robert E. Lee, and by Sherman taking on Joseph Johnston in Georgia. As Sherman summed it up, Grant "was to go for Lee and I was to go for Joe Johnston. That was the plan."

Lincoln had urged just such an approach on his generals since the first year of the war, stressing the need to take advantage of the North's superior numbers. Hearing Grant spell out the notion that even those units not actually engaged in combat could help simply by advancing, the president nodded and cited an old western saying: "Those not skinning can hold a leg."

Grant knew that many of the veterans in the 120,000-man Army of the Potomac—those who would be responsible for doing the skinning—were convinced that they had seen it all before. After three years of fighting, they were camped only a few miles farther south than when the war began. General after general had sounded the battle cry "On to Richmond!" only to be turned back. Although the old-timers in the East did not yet realize it, Grant had in mind something new: His mission was not merely to conquer territory but also to destroy the enemy army. No matter what the toll was in human lives—Federal or Confederate—he intended to keep hammering away until that terrible goal was achieved. He would head straight south, trying to slip by Lee's eastern flank and get between him and Richmond, thus forcing the Rebel leader to fight rather than maneuver.

won a major battle in the state of Virginia. Not until Grant had met Lee and his army would it be decided whether their new commander's first name was Ulysses or "Useless."

Grant himself exuded nothing but confidence about the upcoming fight with the Southern leader. "I know Lee as well as he knows himself," he told his mother. "I know all his strong points, and all his weak ones. I intend to attack his weak points, and flank his strong ones."

On the morning of May 2, 1864, a small group of gray-clad officers rode to the top of Clark's Mountain. This was the Confederate lookout station, some 700 feet above the south bank of the Rapidan River. From here could be seen the enormous Federal encampment of tents and log huts that were sprawling over an area 10 miles square on the rolling

"I want to push on as rapidly as possible to save hard fighting. These terrible battles are very good things to read about for persons who have lost no friends, but I am decidedly in favor of having as little of it as possible. The way to avoid it is to push forward."

ULYSSES S. GRANT

"Lee's army will be your objective point," he told Meade. "Where Lee goes, you will go also."

As they prepared for the spring campaign, the Union troops who would be taking on Lee's men began to make their assessments of the new leader. One of Meade's staff officers thought that Grant had the expression of a man who had made up his mind to drive his head through a stone wall. A private thought that the general "rode his horse like a bag of meal" but liked "the look of his eye." Another of the soldiers was reassured by "his plain unassuming appearance" and "his habit of going around among the camps frequently." He even felt that "the rumors that he was occasionally subject to the besetting frailty of the soldier, injudicious drinking, tended to popularize him with the men."

Most of the troops reserved judgment, however. They knew that ever since General Lee had taken command of the Southern army in 1862 they had not

plain to the north. This sunny spring morning a dozen of the top officers of the Army of Northern Virginia—virtually the entire high command—had made the journey up the mountain. In the middle of them was Robert E. Lee.

Seated ramrod straight astride his horse, Traveller, Lee looked every inch the general. No hotel desk clerk, North or South, would have mistaken him for anything else. He was 57 years old—15 years Grant's senior—and to General John Gordon, who was riding up Clark's Mountain with him, he was "as genial as the sunlight of this beautiful day." He was held in awe just as much by the enlisted men. Indeed, the mystical bond that linked Lee and his soldiers had never been greater. He seemed to command their souls as well as their gaunt bodies. When a religious revival recently swept their camps, Lee had climbed down from Traveller and knelt among them to pray for victory. When he had reviewed one unit of troops, the outpouring of affection from the soldiers—who were ragged, ill-fed, poorly equipped, and in many cases barefoot—brought tears streaming down his cheeks.

It was Lee, above all, who sustained the faith of leaders and soldiers alike that they could still stave off the defeat of their beloved Southland. They could do this, he believed, by making Grant's coming offensive so costly that the citizens of the North would refuse to keep on paying the price. Then, in the November election, the war-weary Union would reject Lincoln and replace him with somebody who was willing to negotiate peace with the Confederacy. To defeat Lincoln, Lee decided, it would be necessary for him to wear down Grant and the Army of the Potomac. "We have got to whip them," he told one of his aides, Colonel Walter Taylor. "We *must* whip them." Then he added with a hint of his characteristic vigor: "And it has already made me feel better to think of it."

It was in order to get his generals ready to whip "the present idol of the North"—as Taylor called Grant—that Lee took them to the top of Clark's Mountain on May 2. He had been thinking hard upon the problem of where Grant would strike, and he wanted his commanders to get a feel for the terrain—and for the magnitude of the enemy army, which outnumbered them nearly two to one. "I think those people over there are going to make a move soon," he said. Then he surveyed the river with his field glasses and pointed downstream. About a dozen miles to the east Germanna Ford crossed the river; a few miles farther east was Ely's Ford. "Grant," he said, "will cross by one of those fords."

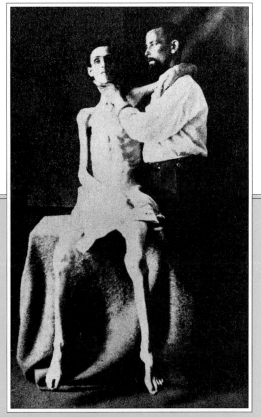

PRIVATION AND DEATH IN PRISONS

"Can those be *men?*" Walt Whitman cried when he saw Union soldiers returned from Confederate prison. Many, such as the one above, were living skeletons. The misery of prisoners on both sides resulted from neglect, especially lack of food. A Southerner imprisoned in Maryland wrote, "The writer has known large, stout men to lay in their tents at night and cry like little babies from hunger." The camps were filthy and disease ridden. Because they were so malnourished, the men had little resistance to disease; even preventive measures could harm them. For instance, vaccinations sometimes became so infected that areas of flesh the size of an orange were destroyed.

For many, the exchange of prisoners that took place near the end of the war was too late. Fifty thousand had died, and Whitman said sadly that many of the survivors **"are mentally imbecile, and will never recuperate."**

Lee based his prediction of Grant's moves on the reputation the Union leader had as someone who would take the bold, straight-ahead approach. And he hoped his hunch was right, for these fords had special geographic and strategic significance. They funneled into the region just south of the Rapidan known as the Wilderness. Lee and Stonewall Jackson had scored a great victory there a year before, at the Battle of Chancellorsville, and Lee felt he could do it again. He figured that the huge Federal army would be unable to maneuver effectively in the difficult terrain of the Wilderness. A fight there could help to even out Grant's superiority in numbers and artillery, which would have little room in which to operate. Lee intended to let Grant cross the Rapidan unopposed, then strike eastward against the Union right flank with his faster-marching army.

On the morning of May 4, two days after Lee's prediction to his top generals, the wigwagging of signal flags from his lookouts atop Clark's Mountain proved him right. Grant was crossing the Rapidan just where Lee had said. The news reached Lee at his headquarters, 20 miles southwest of Germanna Ford at the small town of Orange Court House. Usually cheerful at mealtimes, he seemed positively ecstatic over breakfast as he said grace and then gave the news to his staff. Of Grant, he quipped: "We might have him to breakfast with us."

For the moment, Lee's army was without the presence of James Longstreet and his men. Lee's "Old Warhorse" was marching in from a camp 40 miles to the southwest and was expected that night. But the Confederate commander could not wait. By noon, Lee had two columns of troops heading eastward into the Wilderness on the Orange-Fredericksburg turnpike and the Orange Plank road—little more than wide paths through the thickets, despite their names—running roughly parallel with the river. Their paths led the Confederates straight toward the Federal army inching its way south.

While Lee rode with his southern column along the Orange Plank road around noon on May 4, his Union counterpart was crossing the Rapidan River at Germanna Ford. Grant, sitting easily on his bay mount, Cincinnati, was uncharacteristically dressed up for the occasion. Instead of his customary plain-looking private's uniform, he wore a sword and sash, black felt hat with gold officer's cord around it, and his best dress coat. The three stars on his shoulder straps glinted in the sunlight. Accompanying the general as his guest for the opening of the campaign was Elihu Washburne, the Illinois congressman who had introduced the bill resulting in the revival of the rank of lieutenant general. The congressman was dressed in black with a stovepipe hat, giving rise to the rumor in the passing ranks that Grant had brought his own undertaker with him.

Once on the south bank of the river, Grant established temporary headquarters at a deserted farmhouse on a bluff with a view of the ford. He sat in the afternoon sun on the front steps of the house smoking a cigar and contentedly watching the steady procession of troops tramping across two bridges made of canvas pontoons and disappearing into the Wilderness. He had half expected Lee to hit him at the river crossings, and he was pleased that things were going so well. He was in such good humor, as a matter of fact, that he did not bark when a newspaper correspondent stepped forward and asked the question even Lincoln had hesitated to raise: "General Grant, about how long will it take you to get to Richmond?"

"I will agree to be there in about four days."

Then, seeing disbelief on the reporter's face, Grant added wryly, "That is, if General Lee becomes a party to the agreement. But if he objects, the trip will undoubtedly be prolonged."

Confirmation that Lee did indeed object came that afternoon when a Federal signal officer deciphered a Confederate message from Clark's Mountain. It indicated the enemy was on the move. But where was it moving? Grant fired off orders to the rear elements of his column—which were still 20 miles or more behind—to march to the river crossing. He did not, however, revoke his instructions that all the infantry on the south bank halt and camp in the Wilderness that night to await the arrival of the slow-moving supply train. The 4,000 wagons and ambulances—which, if lined up single file, would stretch out for 65 miles—were not due until the following afternoon. Grant realized the danger of delaying his advance out of the Wilderness, but his supplies had to be protected.

The Army of the Potomac crossed the Rapidan River near the Wilderness on May 4, 1864. Five temporary bridges, each one assembled from a number of pontoon boats like those shown in the inset above, were put in place by Union engineers in less than two hours.

Some of Grant's advance units bivouacked on the eastern edge of the Wilderness near Chancellorsville amid grim reminders of the battle that had been fought there only one year previously. The colonel of a Pennsylvania regiment found the burial sites of fallen comrades sprouting wildflowers and sweet-smelling forget-me-nots. The officer, who would go to his own grave just 10 days later, spoke of the goodness of a Creator who could drape these last resting places of brave men with beauty and perfume.

Elsewhere in the area, shallow graves that had been eroded by winter rains yielded the bones of last year's dead. One soldier counted 50 skulls in a spot less than 300 yards square. Troops from New Jersey, stumbling upon a skull still wearing its cap, looked under the visor and found the name of a sergeant who had served with their regiment at the Battle of Chancellorsville.

A rookie private from New York, Frank Wilkeson, listened intently as old hands described the grim details of the battle. Wilkeson, seized by "the war fever," had run away from his home in the Hudson River Valley the previous year at age 16 to join an artillery outfit. Now, as he contemplated the possibility of actual combat, his war fever was fading rapidly. The youth's fellow artillerymen had built a fire by which to light their pipes, and they sat around it talking. The flames lent searing truth to the story of one veteran who told about how the woods had caught fire, cremating some of the wounded soldiers lying helpless on the ground.

Wilkeson grew uneasy. "The dead were all around us," he wrote. "Their eyeless skulls seemed to stare steadily at us."

As the men sat silently smoking and listening to the veteran's story, another soldier had been prying in the dirt with his bayonet. Rolling a skull on the ground in front of them, he said in a deep, low voice, "That is what you are all coming to, and some of you will start toward it tomorrow."

The next day, May 5, the opening shots in the Battle of the Wilderness were fired shortly after dawn. Around 6:00 a.m., near the intersection of the Orange-Fredericksburg turnpike and the Germanna Ford road, the lead Federal troops came under attack from the west. The Rebels were on the Union flank. For nearly six hours the two sides skirmished with each other before 12,000 Union soldiers finally launched an assault along both sides of the turnpike. They plunged into the thicket—and into what was perhaps the most confused and chaotic battle of the entire war.

Trying to fight in the Wilderness, troops could see barely 50 feet in front of them. Almost immediately the attacking units lost touch with one another, their carefully dressed lines of battle swallowed up in the underbrush. Their line of sight cut short by the tangles of briers, vines, and trees, officers lost all sense of direction and tried to maneuver their units by compass. Soldiers became separated from their units and found themselves fighting alone or in small clusters. Unable to get opponents in their musket sights, troops would listen for the enemy's shot and then fire wildly in that direction—shooting by "ear-sight," the Federals called it. Sometimes, in the confusion, soldiers struck down their own comrades.

Seated on a log beside the Rapidan River, General Grant prepares a telegram to Washington in this contemporary drawing by Alfred R. Waud. "Crossing of the Rapidan effected," the message read. "Forty eight hours will now demonstrate whether the enemy intends giving battle this side of Richmond." The Battle of the Wilderness erupted the following day.

It was, said one Union private, "a blind and bloody hunt to the death, in bewildering thickets, rather than a battle."

But despite the problems that went along with advancing in such rugged terrain, the overwhelming numbers taking part in the Union attack began to drive the Confederate troops back. As the Rebels broke and ran to the rear, Yankees drove forward along both sides of the Orange-Fredericksburg turnpike.

This sudden crisis galvanized into action the Confederate commander on the turnpike, General Richard Ewell. A thin, pale man of 47 with a beak of a nose and precious little hair, Ewell was known to the troops as Old Baldhead. He rode a flea-bitten gray named Rifle whom an old friend thought "singularly like him—so far as a horse could be like a man." As a result of a battle in 1862 Ewell had lost a leg and now had to be lifted into the saddle and strapped on. But he was still a superb horseman. Seeing the center of his line collapsing, Ewell rode Rifle hellbent toward the rear in search of reinforcements to plug the gap. Coming up the turnpike he spotted just the kind of outfit he was looking for, the Georgia Brigade of General John Gordon. These Georgians and their gallant young leader, who was not yet 32, had helped save the day time and again when the Confederates needed it most. Now was one of those occasions.

Ewell galloped up to the oncoming troops and abruptly reined in Rifle, nearly banging his wooden leg into Gordon's knee. He did not need to explain the situation. Gordon had followed the progress of the fight by the battle cries of the opposing sides, the Rebel yell and then the huzzahs of the Yankees. "As these ominous huzzahs grew in volume we knew that Grant's lines were moving forward," recalled Gordon. "The raining of Union bullets as they whizzed and rattled through the scrub-oaks and pines, rendered explanations superfluous." Without preamble, Ewell announced, "General Gordon, the fate of the day depends on you, sir!"

Gordon, a former lawyer who possessed a flair for the flamboyant gesture, spoke boldly both to reassure Ewell and to rouse the pride of his troops, who had crowded up close to hear what the two officers had to say to each other. "These men will save it, sir!" Turning to them, Gordon began to snap out orders. And as his soldiers went charging straight up the turnpike, he called out words to encourage them. "Boys, there are Yankees in front and lots of them," he shouted. "*We* must move them. Now all who are faint-hearted fall out." He continued, "We do not want any to go but heroes—we want brave Georgians!"

Bones washed out of the shallow graves of men killed in the Battle of Chancellorsville in 1863 gave macabre welcome to Union soldiers entering the Wilderness the following year. "It grew dark and we built a fire," recalled one private. "The dead were all around us; their eyeless skulls seemed to stare steadily at us."

As he moved to the attack, a private heard the weird cry of one of his fellow Confederates. "He could halloo the queerest that I ever heard anyone," he remembered. "It was a kind of a scream or low, like a terrible bull, with a kind of neigh mixed along with it, and it was nearly as loud as a steam whistle." Then all the men took up a yell so loud that it drowned out the din of gunfire, and the private could tell when his own musket fired only by the kick of its recoil against his shoulder.

The suddenness of the Confederate counterattack blunted the Union breakthrough and turned the Yankees back. But sparks from gunpowder ignited the dry underbrush, and fires began to flare up everywhere. As the flames intensified, they trapped the wounded of both sides, licking at the cartridge boxes strapped to their bellies. A New York Zouave

heard the pop! pop! of cartridges exploding. He thought the sounds "almost cheerful" at the time, as they gave "no hint of the almost dreadful horror their noise bespoke." The explosions were blowing holes in the helpless screaming victims, and he later saw that "the bodies of the dead were blackened and burned beyond all possibility of recognition."

A mile or so east of the battle on the turnpike, on a knoll near the intersection with the Germanna Ford road, Ulysses Grant sat on a stump whittling a small stick with his penknife. That morning he had partaken of his usual breakfast, coffee and a sliced cucumber dipped in vinegar, then supplied himself with enough cigars to last the day. While the fighting raged, he smoked one cigar after another, his head wreathed in smoke. Despite his earlier reluctance to fight it out in the Wilderness, once the engagement began he ordered his men to press the attack on Lee's army. Sitting there with his coat unbuttoned in the afternoon heat, cutting sticks into small chips, he was an island of calm in a turbulence of staff officers and couriers coming and going.

Much to the disappointment of the young New York artilleryman, Frank Wilkeson, the big Union guns that could have proved so decisive against the Rebels were largely silent. As Lee had known, there was only enough open ground to employ a few cannon. Wilkeson's battery was placed in reserve several miles to the rear of the fighting over on the Orange-Fredericksburg turnpike. But "wild with curiosity," the young soldier decided to sneak away from his unit and go to the front. Hurrying west on the turnpike, he passed hundreds of wounded men leaving the field of battle. He also discovered to his surprise that provost guards were posted along the road with orders to prevent anyone from going to the rear—at gunpoint, if necessary—unless they could "show blood."

"Can I go past you?" Wilkeson asked one of the sentinels, seeking permission to move to the front.

"Yes, you can go up," the man replied. Then he added a warning. "If you go up, you may not be al-

lowed to return, and then"—he shrugged his shoulders—"you may get killed. But suit yourself."

Wilkeson did. But soon he found himself thinking that the guard's prediction was about to come true. Huddling 40 yards from the battle line behind a large oak tree, he listened with horror as bullets smashed into the bark on the other side of the tree trunk. "My heart thumped wildly for a minute," he remembered, "then my throat and mouth felt dry and queer." He looked down and saw at his feet a dead sergeant with a hole in his forehead. Wilkeson bent down and unbuckled the cartridge belt from the man's still-warm body and picked up his rifle. Before he knew it, he was in the thick of the fighting, "blazing away at an indistinct smoke-and-tree obscured line of men clad in gray." At times he could not even see the Confederates in front of him, but that made no difference—"we kept on firing just as though they were in full view."

Wilkeson watched as one of his newfound comrades, a youth of about 20, took a bullet in the thigh. The man gingerly tried walking on the wounded leg, found it still worked, and resumed firing. A few minutes later, when another bullet gashed his arm, he tied his handkerchief around the wound and stepped back into line alongside the young artilleryman. "You're fighting in bad luck today," Wilkeson told him. "You'd better get away from here." The man's luck was not about to improve, however. Just as he turned to answer Wilkeson, his head jolted back as a bullet smashed through his jaw. "A tiny fountain of blood and teeth and bones and bits of tongue burst out his mouth," Wilkeson recalled. "I looked directly into his open mouth, which was ragged and bloody and tongueless. He cast his rifle furious on the ground and staggered off."

During the late afternoon, the violence along the turnpike subsided into stalemate, and a separate battle rose in wrath three miles to the south. Here, too, the focus was a key road junction, the intersection of the Orange Plank road and the Brock road, the continuation of the Federal route south from Germanna Ford. If General A. P. Hill's column of

Confederates, pushing eastward along the Orange Plank road—so named because it was paved with wooden planks—could reach the junction, it could slice through the middle of Grant's columns strung out along the Brock road.

The critical nature of the fighting here already had been demonstrated in a dramatic incident that had taken place earlier that afternoon. Lee, riding at the head of Hill's men, had selected for his headquarters a field at the little farm of the widow Tapp about a mile west of the junction. He rode into a small clearing there on the left-hand side of the Orange Plank road, dismounted, and sat in the shade of a grove of trees conferring with Hill and his cavalry chief, Jeb Stuart. Lee was worried about the separation of his two forces. There was a gap of two miles to the north between Hill's troops on the Orange Plank road and Ewell's soldiers fighting along the turnpike. Lee was concerned that the Federals might find it and come between his two wings.

The danger Lee perceived was closer than he could have imagined. Out of a stand of pines located just to the north emerged a party of blue-clad soldiers deployed in a skirmish line, muskets at the ready. Hill sat stunned. Stuart jumped up and stared in disbelief. Only Lee had the presence of mind to seek help. He hurried off, loudly calling for his adjutant to order up troops to deal with the intruders. The Yankees paused on the edge of the woods within musket range of the Confederate generals, close enough, certainly, to rush forward and capture Robert E. Lee. But the Union officer evidently did not realize that he had the war's greatest prize within his grasp. He hesitated there, startled to find himself in the presence of a cluster of men in gray. Then he gave the command "Right about!" and his men faded back into the timber without firing a shot. Lee blessed his good fortune and then set about redeploying troops. While half of Hill's men covered the road, the rest were to fill the gap to the north, linking up with Ewell's line below the turnpike to ensure that no more Federals filtered through to the widow Tapp's farm.

"[I] stumbled and fell, and my outflung hands pushed up a smolder of leaves. The fire sprang into flame, caught in the hair and beard of a dead sergeant, and lighted a ghastly face and wide open eyes. I rushed away in horror."

MAJOR ABNER SMALL, 16TH MAINE

As some of Hill's units moved into position just north of the Orange Plank road, a chaplain took advantage of a lull in the fighting there to conduct a prayer service. To a lieutenant from South Carolina it was one of the most impressive scenes that he had ever witnessed. He looked up at "the blue, placid heavens," around him at the early green foliage of spring, and then at his men in prayer. "And here knelt," he wrote, "browned veterans striving for another struggle with death." The rapid and severe blast of musketry roused the lieutenant from his reverie. The troops fell into line and headed in the direction of the firing.

It was almost 5:00 p.m., and the Union troops were attacking in force along the Orange Plank road and on both sides of it. Lee's men, numbering perhaps 14,000, faced odds here of at least two to one. But they possessed the advantage of defensive positions. The blue-clad foe stumbled through the thicket, with briers tearing at their clothes and slashing their faces and the low branches ripping the muskets from their hands.

Meanwhile, the Rebel defenders hid behind trees, flopped down prone in the underbrush, or even climbed trees in order to unleash a storm of musket fire. On both sides, the stretchers carried the wounded to the rear and returned laden with fresh cartridge boxes for the men at the front. A wounded Confederate walked back from the fighting saying, "Dead Yankees were knee deep all over about four acres of ground."

But Grant did not have any intention of easing the pressure on the Rebels. Indeed, he kept feeding the fight, sending additional troops into the inferno along the Orange Plank road. Lee and his generals had never seen the Army of the Potomac press the attack with such vigor. And around 6:00 p.m. a courier came racing back to Lee and Hill's headquarters on the Tapp farm bringing with him alarming news. The hole between the forces of Hill and Ewell had reopened a half-mile or so north of the Orange Plank road, and the Yankees were again on the brink of breaking through. Hill had not a sin-

gle unit available to prevent it, except 125 Alabamans who were detailed to guard the swelling ranks of blue-clad prisoners in the rear. Hill scraped up enough wounded and other noncombatants to handle the guard duty and then brought the Alabamans forward. He ordered them to move into the gap on the left, raising enough of a ruckus by firing their weapons and yelling to suggest far greater numbers.

Hill's ploy worked. The Yankees, who were blinded by the underbrush, took the bait, obeying the evidence of their ears. Their attack bogged down, and when darkness fell the battle lines remained essentially where they had been early that afternoon.

Soon after dark, the Union artilleryman Frank Wilkeson was resting among the front-line infantry near the Orange-Fredericksburg turnpike when he heard the news of the Orange Plank road battle. The information came from visiting "campwalkers" or "newsmongers," soldiers who took it upon themselves to gather and disseminate stories from the day's fighting. These shadowy forms hurried through the woods and along the roads, carrying the news from unit to unit. It was supposedly a soldier's point of honor never to lie to them. "Privates of the army," wrote Wilkeson, "never believed a report that was published from headquarters, unless it corresponded with the information the 'campwalkers' had gathered." Intrigued by the accounts of the fighting that day to the south, the young man decided to wander down to the lines of a regiment from his own state of New York in the Orange Plank road vicinity.

Stumbling in the dark over the dead and the wounded—who cursed him roundly—Wilkeson made his way through the woods. Finally, he found his fellow New Yorkers and began to settle down for the night. As he lay down in a pair of blankets that had been confiscated from a corpse, he felt haunted—by memories of the grim stories that were told around the campfire on the previous night, by this day's terrible scenes in the blazing woods, and by the agonizing cries of the wounded. "The prospect of fire running through the woods where they lay helpless, unnerved the most courageous of men," he re-

called. "I saw one man, both of whose legs were broken, lying on the ground with his cocked rifle by his side and his ramrod in his hand. I knew he meant to kill himself in case of fire—knew it as surely as I could read his thoughts."

The following morning, May 6, opened with a full-scale Union assault along the Orange Plank road. At 5:00 a.m., precisely at the hour ordered by Grant, more than 20,000 Federals surged forward on a front more than a mile wide, and the Battle of the Wilderness was on again. Among them, and most unwillingly on this cool and cloudless morning, was Frank Wilkeson. Awake long before dawn, Wilkeson had attempted to return to his artillery battery. But in the road he was stopped by one of the sentinels posted to keep combatants who could not "show blood" from ducking the fight. Wilkeson explained that he had gone to the front the day before just to see the battle. "You have a rifle," the guard replied. "You have a belt and a cartridge box. Your mouth is powder-blackened. You have been fighting as an infantryman, and you shall so continue to fight."

So Wilkeson, fortifying himself with a plug of tobacco and two canteens confiscated from the dead, rejoined the foot soldiers and found himself swept up in the dawn attack. He soon overcame his fears, however, when the Confederates ahead of him began to withdraw. "We charged, and charged, and charged again," he remembered, "and had gone wild with battle fever. We were doing splendidly."

Leading the Union attack was the capable Winfield Scott Hancock. He was still bothered by a wound in the groin suffered in the repulse of Pickett's Charge at Gettysburg, and General Meade had given him permission to ride in an ambulance. But this morning he was on horseback, his commanding figure towering high as he stood up in the stirrups to see the way forward, his face flushed with the excitement of battle. When one of Meade's aides came down to check on the progress of the offensive, Hancock exulted, "We are driving them, sir! Tell General Meade we are driving them most beautifully."

Out in front of a brigade of Federal infantry, Union skirmishers advance cautiously through the Wilderness in this painting by Civil War veteran Julian Scott. The thick underbrush of the Wilderness impeded the skirmish line, one officer reported, "often breaking it completely."

The early assault had caught the Confederates in a state of disarray. Their jumbled lines, pummeled in the previous day's fighting, resembled "a worm fence" in the judgment of one of General A. P. Hill's aides. The army had slept on its arms, most of the men passing the night right where they had fired their last shot. Hill had not tried to straighten them out during the night; his men were exhausted and should get what rest they could. Besides, James Longstreet was expected to arrive by daybreak and relieve the front-line troops. But morning had come, and Longstreet and his force were still on the road. Unrelieved, the battle-weary Rebels retreated. "There was no panic and no great haste," said one soldier. "The men seemed to fall back from a deliberate conviction that it was impossible to hold the ground, and, of course, foolish to attempt it."

But Lee, sitting astride Traveller at the widow Tapp's farm watching his troops streaming to the rear, could not believe his eyes. Never had he been pressed this hard. He rode out to an officer and demanded, with rising anger, "Is this splendid brigade of yours running like a flock of geese?"

"These men are not whipped," the officer said in defense of his men. "They only want a place to form and they will fight as well as they ever did."

Lee clearly saw the danger. Only a dozen cannon deployed along the Tapp farm's western edge stood between him and the onrushing Yankees. The guns, with General A. P. Hill helping man the weapons himself, began shelling the woods in front of them. As a blue-clad line emerged from the trees, the cannon cut through the enemy ranks like a scythe. Lee, meanwhile, sent an aide to the rear to prepare the supply wagons for retreat in case the Federals broke through. He sent another aide back to find Longstreet and hasten forward the reinforcements who were now his last desperate hope.

The famous Texas Brigade under Lieutenant General James Longstreet carried this flag into battle as they rushed into the faltering Confederate center following a 30-mile march to the Wilderness front. "Hurrah for Texas," Lee shouted as they passed. The brigade rolled back the Union advance, but at a cost of nearly half of its men in the first 10 minutes of fighting.

James Longstreet was coming, and he had his old friend Grant very much on his mind. No general in the Confederate army knew the Union commander better than Lee's "Old Warhorse." He had gone to West Point with Grant, had been a guest at his wedding, and had served with him in Mexico. Moreover, he had studied Grant's methods of warfare. "We cannot afford to underrate him and the army he now commands," Longstreet had told an officer who suggested the new lieutenant general would be easy pickings. "That man will fight us every day and every hour till the end of the war."

Longstreet's 10,000-man force had been on the march for a day and a half, with only a few hours out for sleep. Tramping through the dark since 1:00 a.m., they had gotten lost when an overgrown trail simply petered out in the thicket. Longstreet had taken advantage of the delay to form his troops into double columns, which would result in faster deployment when they reached the battlefield. The veteran Texas Brigade led the way.

At last, around 6:00 a.m., a cheer went up from the rear of the Confederate lines, echoing all the way to Lee's post at the Tapp farm. "Here they come! Here's Longstreet! It's all right now!" In two columns, muskets at the ready, they marched up the Orange Plank road through the retreating ranks of their comrades with a precision that, to one admiring onlooker, was "wonderfully beautiful." Caught up in the excitement, Lee rode out to meet Longstreet's advance guard. "Who are you, my boys?" he yelled.

"Texas boys!"

"Hurrah for Texas!" Lee shouted, waving his hat in circles above his head. "Hurrah for Texas!"

He formed the lead 800 men into line of battle and then, giving way to the emotion of the moment, spurred Traveller forward and tried to lead the charge himself: a lone horseman and a line of foot soldiers. When the troops realized what he was doing, they cried, "Lee to the rear! Lee to the rear!" He paid them no heed, and the men, horrified that "Marse Robert" would needlessly expose himself to Yankee fire, slackened their pace, shouting, "We won't go on unless you go back."

Red-faced, eyes ablaze, Lee was behaving like a man possessed. The instincts of the warrior threatened to overwhelm the duties of the commander. It was as if he were trying to get at Grant himself. An officer tried to head him off, and a tall sergeant grabbed Traveller's reins. But only when an aide rode up and shouted that Longstreet had come up and awaited his pleasure did Lee emerge from his trance. Glaring over his shoulder toward the enemy, he reluctantly turned his horse away as the Texans were swallowed up in the forest. The commander of an Alabama regiment just then arriving at the front saw the Confederate leader watch his men sweep past. Lee's face was still flushed and full of animation. "I thought him at that moment the grandest specimen of manhood I ever beheld," he said of his commander. "He looked as though he ought to have been and was monarch of the world." Said a courier riding nearby, tears streaming down his face, "I would charge hell itself for that old man."

Longstreet assured Lee that his men would recover all the lost ground if the commanding general would just permit him to take charge of the troops. He delivered on his promise. The Texas Brigade, boasting that they had "put General Lee under arrest and had sent him to the rear," broke the force of the Federal advance, though at a cost of half their numbers dead or wounded in less than 10 minutes.

The South lost one of its most gifted officers, General Micah Jenkins, on the second day of fighting in the Wilderness when friendly fire from Virginia troops swept through a party of Confederate officers as they were planning an assault on the Union flank. Jenkins, who had once boasted that no Yankee bullet could kill him, was mortally wounded. His battle-damaged sword and scabbard are shown above.

One Confederate officer recalled, "There was a terrible crash, mingled with wild yelling which settled down into a steady roar of musketry."

But Longstreet—with none of the reluctance for the offensive that he had shown at Gettysburg—was at his combative best. He coolly poured in his units against the Yankees. The hail of Rebel bullets was so intense along the Orange Plank road that over on the receiving end Frank Wilkeson swore he could catch a pot full of them if he just had "a strong iron vessel rigged on a pole as a butterfly net." Fearing the Union line would break—Wilkeson could hear officers steadying their regiments "as one speaks to frightened and excited horses"—he and his comrades kept firing and ripping open new cartridges of gunpowder with their teeth until they ached. Still the Confederates came on. Restoring the previous front line by the middle of the morning, Longstreet then went on the attack. Around noon he sent a large force off to the right along an unfinished railroad bed several hundred yards south of the Orange Plank road. These troops, swinging north, smashed Hancock's unprotected southern flank—and in the Union general's words, "rolled it up like a wet blanket." Longstreet felt certain he had pulled off "another Bull Run" on the Yankees. Then, about an hour later, Longstreet rode forward on the Orange Plank road to prepare for a follow-up assault all along the line that he felt could rout his old friend Grant and drive the Federals back against the fords of the Rapidan. One of Longstreet's officers, Micah Jenkins, a 28-year-old South Carolina aristocrat, shared Longstreet's optimism. "I am happy," he told his commander. "I have felt despair for the cause for some months, but am relieved, and feel assured that we will put the enemy back across the Rapidan before night."

Only minutes after Jenkins had finished speaking, shots rang out from the woods on the right side of the road. In the confusion of preparing for the advance, Virginians there had seen fellow Confederates up ahead on the road and mistaken them for Yankees. Longstreet's party was caught in the volley. "Friends! We are friends!" an officer shouted, and the firing stopped. But it was moments too late. A courier and staff captain were killed instantly. Micah Jenkins was hit in the head and fell to the ground, his body in convulsions. And a bullet struck Longstreet between the neck and the right shoulder with such impact that it lifted his heavy frame out of the saddle momentarily. He settled heavily back and instinctively started to ride on before staff members could stop his horse and ease him to the ground. Blood bubbling from his mouth, he gasped instructions to continue the attack.

As Longstreet was borne to the rear on a stretcher, his hat over his face to shield his eyes, stunned onlookers remarked upon the bitter irony. It had been almost exactly a year before, just five miles up the road in this same Wilderness during the Battle of Chancellorsville, when the great Stonewall Jackson was shot. And, like today, he had been fired on by his own men after making a successful flanking maneuver. Seeing Longstreet's hat over his face, soldiers by the roadside concluded, "He is dead, and they are telling us he is only wounded." Longstreet, hearing his premature death pronounced, reached up with his left hand and raised his hat. A great outburst of cheers followed him to the rear. The Old Warhorse would survive. Micah Jenkins would not.

Despite Longstreet's instructions to keep up the offensive, his removal from the field delayed the planned Confederate attack until late afternoon. By that time Hancock had his men well entrenched behind chest-high walls of logs at the Brock road intersection. But Hancock was nervous. He believed

that a general should be seen—by his own men as well as by the enemy—and he thrived on the ability to ride up and down the lines, the way he had done on Cemetery Ridge at Gettysburg. This was impossible in the Wilderness, however, where the enemy was often hidden from sight. Here, where moving figures were glimpsed only at intervals, it was, said one veteran, "a battle of invisibles with invisibles." Moreover, Hancock and his men were facing a second foe: In addition to the Rebel assault, a forest fire was moving toward them.

Dry leaves and underbrush had been ignited that morning during the fighting to the west. Fanned by a stiff wind, the inferno had roared eastward, suffocating wounded soldiers trapped between the lines. Through the flames came masses of yelling South Carolinians and Georgians, "advancing like so many devils," thought a Pennsylvania soldier. Blistered by the fire and blinded by billowing black smoke, the two sides stood and blazed away at each other—in places only a dozen paces apart.

To a New Yorker trapped in this nightmare, "the fire was the most terrible enemy our men met that day." He watched as logs south of the Orange Plank road caught fire, forcing some of the Federals to fall back. Then he saw Southerners leap into the burning breastworks to plant their regimental flags, only to be hurled back by a combination of artillery firing at point-blank range, a counterattack by Union infantry, and the still-raging flames that seared and killed impartially.

An hour or so later, the Federal commanders' attention was drawn to Rebel action several miles to the north, on the other end of the line. The turnpike sector had been relatively quiet until near sundown, when John Gordon finally got permission from Lee to mount an attack Gordon had been urging upon his immediate superiors all day. With his Georgians

Union soldiers carry a wounded comrade from the burning battlefield on a stretcher rigged from muskets and a blanket in this drawing by eyewitness Alfred R. Waud. Nearly 200 wounded soldiers were burned alive when the Wilderness was swept by brush fires ignited during the fighting.

In the burning woods of the Wilderness —

and a brigade of newly arrived North Carolinians, Gordon made a wide swing to his left and came down upon the exposed Union flank more than a mile north of the turnpike.

News of the surprise attack started pouring in to Grant's headquarters shortly after 7:00 p.m.: In less than an hour, the Rebels had taken 600 prisoners and killed or wounded 400. But there were reports of even greater disasters—that the entire right flank had collapsed and that a high-ranking general had been captured—and these, Grant was positive, had to be exaggerations. The Union leader calmly interrogated each of the couriers in order to sift out the kernel of truth from the rumors. Unruffled, he was seated on a stool in front of his tent smoking a fresh cigar and whittling sticks—his new cotton gloves now in tatters—when a high-ranking officer rode up and excitedly predicted imminent disaster. "I know Lee's methods well by past experience," the officer told him. "He will throw his whole army between us and the Rapidan, and cut us off completely from our communications!"

Grant rose from the stool and took the cigar out of his mouth. "Oh, I am heartily tired of hearing about what *Lee* is going to do," he retorted angrily. "Some of you always seem to think he is suddenly going to turn a double somersault, and land in our rear and on both of our flanks at the same time. Go back to your command, and try to think what we are going to do ourselves, instead of what *Lee* is going to do!" The officer—who was rumored among the ranks to be General Meade himself—walked off without saying a word.

Grant's uncharacteristic flareup reflected the unbearable tension of that terrible day. Even as his troops stabilized the threatened northern flank, and darkness closed in to end the fighting, he knew that the toll of casualties would be high. In fact, two days of battle had cost the Federals as many men as had the Battle of Chancellorsville. Grant had not seen such fighting since the first day at Shiloh.

But the lieutenant general had precious little to show for his losses. All of his attacks had been repulsed, and both of his flanks had narrowly escaped collapse. By 8:00 p.m. Grant was even running out of cigars—he had smoked 20 that day, a record. But to the astonishment of his oldest aides, he went into his tent, pulled down the flap, and lay down on his camp bed.

Just 10 minutes after Grant entered his tent, another alarming report was received of the fighting on the right. One of Grant's aides, Colonel Horace Porter, went to inform the general—and found him sleeping soundly. Porter roused him and told him the news. But Grant was convinced the report was a gross exaggeration. In any case, he had already strengthened his defenses in that part of the field. Grant turned over on his bed and went back to sleep. Porter would remember the incident 21 years later, as he sat by his old commander's deathbed. Grant was dying of cancer then, enduring terrible pain, and suffering from insomnia. He remembered that night too. "Ah, yes," he told Porter. "It seems strange that I, who always slept so well in the field, should now pass whole nights in the quiet of this peaceful house without being able to close my eyes."

While Grant resettled himself on his camp bed on the night of May 6, his soldiers were speculating about what would come next. Many guessed their new commander would follow the precedent that had been set by his predecessors and pull back after a hard battle. But Grant had made up his mind: Whatever happened, he had decided, there would be no turning back.

The morning of May 7 Robert E. Lee made a tour of the battlefield with General John Gordon. There had been a standoff between the two armies for two days now, and Lee felt sure he knew what the Union leader would do next. Even though the Northerners had suffered twice as many casualties as the Confederates, Lee predicted that Grant would not retreat. Instead, he would move his army to Spotsylvania, a tiny hamlet a dozen miles to the southeast. Surprised, the Georgian wondered if Lee had some sort of intelligence about such a move-

Officers of the Army of the Potomac relax on pews carried out to their temporary headquarters, Massaponax Church in Spotsylvania County, on May 21, 1864. At left, General Grant peers over General Meade's shoulder as the two men consult a map while planning their attack on Lee's forces at Cold Harbor.

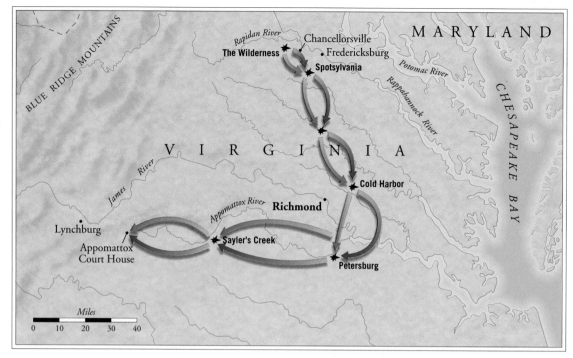

During six weeks of fighting that moved in a southeasterly direction along a 100-mile-long course, Grant *(blue arrows)* tried again and again to maneuver around the Rebel right flank *(red arrows).* At Petersburg, the out-numbered Confederates entrenched themselves to wait out a relentless Yankee siege.

ment. "Not at all, not at all," Lee told him. "But that is the next point at which the armies will meet. Spotsylvania is now General Grant's best strategic point. I am so sure of his next move that I have already made arrangements to march by the shortest practicable route, that we may meet him there."

But Lee did not share this prediction with his rank and file, and when word came after the sun had set that the Federal artillery was on the move, most of the Confederates thought that the Yankees were withdrawing. The Rebel yell arose among Long-street's men on the Orange Plank road, spread up to the turnpike, and rippled back again with renewed fervor. As a South Carolina officer recalled, "The effect was beyond expression. It seemed to fill every heart with new life, to inspire every nerve with might never known before."

Listening to the spine-tingling yell—which was made all the more eerie by the lurid glow of the burning woods lighting the night—many Union troops were more convinced than ever that Grant intended to retreat, to skedaddle, as they put it. It looked like the end of another "On to Richmond!" The pessimism reached back to the reserve artillery,

where Frank Wilkeson had finally rejoined his battery and was in a sour enough mood anyway. Instead of being praised for his two days of service with the infantry, Wilkeson had been punished for being absent without leave. He had to walk around camp that morning with a log across his shoulders, urged on by a guard who pricked him with the point of a sword when he lagged.

Wilkeson's artillery battery pulled out after dark on May 7. As he and the rest of his unit marched eastward on the Orange Plank road, retracing their steps toward Chancellorsville, the veterans in the outfit speculated about which direction they would turn when they reached a key intersection. Left—north—would mean the old familiar retreat; right—toward the Confederate capital—would be something new. The column swung right. "Our spirits rose," Wilkeson recalled. "We marched free. The men began to sing. That night we were happy."

The whole Army of the Potomac was moving out. Through its ranks came Ulysses S. Grant, who was riding his horse Cincinnati at an easy trot south along the Brock road. Spotting the stoop-shouldered figure, the troops set off an uproarious celebration, pressing forward, shouting, waving their hats in tribute to his decision to keep heading toward Richmond. Watching the spectacle, Horace Porter thought that the night march through the burning woods represented a triumphal procession for the Union leader. But Grant muttered, "This is most unfortunate. The sound will reach the ears of the enemy, and I fear it may reveal our movement." Staff officers rode ahead to urge the men to cease their demonstration. But the noise did not really die away until the general rode on out of sight.

Grant's decision to push south was, in his friend Sherman's phrase, "the supreme moment of his life." It was also a turning point in the war. From the first day of the Battle of the Wilderness, Grant was determined to keep a death grip on the Confederates and not let go until he or his enemy prevailed; Lee would never be able to shake him loose. During the next month Grant pressed on relentlessly, forcing battles with Lee at Spotsylvania, just as the Confederate commander had predicted, and at Cold Harbor. The Union losses were so great—an average of 2,000 a day—that some in the North began to have doubts about his brand of warfare. But he stayed on the offensive, preventing Lee from executing the maneuvers that had so awed and intimidated Grant's predecessors. He joined up with another Union army that had come up the Virginia Peninsula, and the combined force closed in upon the capital and the vital rail center of Petersburg, 20 miles to the south.

Former slaves await Federal transport out of Richmond after its capture in April 1865. Lincoln visited the city on April 3 and was mobbed by throngs of freedmen. When some of them knelt before him in gratitude, he protested, "Don't kneel to me. You must kneel to God only, and thank him for your freedom."

For nearly nine months Grant hammered away at the defenses of Richmond and Petersburg until Lee finally gave way on April 3, 1865. The capital fell, and the Confederate president, Jefferson Davis, fled the city, pledging to carry on the fight. The next day, Abraham Lincoln, who had traveled to Richmond to celebrate Grant's triumph, tried out Davis's chair in the executive mansion.

After the fall of Richmond, Lee and the remnants of his Army of Northern Virginia struggled westward, in the hope of eventually turning south and connecting up with what remained of Joe Johnston's 80,000-man army in North Carolina. Grant was in pursuit of the Confederates, and on April 6, at Sayler's Creek, Lee suffered the loss of 7,000 men, most of whom were taken prisoner, including one of his senior generals, "Old Baldhead" Ewell. Outnumbered five to one by Yankees who were closing in on all sides, Lee and his remaining 25,000 troops pressed on, many of them so enfeebled by hunger, sickness, and exhaustion that only a third of them could actually fight. Then, on the night of April 8, Lee's last hope for resupply faded when Union cavalrymen raced ahead to the rail station near the village of Appomattox Court House, captured four trainloads of Confederate provisions, and cut off his line of retreat to the west.

News of the cavalry's coup did little to ease the pain being endured by the Federal commander. For Ulysses S. Grant had a headache. It was 4:00 a.m. on April 9 and the general was pacing back and forth in front of

SHERMAN'S MARCH TO THE SEA

In the fall of 1864 William Tecumseh Sherman *(above)* telegraphed Grant from occupied Atlanta with a daring proposal: He would go on the offensive again and march his 62,000-man army across Georgia to Savannah, "smashing things to the sea." His grasp of the Southern mentality told him that a successful march would thoroughly demoralize the Confederacy. "If the North can march an army right through the South," Sherman argued, "it is proof positive that the North can prevail."

Sherman won Grant's approval and on November 15 abandoned Atlanta after ordering civilians to evacuate and setting it afire. Meeting little military opposition, his army burned courthouses in town after town, raided homes and farms, and destroyed everything of military value in their 285-mile path. One soldier reminisced, "We had a gay old campaign. Destroyed all we could not eat, stole their niggers, burned their cotton & gins, spilled their sorghum, burned & twisted their R. Roads and raised Hell generally."

After a month the army reached the coast, and the Rebels surrendered Savannah to Sherman. His goal had been realized: The march had delivered a devastating blow from which the Confederate spirit would not rebound.

the farmhouse in which he had set up his headquarters, some 20 miles east of Appomattox, which was now occupied by the Federals. The throbbing in his head had begun the previous afternoon, and none of the usual remedies had worked this time: He bathed his feet in hot water that was fortified with mustard and applied mustard plasters to his wrists and to the back of his neck, but to no avail. Not long before dawn his aide Horace Porter found him outside, gripping his head with both hands. Porter tried to cheer him up. "Well, there is one consolation in all this, General: I never knew you to be ill that you did not receive good news before the day passed." Porter admitted to Grant that he was superstitious about such coincidences and wouldn't be surprised "if some good fortune were to overtake you before night."

"The best thing that could happen to me today," Grant said, forcing a smile, "would be to get rid of the pain I'm suffering."

The two men decided to get some coffee, and the caffeine seemed to ease the throbbing in Grant's head a little. He sat down to write yet another message to Robert E. Lee.

For two days now, the adversaries had been carrying on an extraordinary correspondence by courier that had done nothing but frustrate Grant. On April 7 he had written to the Confederate general, expressing his hope that "further effusion of blood" could be avoided and asking him to surrender. In his response Lee said he did not share Grant's opinion that further resistance was hopeless, but nevertheless he asked what terms Grant would offer. Grant replied that his only condition was that the men who laid down their arms would pledge not to take them up again. These were more generous terms than Lee had expected to come from "Unconditional Surrender" Grant. But the Confederate stalled. In a message that Grant had received at midnight in the midst of his migraine, Lee proposed a meeting the following morning at 10:00 between the lines in order to discuss "the restoration of peace." It was not, Grant noted, to consider the surrender of the Army of Northern Virginia.

Around daybreak, his head still hurting, Grant wrote Lee a message rejecting the proposed meeting. Since Grant possessed "no authority to treat on the subject of peace," the meeting, he said, "could

who had returned to duty six months after being wounded in the Wilderness. They sat on blankets or on saddles resting on exposed tree roots. Rimming the horizon in most directions they could see the campfires of the enemy. As Lee stood in the middle of the gathering, by a low-burning fire, he read aloud Grant's generous terms of surrender and talked about the plight of the Confederate army. John Gordon felt his leader had never conducted himself with such dignity: "We knew by our own aching hearts that his was breaking. Yet he commanded himself, and stood calmly facing and discussing the long-dreaded inevitable."

For two days now, Lee had stood firmly against the idea of surrender, even when he was pressed on

> ## *"Thank God that I have lived to see this! It seems to me that I have been dreaming a horrid dream for four years, and now the nightmare is gone."*
>
> ABRAHAM LINCOLN

lead to no good." He left the door open for continued discussion, however, by expressing his hope "that all our difficulties may be settled without the loss of another life." Grant dispatched the courier and then set off for his cavalry's position across Lee's line of retreat west of Appomattox Court House. He declined the offer of a covered ambulance, which would have kept him out of the sun, and chose to ride Cincinnati, though every jolt of the journey over rough fields and streams renewed the torture in his head.

Grant's headache might have gotten still worse if he had known what his adversary had pledged the night before. While the Union commander had been pacing in front of the farmhouse, Lee was vowing to "strike that man a blow in the morning." The occasion of Lee's declaration was a council of war at his camp in a woods 15 miles west of Grant's headquarters. Much Confederate baggage had been jettisoned in the haste of retreat, and Lee was without benefit of tent, table, or even a stool. His top commanders were there, including James Longstreet,

the issue by some of his own officers. "Oh, no, I trust it has not come to that," Lee told them. "We have too many bold men to think of laying down our arms." He then spoke about the overriding importance of defending "sacred principles, for which we were in duty bound to do our best, even if we perished in the endeavor." When another officer urged him to surrender, Lee responded, "What would the country think of me?"

"Country be damned!" the officer replied to Lee. "There *is* no country. There has been no country, General, for a year or more. You are the country to these men."

But around the fire on that Saturday evening, none of Lee's most senior commanders were ready to give up. Their feelings appeared to echo the determination shown by Longstreet. After reading Grant's first message proposing a Confederate surrender, the "Old Warhorse" answered Lee with just two words: "Not yet." There was fight left in them, and Lee and his generals decided to attempt a breakout from the Federal noose.

At dawn the following morning, the remnant of Ewell's old command—some 4,000 fighting men who were now under Gordon—would attempt to cut through the cordon of Yankee horsemen who were blocking the way west just beyond Appomattox Court House. As long as there was no Union infantry, they had a chance. Longstreet's troops would hold off the Federals who were pushing from behind, then join Gordon in the breakout. They would march on to Lynchburg and from there go on to rendezvous with Johnston in North Carolina.

After the council of war had been completed, Gordon sent an officer to Lee to receive any specific directions about where Gordon and his men should camp the following night. The request assumed that Gordon would be successful in carving out an escape route. Lee's straight-faced reply conveyed the grim irony of the Confederate prospects: "Yes, tell General Gordon that I should be glad for him to halt just beyond the Tennessee line." It was not necessary for anyone to tell Gordon that Tennessee was 200 miles away.

Lee's attempt to "strike that man a blow" was launched just west of Appomattox at 5:00 a.m. on Sunday—not long after "that man," the pain-racked Grant, had given up trying to sleep. As the horizon behind them began to redden, Gordon's men advanced along the main road west of the village. Tattered, footsore, and starving—but with the Rebel yell rising from their throats—the Confederates swept the Union horsemen before them and captured the breastworks that had been set up in the road during the night. Gordon saw with relief that all of the dead and wounded Yankee defenders wore spurs: It looked as though only cavalry

George Armstrong Custer, wearing his signature scarlet necktie, exudes a fearless arrogance in this portrait from the Washington studio of photographer Mathew Brady. The brash young cavalry officer was as famous for his flashy and distinctly nonregulation uniforms as he was for his bravery in battle, prompting one Union officer to comment, "He looks like a circus rider gone mad."

had been standing in the way of the Confederate escape, just as Gordon had hoped. This meant that the road to Lynchburg was open.

But as Gordon watched, the retreating blue-clad cavalrymen scattered to reveal—like a parting theater curtain—a terrifying spectacle on the hillsides located off to the west. Rank upon rank of Northern infantry—30,000 men in all—were coming up following an all-night march. Gordon sent back pleas for help to Longstreet, but the "Old Warhorse" himself faced overwhelming numbers of enemy troops. Gordon and Longstreet were trapped back to back, with the village of Appomattox Court House in between them. No one put it more succinctly than a Federal soldier that day who said of Lee's position: "He couldn't go back, he couldn't go forward, and he couldn't go sideways."

Lee was standing on a knoll near the village early that morning, and he was eager for news of Gordon's breakout attempt. Dressed as if for a grand review, he sported a new uniform, handsomely embroidered belt, yellow silk sash, sword with ornate hilt, leather and gold scabbard, and highly polished boots with gold spurs. When one of his officers expressed surprise at such unaccustomed finery, Lee explained that he would probably be Grant's prisoner. "I must make my best appearance," he said.

While Lee was waiting, an aide returned from the battlefield carrying a message from Gordon: "Tell General Lee I have fought my corps to a frazzle, and I fear I can do nothing unless I am heavily supported by Longstreet's corps." Lee took Gordon's message in and, as though he were speaking to himself, said, "Then there is nothing left me but to go and see General Grant, and I would rather die a thousand deaths." A tearful staff officer asked what history would say of his surrender of an army in the field. "Hard things," Lee answered. "But that is not the question, Colonel. The question is, is it right to surrender this army? If it is right, then I will take all the responsibility."

Thinking that Grant would be expecting him at 10:00 a.m., Lee rode out into the no man's land between the two armies. Beside him was an orderly who was carrying a soiled white handkerchief tied to a stick as a flag of truce. The two came upon a line of Federal skirmishers, who were astonished to find the enemy commander standing in front of them. Their next encounter was with the Union courier who was bearing Grant's message that there could be no meeting except to discuss the capitulation of Lee's forces. The Confederate general now had no choice. He returned to his own lines and directed an aide to write a reply asking for a meeting "to deal with the question of the surrender of my army." Lee then dispatched messages to Gordon and Longstreet to cease firing and send out a flag of truce.

Longstreet responded by sending a staff officer into the Yankee lines carrying a white towel and a message to the cavalry commander, General Philip Sheridan, asking for a suspension of hostilities. Not long afterward, the general's request brought a picturesque visitor to his headquarters. A slender young cavalry officer who was waving a white handkerchief on the tip of his saber rode up at a fast gallop. His long blond curls nearly brushed his shoulders, which carried the largest shoulder straps that one ill-clad Confederate officer there had ever seen. Around his neck he wore a red scarf with a two-inch-wide gold pin. Without dismounting, he called out: "General Longstreet, in the name of General Sheridan I demand the unconditional surrender of this army! I am General Custer."

Crossed sabers, a symbol of Union cavalry, decorate the field of Custer's personal guidon. Custer took this flag into battle while he led the 3rd Cavalry Division in 1864 and 1865.

The "Old Warhorse" bristled at this breach of military etiquette. He frostily reminded Custer that it was Lee, in fact, not Longstreet, who was the commander of the Army of Northern Virginia. Moreover, the Union officer was "within the lines of the enemy without authority, addressing a superior officer." In answer to this rebuke, Custer responded with some heat that Longstreet would "be responsible for the bloodshed to follow."

"Go ahead and have all the bloodshed you want!" Longstreet growled. His bravado rapidly waning, the young Federal replied, "General, probably we had best wait until we hear from Grant and Lee. I will speak to General Sheridan about it. Don't move your troops yet!" Custer then wheeled about on his horse and made his way back toward his own headquarters.

White flags of truce now sprang up along a battlefront that had fallen eerily silent. Lee had requested a one-hour cessation of hostilities, which General Meade agreed to because Grant was not anywhere to be found. Meade sent out a courier to try to locate him.

The Federal commander, who was still in the anguished grip of his headache, had ridden off with his staff officers earlier that morning. Lee, it appeared, meant to keep fighting, so Grant had to study the landscape and decide how he should deploy his troops for the next encounter. Making a wide detour around the front in order to avoid Confederate pickets, the group stopped for a rest shortly before noon at a roadside clearing located eight or so miles east of Appomattox Court House.

Grant and several others were lighting their cigars when Meade's courier came riding up to them on his sweaty stallion, yelling excitedly. He jumped off his horse, saluted, and handed over an envelope containing the Confederate surrender note. Grant read Lee's message without any comment. Nor did his face betray his reaction to the contents of the note. One member of the group said of the general's expression, "It was that of a Sphinx."

Grant asked his chief of staff, General John Rawlins, to read the note aloud. Rawlins's voice quivered as he did so: "I received your note of this morning with reference to the surrender of this army. I now ask an interview in accordance with that purpose." After a brief silence, someone sprang up on a log and attempted to lead the assembly in three cheers. But most of the group were too choked up to venture more than a few feeble hurrahs. Grant sat down on the grass and dashed off a reply to Lee, saying he would "push forward to the front for the purpose of meeting you." Then he swung up into the saddle and set off for Appomattox Court House at a trot. Colonel Porter asked him about his headache. It was gone, said Grant: "The instant I saw the contents of the note I was cured."

About an hour later, the courier carrying Grant's reply found Lee not far from the village lying under an old apple tree on a blanket-covered pallet that had been improvised from fence rails. He mounted Traveller and headed toward Appomattox with his orderly, sending his aide Colonel Charles Marshall ahead to find a suitable place for the surrender conference.

The village did not amount to much—the small county courthouse, a tavern, a jail, a few houses. Apart from a handful of Yankee cavalrymen, its streets were virtually deserted when Marshall arrived. He enlisted the help of the first townsman he saw. His name was Wilmer McLean, and by remarkable coincidence he had already played a small role in the history of the war. Four years before he had owned a farm near Manassas Junction in northern Virginia. During the Battle of Bull Run in 1861 the Confederates had used his house for a hospital and field headquarters, and a Federal shell had crashed through his kitchen roof. A loyal Southerner but sick of war, he moved from Manassas and found refuge in this peaceful village situated on rising ground above the Appomattox River. "Here," he told his family, "the sound of battle will never reach you."

McLean's first suggestion—a vacant, dilapidated building—was completely unsuitable. Somewhat reluctantly, he then offered, and Marshall accepted, the front parlor of his own house as a meeting place. Just as the first great drama of the war had taken place on McLean's farm, so in his house would be enacted its grand but melancholy finale.

It was nearly 2:00 p.m. when Grant rode up to the McLean house with his staff, about a half-hour after Lee. He mounted the half-dozen steps to the porch, entered the house, and went into the parlor. Lee, seated inside the room, rose to his feet. The two generals shook hands. The contrast between both of the men could not have been greater. Here was the son of an Ohio tanner, short, slight, and slouching, dressed in the uniform of a common soldier—one button fixed in the wrong hole—and splattered with mud from his long ride that morning. He was about to accept the surrender of a man whose family was as celebrated as his own was obscure—a man 15 years his senior, five inches taller, resplendent in crisp uniform, sword, and sash.

Grant, who had always felt comfortable in field garb, decided to apologize for his attire. The last thing he wanted was to seem to mock the defeated Confederate commander. In fact, a wave of sadness flowed over him at the prospect of the surrender of such a valiant foe. But as to what Lee's emotions were, Grant could not tell. "It was impossible to say," Grant later wrote, "whether he felt inwardly glad that the end had finally come, or felt sad over the result and was too manly to show it."

Grant was glad for the moment to chat about old army days during the Mexican War. He distinctly remembered Lee, who had been a staff officer to the commanding general there, but thought that Lee might not recall him because of the differences in age and rank. To Grant's surprise, Lee did recall him, and in his relief at having something else to talk about, he went on at such length about the earlier war that Lee had to remind him why they were there. He suggested that Grant write out his surrender terms. An aide brought a small oval table, and

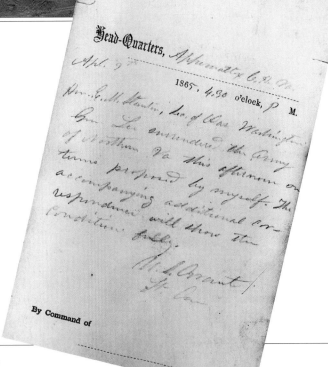

As officers from both armies look on, Lee signs the terms of surrender dictated by Grant on April 9, 1865, in the parlor of Wilmer McLean's house at Appomattox *(above)*. As he rushed to issue follow-up instructions, Grant nearly forgot to inform Washington of the momentous event. He stopped and quickly jotted a message *(right)* to Secretary of War Edwin Stanton.

Grant, after lighting up a cigar, began writing with a pencil in a field order book. Besides spelling out his previous condition that the Rebels lay down their arms and not take them up again, Grant added a new and generous provision: The officers could keep their side arms and the horses they had provided themselves. He felt that confiscation of their pistols and swords would have been an unnecessary humiliation. Lee was pleased. "This will have a very happy effect on my army," he said.

Emboldened by the victor's generosity, Lee asked a further favor. He pointed out that in the Confederate cavalry and artillery the enlisted men, like their officers, furnished their own horses, and most would need them to make a living when they returned home. "These men will want to plow ground and plant corn," he told him. Grant replied that the written terms of the surrender permitted only officers to keep their private property. But then, perhaps reflecting on his own years of hard-scrabble farming before the war, Grant reconsidered. He said he would give orders to allow every Confederate soldier who claimed to own a horse or mule to take it home. Looking relieved, Lee then asked Colonel Marshall to draft a letter of acceptance. He urged him to keep it simple: "Just say, 'I accept these terms.'"

> *"This was our hour of intense humiliation. So long as we carried our guns we felt something of the dignity of soldiers; but when we tramped away leaving these behind, we felt like hoboes stranded on an alien shore."*
>
> A. C. JONES, 3RD ARKANSAS

While both letters were being copied in ink supplied by Marshall from a boxwood inkstand he always carried with him in a little satchel, Grant introduced some of the generals and staff members gathered in the room. One of them was Colonel Ely Parker, his military secretary and a Seneca Indian. The general looked at Parker for a moment and then extended his hand, saying, "I am glad to see one real American here."

"We are all Americans," Parker replied.

Before leaving, Lee raised one final issue. He promised to return the Union prisoners he held and remarked that he had no provisions for them. Then

Lined up opposite Union general Joshua Chamberlain and his men, Confederate soldiers furl their battle colors for the last time in front of their relinquished weapons in this depiction of the formal surrender ceremony on April 12, 1865.

he added: "I have, indeed, nothing for my own men. They have been living for the last few days principally upon parched corn." Grant looked over at his cavalry chief, Philip Sheridan, whose men the day before had intercepted the four trainloads of provisions intended for Lee's army.

"Sheridan, how many rations have you?"

"How many do you want?" asked Sheridan.

"How many can you send?"

"Twenty-five thousand."

Grant then asked Lee if this would be sufficient. "I think it will be ample," Lee replied. "And it will be a great relief, I assure you."

Grant signed his letter. Lee signed his. They exchanged the documents and shook hands. The actual laying down of arms would take place three days later, and the scattered Confederate forces still in the field under other commands would have to be dealt with. But with this spare drama—in Colonel Marshall's words, "the simplest, plainest and most thoroughly devoid of any attempt at effect you can imagine"—the American Civil War effectively came to an end. It had taken four years and more than 620,000 lives to preserve the Union.

Carrying his hat and gloves, Lee emerged onto the front porch and paused before descending the steps. Slowly crossing to the top of the steps, he placed his hat on his head and returned the salutes of several Union officers gathered on the porch. There he pulled on his gloves and distractedly banged the fist of one hand into the palm of the other several times. His eyes looked off in the direction of the little valley beyond the courthouse where his army lay. Then, as if remembering the occasion, he called out, in a half-choked voice, "Orderly! Orderly!"

"Here, General, here," the orderly responded, bringing Lee's horse up to the front of the house as Lee was coming down the steps. While Traveller was being bridled, Lee drew the forelock out from under the browband and patted the gray charger's head. Then he caught up the reins, put his foot in the stirrup, and swung himself slowly into the saddle, emitting what sounded to one witness like a low groan.

Joined by Marshall and the orderly, Lee began to move off at a slow trot. At that moment Grant came out of the house and down the steps. He stopped. Both generals simultaneously raised their hands in salute. When Lee had passed, the Union commander sprang lightly into the saddle of his horse Cincinnati and rode off.

After Lee and Grant had left, the McLean house was swept by a frenzy of souvenir hunting. Union officers offered Wilmer McLean money for everything in the parlor, from a child's doll to pieces of the cane-bottomed chair in which Lee had sat. Philip Sheridan forced two $10 gold pieces on McLean for the little table at which Grant had written the terms of surrender. Sheridan presented it to his dashing young subordinate, George Custer, as a gift for his wife, and Custer rode off with the table perched on his shoulder.

Lee made his way back to his camp at a walk, through a tumult of cheers that turned to cries of despair. The reins hung loose in his hands, and his head was sunk low on his chest. "General, are we surrendered? Are we surrendered?" cried the ragged soldiers who were lining the road. They pressed in close trying to touch him, laying their hands against Traveller as well. Lee stopped, took off his hat, and said softly: "Men, we have fought the war together, and I have done the best I could for you. You will all be paroled and go to your homes." The soldiers sobbed like children. Tears came into Lee's eyes. His lips formed a soundless "Good-bye."

Grant, as he rode toward his own camp, was so preoccupied with the mingled grief and joy of the day's events that he nearly forgot to send notification to Washington. When Porter reminded him, he dismounted his horse, sat down on a large stone, and wrote out a terse telegram: "General Lee surrendered the Army of Northern Virginia this afternoon on terms proposed by myself." Then, hearing Federal guns booming out a victory salute, he sent word to cease firing. He had no desire to rub salt in wounds. "The war is over," he told his staff. "The Rebels are our countrymen again." ◆

THE FINAL ACT

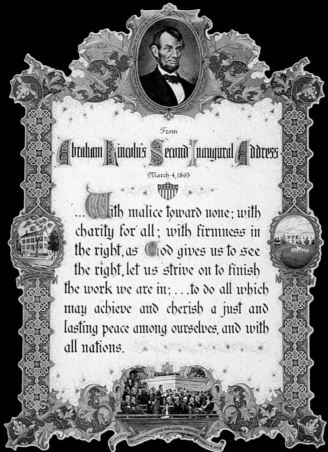

From
Abraham Lincoln's Second Inaugural Address
March 4, 1865

... With malice toward none; with charity for all; with firmness in the right, as God gives us to see the right, let us strive on to finish the work we are in; ... to do all which may achieve and cherish a just and lasting peace among ourselves, and with all nations.

In the wake of the Confederate surrender at Appomattox, Abraham Lincoln seemed like a new man. He confided to his wife, Mary, "I never felt so happy in my life." Senator James Harlan observed, "His whole appearance, poise, and bearing has marvelously changed. He seemed the very personification of supreme satisfaction."

With peace finally at hand, the Union capital had fairly erupted with fireworks, parades, and band music. "Washington was a little delirious," recalled Colonel William Crook, a member of Lincoln's staff. "Everybody was celebrating. Those about the President lost somewhat the feeling that his life was not safe," he noted. "It did not seem possible, now that the war was over . . . after President Lincoln had offered himself a target for Southern bullets in the streets of Richmond and had come out unscathed, there could be danger. For my part, I had drawn a full breath of relief . . . and had forgotten to be anxious since."

Several attempts had been made on Lincoln's life in the course of the war, and on his desk in the White House there was an envelope labeled "Assassination" containing some 80 menacing letters that he had collected during that period. The president had reluctantly accepted the necessity of a personal bodyguard and a cavalry escort when he was traveling, but he disliked altering his daily routine, which invariably meant contact with the public. "I cannot possibly guard myself against all dangers unless I shut myself up in an iron box," he pointed out. "If anyone is willing to give his life for mine, there is nothing that can prevent it."

Although Colonel Crook and others concerned for President Lincoln's safety breathed a sigh of relief on that score with the coming of peace, in reality he was in as much danger as ever. There remained fanatical supporters of the Southern cause whose hatred of the Union and its leaders rendered them deaf to the message of reconciliation the president had delivered in his second inaugural address six weeks before the surrender. These men were as determined as ever to strike a violent blow against the president, and to strike at the first opportunity.

CONSPIRATORIAL DREAMS

*"The world may censure me for what I am about to do;
but I am sure that posterity will justify me."*

JOHN WILKES BOOTH, APRIL 14, 1865

A member of a celebrated family of actors, John Wilkes Booth was known for his good looks and dashing theatrics. Although the Maryland native was an ardent Southern sympathizer, he never enlisted. By 1864 the prospects for a Confederate victory were dimming, and Booth, perhaps pricked by guilt at not having served in the army, decided to undertake a "bold enterprise" with the help of several other Southern sympathizers: They would kidnap the president and demand the release of Confederate prisoners of war as ransom.

The group tried to carry out their plot at least once on March 17, 1865, when Lincoln was scheduled to travel by carriage outside Washington. They lay in wait along his route but they were foiled when his plans changed and he stayed in the city instead.

Soon afterward, Booth was set on a more desperate course by the news that General Grant had arrived in Washington on April 13. The word around town was that the Grants had been invited to attend a play at Ford's Theatre with President and Mrs. Lincoln the following evening. Booth seized on the occasion as an opportunity to kill both the president and the triumphant general.

At 8:00 p.m. on April 14 Booth convened his band of accomplices, but he presented them with a revised plan because General and Mrs. Grant had left town that afternoon. Booth directed Lewis Paine, who had served in the Confederate army, to kill Secretary of State William Seward. David Herold would guide Paine to Seward's house and then out of the city afterward. George Atzerodt had orders to attack Vice President Andrew Johnson. Booth reserved the main target for himself.

The attacks were all scheduled to be made at 10:15 p.m. The assassins would regroup just outside Washington, then flee by way of southern Maryland to safety in the South. By the time the meeting ended, President Lincoln was already seated in a stage-side box at Ford's Theatre.

John Wilkes Booth used the Washington boarding-house run by Mary Surratt *(below, far left)* as a gathering place for his band of anti-Lincoln conspirators. Key men who took part in the assassination plot included, from left to right below, David Herold, Lewis Paine, and George Atzerodt.

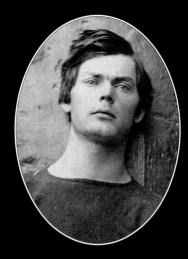

At 27 the handsome John Wilkes Booth *(right)* was a promising actor and Confederate supporter, unlike his more famous brother Edwin, who was a staunch Union man. Asked by his sister Asia why he did not serve in the Rebel army, John replied: "My brains are worth twenty men. My profession, my beloved precious money—oh, never beloved 'til now!—is the means by which I serve the South."

Tragedy at Ford's Theatre

"I had never witnessed such a scene. The seats, aisles, galleries, and stage were filled with shouting, frenzied men and women, many running aimlessly over one another; a chaos beyond control."

SEATON MONROE, FORD'S THEATRE, APRIL 14, 1865

The performance of *Our American Cousin* had begun when President and Mrs. Lincoln arrived with Major Henry Rathbone and his fiancée, Clara Harris, the daughter of a senator. Lincoln's regular bodyguard was in Richmond, so a substitute, John Parker, had been conscripted from the city police force. Parker met the presidential party at the theater, but once they were settled in their box, Parker left his post—to watch the play, he later claimed, though there was suspicion that he had gone to the tavern next door.

Booth left his horse at the back entrance, threaded his way through the building, and slipped into the vestibule outside the unguarded presidential box. At 10:13 p.m. he entered the box, stepped behind the president, and fired a lead ball almost one-half inch in

After shooting the president, who was seated in a rocking chair provided by the solicitous theater manager, Booth dropped this .44 caliber derringer. When Henry Rathbone *(far right)* tried to stop his escape, Booth slashed him from elbow to shoulder with a knife.

diameter into the left side of Lincoln's head. Throwing Major Rathbone aside, Booth scrambled onto the railing and sprang 12 feet to the stage below. As he jumped, his spur caught on the Union flag draped on the outside of the box, throwing him off balance. He landed hard, snapping a bone just above his left ankle. Without missing a beat he turned toward the startled audience and shouted the motto of Virginia: *"Sic semper tyrannis!"*— "Thus always to tyrants." He limped offstage to the back door and his waiting horse.

"The President is in yonder upper right hand private box so handsomely decked with silken flags festooned over with a picture of Washington," wrote Julia Adelaide Shepard, a member of the audience, who was composing a letter to her father during the play. "The young and lovely daughter of Senator Harris is the only one of the party we can see, as the flags hide the rest. How sociable it seems, like one family sitting around their parlor fire."

The Actor's Last Performance

"After being hunted like a dog through swamps and woods, and last night being chased by gun boats till I was forced to return, wet, cold, and starving, with every man's hand against me, I am here in despair."

John Wilkes Booth, April 21, 1865

Lewis Paine struck on schedule, savagely wounding five members of the Seward household and injuring the secretary himself, who was in bed recovering from a serious carriage accident; all of Paine's victims would survive. In the subsequent uproar, David Herold panicked and fled, abandoning Paine. George Atzerodt did not have the stomach even to begin his assignment. Instead, he spent the evening drinking before fleeing to the home of a cousin in Germantown, Maryland.

Despite the pain of his broken leg, Booth pressed on to Maryland, where Herold soon caught up with him. Together they rode on to Surrattsville, Mary Surratt's one-time home, in order to collect the supplies that she had left there for the fleeing conspirators. Their next stop was the home of Samuel Mudd, a physician Booth had met some months before. Mudd treated Booth's leg and sheltered the two men for the night. For more than a week the fugitives hid in the woods waiting for a chance to cross the Potomac to Virginia, while Federal troops searched the countryside.

The other conspirators proved to be less successful at evading the authorities. Lewis Paine showed up at Mary Surratt's just as police were arresting the entire household, and Atzerodt was taken into custody at his cousin's house. When Federal officers learned that Dr. Mudd had tended the wounded Booth, he was arrested as a conspirator.

On the night of April 22 Booth and Herold crossed the Potomac in a boat provided by sympathizers. The fugitives, using false names, were introduced by a sympathizer to a man named Richard Garrett, who agreed to let them stay on his farm. But Federal troops were not far behind. At 2:00 a.m. on April 26 they surrounded the barn where the two men were sleeping. Herold gave himself up, but Booth had vowed never to be taken alive. "Draw up your men before the door, and I'll come out and fight you," Booth called to the party's commander. In answer, the troops set the barn on fire. Peering through a chink in the wall, they saw that Booth was armed. He was limping toward the barn door when he was felled by a bullet through the neck. The actor was carried out of the burning barn and died at about 7:00 a.m., close to the hour that the president died 11 days before.

Along the route Booth and Herold took from Washington to Virginia, Rebel sympathizers gave them food and newspapers, from which Booth was astounded to learn that he was being condemned in North and South alike.

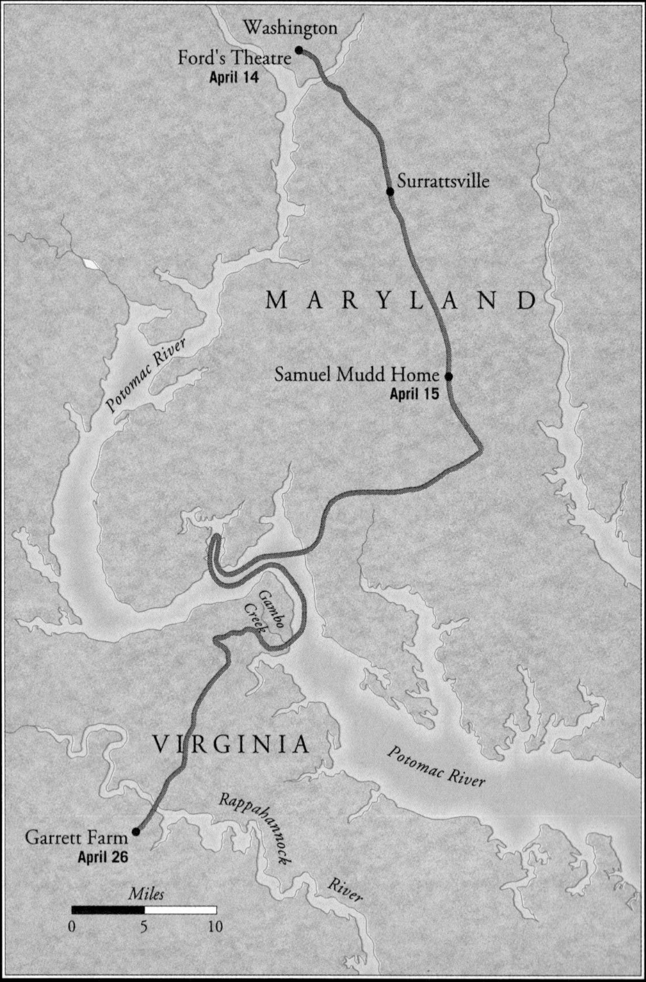

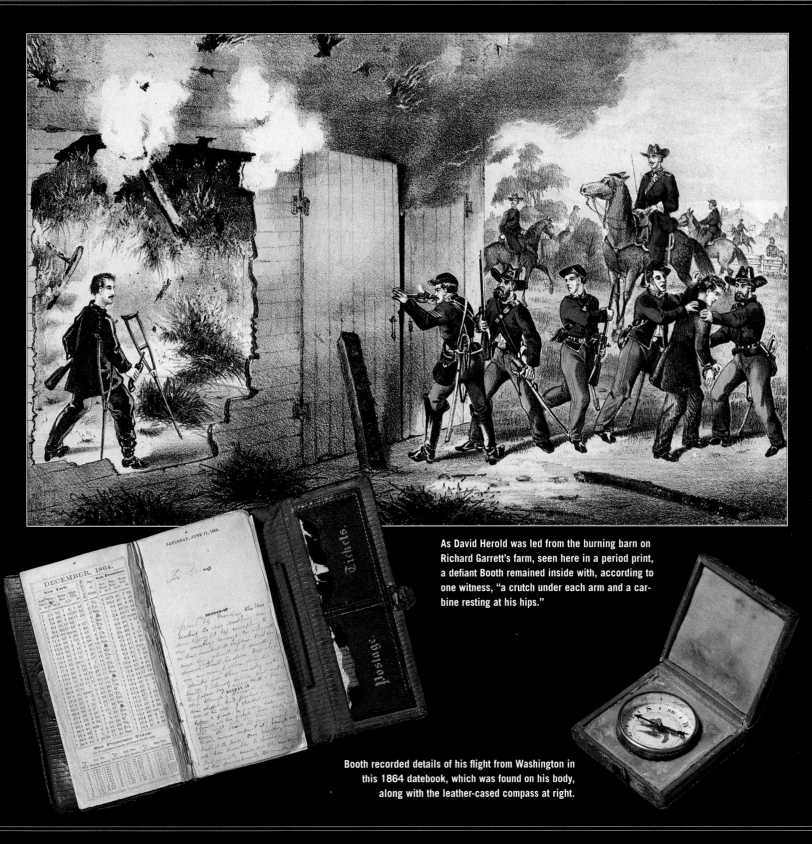

As David Herold was led from the burning barn on Richard Garrett's farm, seen here in a period print, a defiant Booth remained inside with, according to one witness, "a crutch under each arm and a carbine resting at his hips."

Booth recorded details of his flight from Washington in this 1864 datebook, which was found on his body, along with the leather-cased compass at right.

Carried to this tiny chamber in a rooming house across 10th Street from Ford's Theatre, the mortally wounded president had to be laid diagonally on the bed because it was too short for his great frame. The bloodstained pillow on which his head rested was still on the bed hours after he died, when this photograph was taken.

THE LAST FULL MEASURE

"A look of unspeakable peace came over his worn features. Stanton broke the silence by saying, 'Now he belongs to the ages.'"

CHAUNCEY DEPEW, APRIL 15, 1865

"Oh, doctor," Mary Lincoln screamed, "What can you do for my poor husband? Is he dead? Can he recover?" Charles Leale, a young army physician who rushed from his nearby seat to the unconscious president's side, gave orders for him to be carried to a house across the street. There Lincoln's family doctor agreed sadly with Dr. Leale that the wound was fatal: "He is tenacious and he will resist, but death will close the scene." Less than 10 hours later, at 7:22 on the cold, rainy Saturday morning of April 15, Abraham Lincoln died at the age of 56.

At the funeral in the East Room of the White House on April 19, Grant wept. "It seemed as if the whole world had lost a dear, personal friend," one mourner lamented. The whole nation grieved—even

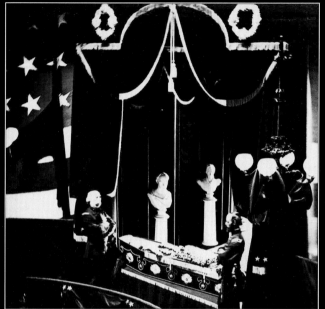

Lincoln's body lay in state in several cities along the funeral train's route. This photograph, taken in New York's City Hall, is the only one of the president after his death.

the South, where many agreed with Confederate general Joseph Johnston when he called Lincoln "the best friend" the South had.

After lying in state at the Capitol, Lincoln's body, along with that of his 12-year-old son Willie, who had died in 1862, was placed on a flag-draped train that steamed 1,700 miles from Washington to Springfield, Illinois, where Lincoln had practiced law before coming to Washington. Cities along the route held solemn parades and memorial services, while at country crossroads and small towns an estimated 7,000,000 people sang and prayed while they patiently waited to see the train go by. On May 4 Abraham Lincoln and his son were laid to rest in a burial vault in Oak Ridge Cemetery in Springfield.

THE CRY FOR VENGEANCE

"I gave the signal, the two drops fell with a sickening thud, and as one, the four bodies shot down and hung in mid air."

CAPTAIN CHRISTIAN RATH, JULY 7, 1865

Andrew Johnson, now president of the United States, ordered that the alleged conspirators be tried in a military court. The trial began on May 9, less than one month after Lincoln's assassination. In all, 198 witnesses for the prosecution and 163 for the defense were called. The officers of the court began their deliberations on June 29 and quickly reached their decisions: Lewis Paine, David Herold, George Atzerodt, and Mary Surratt were condemned to death; Samuel Mudd was sentenced to life in prison. Several of the judiciary officers rec-ommended commuting Mrs. Surratt's sentence to life imprisonment, but President Johnson refused to intervene.

Although a few critics questioned the fairness and legality of a military trial because of its looser standards for evidence and procedure compared with a state or federal court, a newspaper summed up the more general feeling about the conspirators: "We wish to hear their names no more, but to think of our dead President only as a great and good man and patriot gone to his rest." The hanging was scheduled for July 7.

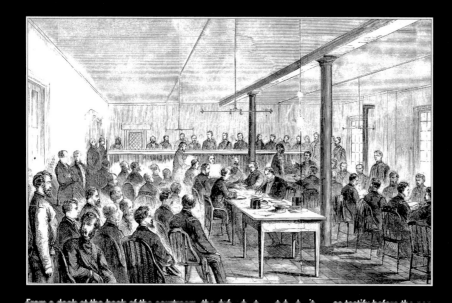

Executioner Christian Rath made the four nooses used; the one above was for Lewis Paine. Paine's last words were, "Mrs. Surratt is innocent. She doesn't deserve to die with the rest of us." Moments later those in the Old Penitentiary's courtyard, some shielding themselves from the July sun, saw Surratt, Paine, David Herold, and George Atzerodt hanged.

A NATION REUNITED

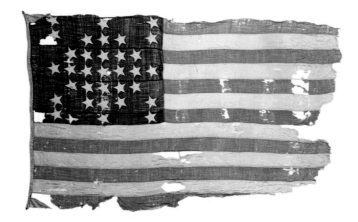

The day that Abraham Lincoln made his fateful visit to Ford's Theatre, a simple ceremony took place at Fort Sumter in the harbor of Charleston, South Carolina. More than 4,000 people—most of them from the North but some of them blacks from nearby plantations—had been ferried out to the island stronghold for the event. After a chaplain said a short prayer and led a responsive reading from the Psalms—"When the Lord turned again the captivity of Zion"—a sergeant who had been stationed at Sumter at the time of the bombardment stepped forward. From a leather pouch he drew the scorched and frayed United States flag *(shown above)* that had flown over the fort on the day that it surrendered. Two sailors attached the flag to the rope that would run it up a tall new flagstaff in the middle of the fortress.

"We all held our breath for a second," wrote one of those in attendance, a young woman who was from Philadelphia, "and then we gave a queer cry, between a cheer and a yell; nobody started it and nobody led it; I never heard anything like it before or since, but I can hear it now."

As the crowd watched, the man who as a major in the United States Army had been forced to lower the flag on April 14, 1861—four years ago to the day—rose to speak. "I thank God that I have lived to see this day," said now general Robert Anderson. "I restore to its proper place this dear flag." After a few more words, he began to hoist the Stars and Stripes in the still, mild spring air. Hanging limp against the staff, the flag had risen above the walls of Fort Sumter when a gust of wind shook its folds and it flared out straight above the watching crowd.

Soldiers and sailors saluted instinctively. The crowd stood up. Someone led off with the first stanza of "The Star-Spangled Banner." Then one of Sumter's cannon thundered out a salute, which was followed by the firing of every one of the Charleston batteries that had bombarded the fort in 1861. A fleet of warships in the harbor loosed a salute, and the air turned black with smoke.

For Robert Anderson, the flag raising was "perhaps the last act of my life, of duty to my country," and he had a somewhat let-down feeling as the ceremony ended and he took leave of Fort Sumter.

That same day, Confederate generals Joseph Johnston and P. G. T. Beauregard began negotiations with the Union army in North Carolina commanded by William Tecumseh Sherman, against the will of their president, Jefferson Davis. Davis, who was also in North Carolina, was trying to run the Confederate government from the railroad cars in which he and his staff had fled Richmond. On hearing the news of Robert E. Lee's surrender at Appomattox, Davis had summoned Johnston and Beauregard to a meeting at Greensboro.

To the amazement of his generals, the president had talked at length of his plans to raise new troops and keep up the fight. He proposed to make up for the loss of Lee's army by rounding up deserters. Many missing Rebel soldiers, Davis felt sure, had simply gone home so that they could care for their families, and they would soon be back.

When the president finally asked Johnston's opinion, the commander of the Confederate army in North Carolina was direct. "My views are, sir," he began, "that our people are tired of war, feel themselves whipped, and will not fight. Our country is overrun, its military reserves greatly diminished, while the enemy's military power and resources were never greater, and may be increased to any extent desired." Moreover, Johnston went on, the situation was growing steadily worse. His troops regarded Lee's surrender as the end of the war, and he predicted that soon no soldier would be found anywhere "beyond the by-road or cowpath that leads to his house." Home was where they wanted to be, and home was where they were heading. "My small force is melting away like snow before the sun," Johnston said, "and I am hopeless of recruiting it."

A long pause followed. Then, in a low voice, Davis asked, "What do you say, General Beauregard?" Beauregard replied steadily, "I concur in all General Johnston has said."

The military men could see no way out. On April 14 Johnston and Beauregard—both of them victors of the war's first battle, at Bull Run—asked Sherman for a cessation of hostilities until a peace could be worked out. But Jefferson Davis still held out hope. While there were Rebel forces in the field, Davis pledged to continue the struggle.

One of the men the president might well have expected to fight on to the end was cavalry commander Nathan Bedford Forrest. Forrest was in the backwoods of Alabama when the Confederate forces in that state surrendered, on May 8. Rather than submit to the Yankees, he toyed with the notion of riding all the way to Mexico. "Which way, General?" one of his officers asked when he and his cavalrymen came to a fork in the road.

"Either," replied Forrest. "If one road led to hell and the other to Mexico, I would be indifferent which to take."

But after further thought, Forrest decided on a different course: He could serve the South best by leading his men back into the restored Union. He addressed his troops one last time. "I have never on the field of battle sent you where I was unwilling to go myself," he told them, "nor would I now advise you a course which I felt myself unwilling to pursue. You have been good soldiers. You can be good citizens. Obey the laws, preserve your honor, and the government to which you have surrendered can afford to be and will be magnanimous."

Forrest liked to say, "War means fighting. And fighting means killing." The time for fighting was past. By June 23, 1865, all remaining Confederate troops had laid down their arms.

The bloodiest war in the history of the United States had at last ended. More Americans perished in this fratricidal conflict than in all of the nation's other wars combined. More than 600,000 men were dead—at least 250,000 Southerners and more than 350,000 Northerners, fully two percent of the country's population. One hundred ninety thousand black soldiers and sailors had fought on the Union side, and about 32,000 of them had died in uniform. Whole cities were in ruins, vast stretches of countryside were ravaged, and a way of life had vanished forever. But the war between brothers was over, and the Union was restored.

LAST DAYS

The Civil War was a defining moment in the American story, changing forever the lives of those who experienced it. The brief accounts below describe the last days of some of the war's personalities.

✦ **PIERRE GUSTAVE TOUTANT BEAUREGARD** In the years immediately following the war, Beauregard considered offers of high command in the armies of Romania, Argentina, and Egypt. But a promising future as a railroad executive kept him from emigrating, and in 1877 his financial well-being was assured when he accepted the post of supervisor of the controversial Louisiana Lottery. His antagonism to ex-Confederate president Jefferson Davis continued until the end. When invited to ride at the head of Davis's funeral procession in 1889, Beauregard declined.

✦ **GEORGE ARMSTRONG CUSTER** The flamboyant Custer became lieutenant colonel of the newly formed 7th Cavalry, trading his blue-and-gold uniform for buckskins. Always seeking opportunities for self-promotion, Custer chronicled his adventures in articles for eastern newspapers and in his book, *My Life on the Plains*. He got more fame than he bargained for when he took on a far superior force of Sioux and Cheyenne warriors at the Battle of the Little Bighorn in 1876. Custer and all 210 men under his immediate command were killed, and a legend was born.

✦ **CHARLES DANA** Dana returned to journalism after the war, and under his stewardship the *New York Sun* became that city's best-selling morning daily. Although he endorsed Ulysses S. Grant for president in 1868, Dana became one of the fiercest critics of Grant's administration.

✦ **JEFFERSON DAVIS** Davis was captured by Union troops in Georgia on May 10, 1865. After serving a two-year imprisonment, he lived a vagabond existence, spending time in such places as Montreal, Havana, and London, before returning to his beloved Mississippi. Failure and loss were a constant theme: Two of Davis's children died, his forays into railroading, mining, and insurance came to nought, and the family plantation had to be sold.

✦ **FREDERICK DOUGLASS** After the war, Douglass crisscrossed the country, promoting the cause of civil rights for blacks and putting his oratorical gifts at the service of a succession of Republican politicians. President Rutherford Hayes named him the first black marshal of the District of Columbia, and from 1889 to 1891 Douglass served as the U.S. minister to Haiti.

✦ **NATHAN BEDFORD FORREST** Reputed to be the Grand Wizard of the Ku Klux Klan during its early years, Forrest later disassociated himself from the organization and denied ever having been a member. In 1875 he underwent a religious conversion that was sparked by a chance encounter on a Memphis street with a former subordinate turned preacher. Forrest died of diabetes in Memphis in 1877, and 28 years later his remains were reinterred in the city's Forrest Park, an area dedicated to his memory.

✦ **FREDERICK DENT GRANT** Following in his father's footsteps, the younger Grant attended West Point, although his record at the academy was less than impressive. Two years after his graduation, he joined the U.S. cavalry and went on two of George Custer's frontier expeditions. Grant was appointed minister to Austria under President Benjamin Harrison in 1889, and served as New York City's commissioner of police from 1895 to 1897.

✦ **ULYSSES S. GRANT** Although the great Union commander won the Republican presidential nomination in 1868, President Grant showed little of the judgment and forcefulness that had characterized the career of General Grant. During his two terms in office, his administration was plagued by corruption and political infighting, although scandal never touched Grant himself. After he left the White House he began to write his memoirs, completing them just days before he died of throat cancer in 1885. More than a million and a half people attended his funeral in New York City.

✦ **JOSEPH HOOKER** "Fighting Joe" sat out the last six months of the war at a post in Ohio and retired from military service in 1868, after suffering a paralytic stroke related to injuries he sustained at Chancellorsville. He spent his retirement traveling, entertaining at his Long Island home, attending veterans' reunions, and indulging in public criticism of his former superiors.

✦ **JOSEPH E. JOHNSTON** After hostilities ended, Johnston served as a Democratic congressman for one term and as commissioner of railroads under President Grover Cleveland. While he was acting as a pallbearer at the funeral of his old adversary, William Tecumseh Sherman, in February 1891, Johnston caught the cold that resulted in his death. Admonished to put on his hat so that he would not catch a chill, the 84-year-old Johnston replied, "If I were in his place and he were standing here in mine, he would not put on his hat."

✦ **ROBERT E. LEE** Unlike many former generals, Lee refused to capitalize on his military reputation by entering politics, publishing his memoirs, or lending his name to business enterprises. Instead, in the fall of 1865 he accepted the presidency of impoverished Washington College in Lexington, Virginia. Lee lived for just five years after the war, and during that time he encouraged national reconciliation through both word and deed. But on his deathbed he returned to the war, ordering General A. P. Hill to move up his troops and then issuing one last command: "Strike the tent."

✦ **JAMES LONGSTREET** The war over, Longstreet resumed his old friendship with Ulysses Grant, joined the Republican Party, and secured a string of federal appointments, including that of minister to Turkey. But many Southerners vilified Longstreet for his support of Reconstruction—and for his published criticisms of Lee's generalship at Gettysburg. After his death in 1904, the defense of Longstreet's military record and postwar political activities was taken up by his young second wife, who lived until 1962, the centenary year of the Battle of Antietam.

✦ **MARY LOUGHBOROUGH** The journal that Loughborough kept during the siege of Vicksburg was published in 1864 as *My Cave Life in Vicksburg.* After the war Loughborough moved to Arkansas, which was her native state, and in 1884 she founded the *Arkansas Ladies' Journal,* one of the first women's magazines in the United States.

✦ **GEORGE McCLELLAN** When he lost the 1864 presidential election to Abraham Lincoln, McClellan left with his family for a three-and-a-half-year sojourn in Europe. There was some talk of nominating him for the presidency again, in 1868, but after Ulysses Grant became the Republican candidate, it no longer seemed like a good idea to run "the man who didn't take Richmond against the man who did." McClellan reentered politics in the 1870s and won election as governor of New Jersey. He died of a heart ailment in 1885, at age 58.

✦ **IRVIN McDOWELL** McDowell's defeat at the First Battle of Bull Run had cost him his army command, and his poor performance during the Second Battle of Bull Run ended his field service. He eventually became a parks commissioner in San Francisco and is credited with laying out part of the Presidio, the military base overlooking the Golden Gate Bridge. He died in 1885 and was buried in the Presidio.

✦ **ELY PARKER** President Grant named his former secretary the first Native American commissioner of Indian affairs in 1869. Eventually, he and his young wife, a Washington belle, moved to fashionable Fairfield, Connecticut. After his Wall Street investments went sour in the mid-1870s, Parker worked at a midlevel clerical job with the New York City police department until his death in 1895.

✦ **JOHN PEMBERTON** The Pennsylvanian who fought for the Confederacy took up farming in Virginia after the war. But finding that he could not support his family by agriculture alone, he established a boarding school on his farm, holding classes in a converted shed. Pemberton devoted much of what leisure time he had to writing a defense of what some Southerners considered his traitorous actions at Vicksburg. He spent his last years back in his hometown of Philadelphia, where he died in 1881. No veterans were in attendance at his funeral, and no military escort took part in the service.

✦ **GEORGE PICKETT** For the rest of his life, Pickett would grieve for the men lost during the charge that would forever bear his name—and would blame Lee for the disaster. "That old man had my division slaughtered at Gettysburg," he told another ex-Confederate officer after they paid a courtesy call on Lee in Richmond five years after the war. "Well," his comrade replied, "it made you immortal."

✦ **WILLIAM TECUMSEH SHERMAN** In July 1865 Sherman assumed command of U.S. forces in the West and pursued a harsh policy toward the Plains Indians. President Grant named him general in chief of the army in 1869. But the relationship between the two men—so close during the war—turned sour when Grant gave the secretary of war more authority at Sherman's expense. "Cump" himself refused to become involved in politics, brushing off the suggestion that he run for the 1884 Republican presidential nomination with the famous words "I will not accept if nominated and will not serve if elected."

✦ **JEB STUART** On May 11, 1864, the "Dixie Cavalier" and his badly outnumbered horsemen went head to head with Union cavalry at a battle just six miles outside Richmond. Stuart took a bullet in the stomach during the fighting, and after hours spent in terrible pain, he died on May 12. Just two days earlier, the 31-year-old Stuart had confided to one of his officers that he had never thought he would survive the war—and that he would not want to live if the Confederacy lost.

NATIONAL FIRSTS

• The first Pony Express relay rider sets out, from Saint Joseph, Missouri, to Sacramento, California (1860)

• Yale awards the first American Ph.D. (1861)

• Federal income tax is enacted (1861)

• The telegraph is first used in the field for military communication (1861)

• Balloons are used for military reconnaissance for the first time in an American war (1861)

• Coleman Sellars patents the kinematoscope, one of the earliest motion-picture devices (1861)

• The first football club is established in Boston (1862)

• Thanksgiving is celebrated as a national holiday for the first time (1863)

• The first Congressional Medal of Honor is presented (1863)

• Olympia Brown becomes the first female ordained minister (1863)

• Free home mail delivery is first instituted in cities (1863)

• The first major racetrack for flat racing opens at Saratoga Springs, New York (1863)

• The first Bessemer steel is produced in the United States (1864)

• Vassar, the first true American women's liberal arts college, opens (1865)

• John S. Rock becomes the first black admitted to practice before the Supreme Court (1865)

• The U.S. Secret Service is established (1865)

CIVIL WAR ERA WORDS AND PHRASES

GREENBACKS: popular name given in 1862 to the first U.S. bank notes, which were green in color; Confederate bank notes were called bluebacks or graybacks after their color.

SHODDY: a cheap fabric made from scraps and ravelings processed to look like good woolen cloth; the term was also applied to contractors who profited from selling poor-quality goods to the United States Army.

PASS THE BUCK: a western expression for passing a counter during a poker game; the counter was frequently a knife; "buck" probably refers to buckhorn, a common material for making knife handles.

JAMBOREE: may come from a West African word, *jama,* which means crowd or gathering.

A.W.O.L.: as part of their punishment, Confederate soldiers who had been absent without leave were sometimes required to wear a placard bearing the initials A.W.O.L. while performing hard physical labor.

AMERICA DIVIDED

POPULATION

Union	22,339,989
Confederacy	
Whites	5,449,462
Slaves	3,521,110
Free Blacks	132,760
	9,103,332

RAILROAD MILEAGE

Union	21,625
Confederacy	9,001

HORSES

Union	4,417,130
Confederacy	1,698,328

STRENGTH OF ARMIES

JULY 1, 1861
Union   183,588   Confederacy   112,040

JANUARY 1, 1865
Union   620,924   Confederacy   196,016

104,000 white Southerners fought for the North.

FEDERAL DEBT

1860	$ 65 million
1866	$2,756 million

CONFEDERATE DEBT

1862	$ 163 million
1864	$1,863 million

INFLATION

The Confederacy experienced 20% inflation in 1861 and 5,000% inflation by the end of 1864. The Union experienced 80% inflation over the course of the war.

INFANTRY ORGANIZATION AT THE BEGINNING OF THE WAR

Company	80–100 officers and men
Regiment	10 companies
Brigade	2 or more regiments
Division	2 or more brigades
Corps	2 or more divisions
Army	2 or more corps

Blacks in the Union army	179,000 soldiers
Blacks in the Union navy	10,000 sailors

The Confederacy did not authorize the use of black soldiers until a few weeks before the war's end.

FOREIGN-BORN SOLDIERS IN THE UNION ARMY

Germans	175,000–200,000
Irish	144,000
English	45,000
Norwegians	4,000
Swedish	3,000

There were also substantial numbers of French, Polish, Scots, Canadians, Belgians, and Hungarians. In all, immigrants accounted for roughly 25% of the Union forces.

WOMEN

18,200 women, including around 2,000 black women, were employed in Union hospitals as matrons, nurses, laundresses, and cooks. The Confederates employed 3,300 women in similar roles.

BATTLE CASUALTIES (DEAD, WOUNDED, AND MISSING)

	UNION	CONFEDERATE
Gettysburg	23,049	28,000*
Seven Days'	15,849	20,141
Chancellorsville	17,287	12,764
Antietam	12,469	13,724
Wilderness	17,666	7,500*
Shiloh	13,047	10,694

*Approximate figure

BATTLEFIELD INJURIES

CAUSE	PERCENTAGE OF INJURIES
Bullets	93%
Artillery projectiles	6%
Sabers or bayonets	less than 1%

FATALITY RATES FOR BATTLEFIELD INJURIES

TYPE OF WOUND	PERCENTAGE FATAL
Abdominal	87%
Chest	63%
Skull	60%
Shoulder	33%

DISEASE

Union troops reported 6,000,000 disease cases, including:

	CASES	DEATHS
Diarrhea and dysentery	1,739,135	44,558
Malaria	1,315,955	10,063
Catarrh and bronchitis	283,075	585
Pneumonia	77,335	19,971
Measles	76,318	5,177
Scurvy	46,931	771

AMPUTATIONS

Union medical records report 29,980 amputations.

TYPE OF AMPUTATION	FATALITY RATE
at the hip	90%
thigh or knee joint	50%
upper arm	25%
ankle joint	7%

1860	1861	1862

FROM THE EVE OF WAR TO THE SURRENDER AT APPOMATTOX

CONFEDERATE KEG TORPEDO

NOVEMBER 18 The Georgia legislature appropriates $1 million to arm the state.

DECEMBER 30 The Federal arsenal at Charleston is seized by South Carolina.

MARCH 6 Jefferson Davis calls out 100,000 volunteers for one year.

APRIL 12 Confederates fire on Fort Sumter (South Carolina).

APRIL 15 Lincoln issues a call for 75,000 militiamen for three months' service.

APRIL 19 Lincoln declares a blockade of Confederate ports.

APRIL 22 Robert E. Lee is named commander of Virginia's army.

JUNE 10 Dorothea Dix is commissioned the Union army's first superintendent of women nurses.

JULY 21 First Battle of Bull Run (Virginia).

JULY 27 George B. McClellan is put in command of what will soon be named the Army of the Potomac.

SEPTEMBER 9 Sally Louisa Tompkins becomes the Confederacy's only female commissioned officer.

FEBRUARY 16 Fort Donelson (Tennessee) surrenders.

MARCH 9 The *Monitor* defeats the *Virginia* (formerly the *Merrimac*).

MARCH 23 First battle in Stonewall Jackson's Shenandoah Valley campaign, at Kernstown (Virginia).

APRIL 6-7 Battle of Shiloh (Tennessee).

APRIL 25 Fall of New Orleans to Flag Officer David Farragut.

JUNE 25 Battle of the Seven Days begins (Virginia).

AUGUST 25 Secretary of War Stanton authorizes raising black troops.

AUGUST 29-30 Second Battle of Bull Run (Virginia).

SEPTEMBER 17 Battle of Antietam (Maryland).

DECEMBER 13 Battle of Fredericksburg (Virginia).

THE POLITICS OF SECESSION; THE POLITICS OF UNION

NOVEMBER 6 Abraham Lincoln is elected president.

DECEMBER 14 The Georgia legislature calls for a convention to consider a confederacy of southern states.

DECEMBER 20 South Carolina secedes from the Union.

LINCOLN CAMPAIGN BOOKMARKS

JANUARY 9 Mississippi secedes from the Union.

JANUARY 10 Florida secedes from the Union.

JANUARY 11 Alabama secedes from the Union.

JANUARY 19 Georgia secedes from the Union.

JANUARY 26 Louisiana secedes from the Union.

JANUARY 29 Kansas becomes the 34th state.

FEBRUARY 1 Texas secedes from the Union.

FEBRUARY 18 Jefferson Davis of Mississippi is inaugurated the provisional president of the Confederacy.

FEBRUARY 28 The Colorado Territory is organized.

MARCH 2 Nevada and Dakota Territories are formed.

MARCH 4 Abraham Lincoln is inaugurated (first term).

APRIL 17 Virginia secedes from the Union.

MAY 6 Arkansas and Tennessee secede from the Union.

MAY 13 Queen Victoria issues a proclamation of British neutrality.

MAY 20 North Carolina secedes from the Union.

MAY 20 Confederate Congress votes to move the capital from Montgomery (Alabama) to Richmond.

UNION DRUM WITH EAGLE INSIGNIA

FEBRUARY 22 Jefferson Davis is inaugurated president of the Confederacy.

APRIL 16 Confederate Conscription Act is signed by Davis.

APRIL 16 Slavery is abolished in the District of Columbia.

JULY 17 Federal Confiscation Act frees slaves of disloyal masters who come under Union control, authorizes use of black troops.

MAY 2-6 Battle of Chancellorsville (Virginia).

JULY 1-3 Battle of Gettysburg (Pennsylvania).

JULY 4 Vicksburg (Mississippi) surrenders.

SEPTEMBER 19-20 Battle of Chickamauga (Georgia).

NOVEMBER 23-25 Battle of Chattanooga (Tennessee).

IRISH BRIGADE FLAG

MARCH 2 Grant is officially named general in chief of the Union's armies.

MAY 5-7 Battle of the Wilderness (Virginia).

JUNE 1-3 Battle of Cold Harbor (Virginia).

JUNE 18 Siege of Petersburg (Virginia) begins.

JULY 11-12 Confederates under Jubal Early threaten Washington, D.C.

SEPTEMBER 2 Sherman enters Atlanta.

DECEMBER 15-16 Battle of Nashville (Tennessee).

JANUARY 31 Lee is named general in chief of the Confederacy.

MARCH 13 Davis signs legislation authorizing the use of black soldiers.

APRIL 3 Fall of Richmond and Petersburg.

APRIL 9 Lee surrenders to Grant at Appomattox Court House.

APRIL 26 Joseph E. Johnston's final surrender to Sherman, near Durham Station, North Carolina.

MAY 10 Jefferson Davis captured in Georgia.

MAY 26 E. Kirby Smith's Army of the Trans-Mississippi surrenders at New Orleans.

JUNE 23 Stand Watie, commander of the Confederacy's Indian forces, surrenders in Indian Territory.

JANUARY 1 The Emancipation Proclamation takes effect.

FEBRUARY 24 The Arizona Territory is formed.

MARCH 3 The Federal draft law is enacted.

MARCH 3 The Idaho Territory is organized.

MARCH 26 The Confederate Congress authorizes impressment of private property by armies in the field.

JUNE 20 West Virginia becomes the 35th state.

JULY 13-16 New York City draft riots.

NOVEMBER 19 Lincoln delivers the Gettysburg Address.

MAY 26 Montana is organized as a territory.

JUNE 28 Fugitive Slave Act is repealed by Congress.

OCTOBER 31 Nevada becomes the 36th state.

NOVEMBER 8 Lincoln is reelected president, defeating McClellan.

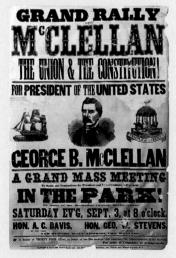

CAMPAIGN POSTER

FEBRUARY 3 Confederate commissioners meet Lincoln at Hampton Roads, Virginia, to discuss peace terms.

MARCH 3 The Freedmen's Bureau is created.

MARCH 4 Abraham Lincoln is inaugurated (second term).

APRIL 14 Abraham Lincoln is assassinated.

APRIL 15 Andrew Johnson is sworn in as president.

MAY 9 Trial of Lincoln assassination conspirators begins.

DECEMBER 18 The 13th Amendment is ratified, abolishing slavery.

Dawson, ©1913 Houghton Mifflin, Boston. 128, 129: Library of Congress; Western Reserve Historical Society, Cleveland, Ohio; Stowe-Day Foundation, Hartford, Conn. 130, 131: Department of Archives and Manuscripts, Louisiana State Univeristy, Baton Rouge. 132, 133: Courtesy Meserve-Kunhardt Collection; Library of Congress. 134: ©White House Historical Association. 135: National Museum of Natural History. 136: Library of Congress. 137: Collection of New-York Historical Society. 139-141: Library of Congress. 140, 141: Library of Congress. 142: Drawing by Alfred R. Waud/Library of Congress. 143: Library of Congress, no. B8151-5018. 146: Painting by Julian Scott, courtesy Robert A. McNeil/photograph by Sharon Deveaux. 148: Archives Division-Texas State Library. 149: Confederate Museum, Charleston, S.C./photograph by Harold H. Norvell—Larry Sherer. 150, 151: Drawing by Alfred R. Waud/Library of Congress. 153: Courtesy Meserve-Kunhardt Collection. 154: Map by Maryland CartoGraphics, Inc. 155: Library of Congress, no. B8121-948. 156: Library of Congress, no. B8171-3623. 158: Courtesy Meserve-Kunhardt Collection. 159: Courtesy Butterfield & Butterfield. 161: Thomas Lovell/courtesy National Geographic Society—Rosenbach Museum and Library, Philadelphia. 162, 163: Ken Riley, courtesy West Point Collection, no. 71414. 165: Smithsonian Institution. 166: Courtesy Meserve-Kunhardt Collection; Library of Congress, no. B8171-7784; Library of Congress, no. B8171-7773; Library of Congress, no. B8171-7781. 167: Richard J. S. and Kellie O. Gutman Collection. 168: Courtesy Ford's Theatre/photograph by Edward Owen; Frank and Marie-Thérèse Wood Print Collections, Alexandria, Va. 169: Courtesy Lloyd Ostendorf Collection, Dayton, Ohio. 170: Map by Maryland CartoGraphics, Inc. 171: David Buffington Photography—courtesy Ford's Theatre/photograph by Edward Owen (2). 172: Courtesy Lloyd Ostendorf Collection, Dayton, Ohio. 173: Illinois State Historical Library—map by Maryland CartoGraphics, Inc. 174, 175: Frank and Marie-Thérèse Wood Print Collections, Alexandria, Va.; noose courtesy Dr. John K. Lattimer/photograph by Henry Groskinsky; courtesy Meserve-Kunhardt Collection. 176: National Park Service. 178: Library of Congress—Granger Collection, New York; Library of Congress, no. USZ62-21561. 179: Library of Congress, no. USZ62-63483; Fairfield Historical Society. 182: Private Collection/photograph by Henry Groskinsky—courtesy National Museum of American History, Smithsonian Institution, Washington, D.C./photograph by Larry Sherer; Seventh Regiment Fund, Inc./photograph by Al Freni. 183: Hall of Flags, State House, Boston/photograph by Jack Leonard—courtesy National Museum of American History, Smithsonian Institution, Washington, D.C./photograph by Larry Sherer.

BIBLIOGRAPHY

BOOKS

Alexander, E. P. *Military Memoirs of a Confederate: A Critical Narrative.* Dayton: Press of Morningside Bookshop, 1977 (reprint of 1907 edition).

Alleman, Tillie Pierce. *At Gettysburg, or What a Girl Saw and Heard of the Battle: A True Narrative.* New York: W. Lake Borland, 1889.

Andrews, W. H. *Footprints of a Regiment: A Recollection of the 1st Georgia Regulars, 1861–1865.* Atlanta: Longstreet Press, 1992.

Armstrong, William H. *Warrior in Two Camps: Ely S. Parker, Union General and Seneca Chief.* Syracuse, N.Y.: Syracuse University Press, 1978.

Bailey, Ronald H., and the Editors of Time-Life Books. *Forward to Richmond* (The Civil War series). Alexandria, Va.: Time-Life Books, 1983.

Ball, Douglas B. *Financial Failure and Confederate Defeat.* Chicago: University of Illinois Press, 1991.

Ballard, Michael B. *Pemberton: A Biography.* Jackson: University Press of Mississippi, 1991.

Bateman, Fred, and Thomas Weiss. *A Deplorable Scarcity: The Failure of Industrialization in the Slave Economy.* Chapel Hill: University of North Carolina Press, 1981.

Billings, John D. *Hardtack and Coffee, or The Unwritten Story of Army Life.* Boston: George M. Smith, 1887.

Borreson, Ralph. *When Lincoln Died.* New York: Appleton-Century, 1965.

Bradford, Ned (ed.). *Battles and Leaders of the Civil War.* New York: Dutton, 1956.

Brother against Brother: Time-Life Books History of the Civil War. Alexandria, Va.: Time-Life Books, 1990.

Bruce, Robert V. *Lincoln and the Tools of War.* Urbana and Chicago: University of Illinois Press, 1989.

Burgess, Lauren Cook (ed.). *An Uncommon Soldier.* Pasadena, Maryland: MINERVA Center, 1994.

Carruth, Gorton. *The Encyclopedia of American Facts & Dates.* New York: Harper & Row, 1987.

Carter, Samuel, III. *The Final Fortress: The Campaign for Vicksburg, 1862–1863.* New York: St. Martin's Press, 1980.

Catton, Bruce:
The Civil War (The American Heritage Library). Boston: Houghton Mifflin, 1960.
Grant Moves South. Boston: Little, Brown, 1960.

Cauble, Frank P. *The Surrender Proceedings: April 9, 1965, Appomattox Court House.* Lynchburg, Va.: H. E. Howard, 1987.

Chaitin, Peter M., and the Editors of Time-Life Books. *The Coastal War* (The Civil War series). Alexandria, Va.: Time-Life Books, 1984.

Channing, Steven A., and the Editors of Time-Life Books. *Confederate Ordeal* (The Civil War series). Alexandria, Va.: Time-Life Books, 1989.

The Civil War, 1861–1865: A Collection of U.S. Commemorative Stamps. The Editors of Time-Life Books. Washington, D.C.: U.S. Postal Service, 1995.

Civil War Naval Chronology: 1861–1865. Compiled by Naval History Division, Navy Department. Washington, D.C.: Government Printing Office, 1971.

Clark, Champ, and the Editors of Time-Life Books:
The Assassination: Death of the President. Alexandria, Va.: Time-Life Books, 1987.
Decoying the Yanks. Alexandria, Va.: Time-Life Books, 1984.
Gettysburg: The Confederate High Tide. Alexandria, Va.: Time-Life Books, 1985.

Coggins, Jack. *Arms and Equipment of the Civil War.* New York: Doubleday, 1962.

Conklin, E. F. *Women at Gettysburg, 1863.* Gettysburg, Pa.: Thomas Publications, 1993.

Cornish, Dudley Taylor. *The Sable Arm: Black Troops in the Union Army, 1861–1865.* Lawrence: University Press of Kansas, 1987.

Cowan, Tom, and Jack Maguire. *Timelines of African-American History: 500 Years of Black Achievement.* New York: Roundtable Press/Perigee, 1994.

Crummer, Wilbur F. *With Grant at Fort Donelson, Shiloh and Vicksburg.* Oak Park, Ill.: E. C. Crummer, 1915.

Cullen, Joseph P. *The Peninsula Campaign, 1862.* New York: Bonanza Books, 1973.

Cullinan, Gerald. *The Post Office Department.* New York: Frederick A. Praeger, 1969.

Current, Richard Nelson. *Lincoln's Loyalists: Union Soldiers from the Confederacy.* Boston: Northeastern University Press, 1992.

Current, Richard N. (ed.). *Encyclopedia of the Confederacy*

(Vol. 1). New York: Simon & Schuster, 1993.

Dana, Charles A. *Recollections of the Civil War: With the Leaders at Washington and in the Field in the Sixties*. New York: D. Appleton, 1902.

Davis, Burke. *Jeb Stuart: The Last Cavalier*. New York: Rinehart, 1957.

Davis, William C.:
Battle at Bull Run: A History of the First Major Campaign of the Civil War. Baton Rouge: Louisiana State University Press, 1977.
Brothers in Arms. New York: Smithmark, 1995.
The First Battle of Manassas (National Parks Civil War series). Conshohocken, Pa.: Eastern National Park and Monument Association, 1995.
The Image of War, 1861–1865, Volume 4: Fighting for Time. Garden City, N.Y.: Doubleday, 1983.
Jefferson Davis: The Man and His Hour. New York: HarperPerennial, 1992.

Davis, William C., and the Editors of Time-Life Books:
Brother against Brother (The Civil War series). Alexandria, Va.: Time-Life Books, 1983.
First Blood (The Civil War series). Alexandria, Va.: Time-Life Books, 1983.

Davis, William C. (ed.):
The Confederate General (6 vols.). Gettysburg, Pa.: National Historical Society, 1991.
The Image of War, 1861–1865, Volume 1: Shadows of the Storm. Garden City, N.Y.: Doubleday, 1981.

Donald, David Herbert. *Lincoln*. New York: Simon & Schuster, 1995.

East, Charles (ed.). *The Civil War Diary of Sarah Morgan*. Athens: University of Georgia Press, 1991.

Echoes of Glory (3 vols.). Alexandria, Va.: Time-Life Books, 1991.

Elting, John R., Dan Cragg, and Ernest L. Deal. *A Dictionary of Soldier Talk*. New York: Charles Scribner's Sons, 1984.

Esposito, Vincent J. (ed.) *The West Point Atlas of the Civil War*. Compiled by the Department of Military Art and Engineering, the United States Military Academy, West Point. New York: Frederick A. Praeger, 1962.

Farwell, Byron. *Stonewall: A Biography of General Thomas J. Jackson*. New York: W. W. Norton, 1992.

Faust, Patricia L. (ed.). *Historical Times Illustrated Encyclopedia of the Civil War*. New York: Harper & Row, 1986.

Fellman, Michael. *Citizen Sherman: A Life of William Tecumseh Sherman*. New York: Random House, 1995.

Fleming, Thomas J. *West Point: The Men and Times of the United States Military Academy*. New York: William Morrow, 1969.

Flexner, Stuart Berg. *Listening to America*. New York: Simon & Schuster, 1982.

Flood, Charles Bracelen. *Lee: The Last Years*. Boston: Houghton Mifflin, 1981.

Foote, Shelby. *The Civil War: A Narrative* (3 vols.). New York: Random House, 1958, 1963, 1974.

Freeman, Douglas Southall:
Lee's Lieutenants: A Study in Command, Volume 1: Manassas to Malvern Hill. New York: Charles Scribner's Sons, 1942.
R. E. Lee: A Biography (5 vols.). New York: Charles Scribner's Sons, 1934.

Frobel, Anne S. *The Civil War Diary of Anne S. Frobel*. McLean, Va.: EPM Publications, 1992.

Furgurson, Ernest B. *Chancellorsville 1863: The Souls of the Brave*. New York: Alfred A. Knopf, 1992.

Gallagher, Gary W. *The Battle of Chancellorsville* (National Parks Civil War series). Conshohocken, Pa.: Eastern National Park and Monument Association, 1995.

Gallman, J. Matthew. *The North Fights the Civil War: The Home Front* (The American Way series). Chicago: Ivan R. Dee, 1994.

Geary, James W. *We Need Men: The Union Draft in the Civil War*. De Kalb: Northern Illinois University Press, 1991.

Gettysburg (Voices of the Civil War series). Alexandria, Va.: Time-Life Books, 1995.

Goolrick, William K., and the Editors of Time-Life Books. *Rebels Resurgent* (The Civil War series). Alexandria, Va.: Time-Life Books, 1985.

Gordon, John B. *Reminiscences of the Civil War*. New York: Charles Scribner's Sons, 1903.

Grant, Ulysses S. *Personal Memoirs of U. S. Grant*. Edited by E. B. Long. New York: Da Capo Press, 1982.

Hassler, Warren W., Jr. *Commanders of the Army of the Potomac*. Baton Rouge: Louisiana State University Press, 1962.

Hattaway, Herman, and Archer Jones. *How the North Won: A Military History of the Civil War*. Chicago: University of Illinois Press, 1983.

Hebert, Walter H. *Fighting Joe Hooker*. Indianapolis: Bobbs-Merrill, 1944.

Holloway, Joseph E., and Winifred K. Vass. *The African Heritage of American English*. Indianapolis: Indiana University Press, 1993.

Hurst, Jack. *Nathan Bedford Forrest: A Biography*. New York: Alfred A. Knopf, 1993.

Jackson, Donald Dale, and the Editors of Time-Life Books. *Twenty Million Yankees* (The Civil War series). Alexandria, Va.: Time-Life Books, 1985.

Jackson, Mary Anna. *Memoirs of Stonewall Jackson*. Dayton: Press of Morningside Bookshop, 1976.

Jaynes, Gregory, and the Editors of Time-Life Books. *The Killing Ground* (The Civil War series). Alexandria, Va.: Time-Life Books, 1986.

Johnson, Curt, and Mark McLaughlin. *Civil War Battles*.

New York: Fairfax Press, 1977.

Jones, Katharine M. (ed.). *Heroines of Dixie: Confederate Women Tell Their Story of the War*. Westport, Conn.: Greenwood Press, 1973.

Kane, Joseph Nathan. *Famous First Facts*. New York: H. W. Wilson, 1981.

Kelbaugh, Ross J. *Introduction to Civil War Photography*. Gettysburg, Pa.: Thomas Publications, 1991.

Keylin, Arleen, and Douglas John Bowen (eds.). *The New York Times Book of the Civil War*. New York: Arno Press, 1980.

Korn, Jerry, and the Editors of Time-Life Books:
The Fight for Chattanooga (The Civil War series). Alexandria, Va.: Time-Life Books, 1985.
Pursuit to Appomattox (The Civil War series). Alexandria, Va.: Time-Life Books, 1987.
War on the Mississippi (The Civil War series). Alexandria, Va.: Time-Life Books, 1985.

Kunhardt, Dorothy Meserve, Philip B. Kunhardt Jr., and the Editors of Time-Life Books. *Mathew Brady and His World*. Alexandria, Va.: Time-Life Books, 1977.

Lee, Richard M. *Mr. Lincoln's City: An Illustrated Guide to the Civil War Sites of Washington*. McLean, Va.: EPM Publications, 1981.

Lee Takes Command (The Civil War series). Alexandria, Va.: Time-Life Books, 1984.

Leech, Margaret. *Reveille in Washington: 1860–1865*. Alexandria, Va.: Time-Life Books, 1962.

Lewis, Paul. *Yankee Admiral: A Biography of David Dixon Porter*. New York: David McKay, 1968.

Lewis, Thomas A., and the Editors of Time-Life Books. *The Shenandoah in Flames* (The Civil War series). Alexandria, Va.: Time-Life Books, 1987.

Long, E. B., and Barbara Long. *The Civil War Day by Day: An Almanac, 1861-1865*. Garden City, N.Y.: Doubleday, 1971.

Longacre, Edward G. *Pickett: Leader of the Charge*. Shippensburg, Pa.: White Mane Publishing, 1995.

Longstreet, James. *From Manassas to Appomattox: Memoirs of the Civil War in America*. Edited by James I. Robertson Jr. Bloomington: Indiana University Press, 1981.

Lonn, Ella. *Foreigners in the Union Army and Navy*. Baton Rouge: Louisiana State University Press, 1951.

Loughborough, Mrs. James M. *My Cave Life in Vicksburg with Letters of Trial and Travel*. Spartanburg, S.C.: Reprint Co., 1976.

Lowry, Thomas P. *The Story the Soldiers Wouldn't Tell: Sex in the Civil War*. Mechanicsburg, Pa.: Stackpole Books, 1994.

Lyman, Darryl. *Civil War Wordbook: Including Sayings, Phrases and Slang*. Conshohocken, Pa.: Combined Books, 1994.

McDonald, Cornelia Peake. *A Woman's Civil War: A Diary with Reminiscences of the War, from March 1862.* Edited by Minrose C. Gwin. Madison: University of Wisconsin Press, 1992.

McDonough, James Lee. *Shiloh—in Hell Before Night.* Knoxville: University of Tennessee Press, 1977.

McFeely, William S.:
Frederick Douglass. New York: W. W. Norton, 1991.
Grant: A Biography. New York: W. W. Norton, 1981.

McPherson, James M.:
Battle Cry of Freedom: The Civil War Era. New York: Oxford University Press, 1988.
The Negro's Civil War: How American Blacks Felt and Acted During the War for the Union. New York: Ballantine Books, 1991.
Ordeal by Fire: The Civil War and Reconstruction. New York: McGraw-Hill, 1992.

McPherson, James M. (ed.). *The Atlas of the Civil War.* New York: Macmillan, 1994.

McWhiney, Grady. *Braxton Bragg and Confederate Defeat, Volume 1: Field Command.* New York: Columbia University Press, 1969.

Major, Clarence (ed.). *Juba to Jive: A Dictionary of African-American Slang.* New York: Viking, 1994.

Marszalek, John F. *Sherman: A Soldier's Passion for Order.* New York: Macmillan/Free Press, 1993.

Martin, David G.:
The Chancellorsville Campaign: March–May 1863 (The Great Campaigns series). Conshohocken, Pa.: Combined Books, 1991.
The Peninsula Campaign: March–July 1862 (The Great Campaigns series). Conshohocken, Pa.: Combined Books, 1992.
The Vicksburg Campaign: April 1862–July 1863 (The Great Campaigns series). Conshohocken, Pa.: Combined Books, 1994.

Meredith, Roy. *Mr. Lincoln's Camera Man: Mathew B. Brady.* New York: Dover Publications, 1974.

Miers, Earl Schenck. *The Web of Victory: Grant at Vicksburg.* Westport, Conn.: Greenwood Press, 1955.

Naisawald, L. Van Loan. *Grape and Canister: The Story of the Field Artillery of the Army of the Potomac, 1861–1865.* New York: Oxford University Press, 1960.

Nevin, David, and the Editors of Time-Life Books:
The Road to Shiloh (The Civil War series). Alexandria, Va.: Time-Life Books, 1983.
Sherman's March (The Civil War series). Alexandria, Va.: Time-Life Books, 1986.

Oates, Stephen B. *A Woman of Valor: Clara Barton and the Civil War.* New York: Macmillan/Free Press, 1994.

Paludan, Phillip Shaw. *"A People's Contest": The Union and Civil War, 1861–1865.* New York: Harper & Row, 1988.

Paskoff, Paul F. (ed.). *Iron and Steel in the Nineteenth Century* (Encyclopedia of American Business History and Biography). New York: Facts On File, 1989.

Pemberton, John C. *Pemberton: Defender of Vicksburg.* Chapel Hill: University of North Carolina Press, 1942.

Perry, Milton F. *Infernal Machines: The Story of Confederate Submarine and Mine Warfare.* Baton Rouge: Louisiana State University Press, 1965.

Pfanz, Harry W. *The Battle of Gettysburg* (National Parks Civil War series). Conshohocken, Pa.: Eastern National Park and Monument Association, 1994.

Porter, David D. *Incidents and Anecdotes of the Civil War.* New York: D. Appleton, 1885.

Porter, Horace. *Campaigning with Grant.* New York: Century, 1897.

Quigley, Martin, Jr. *Magic Shadows: The Story of the Origin of Motion Pictures.* Washington, D.C.: Georgetown University Press, 1948.

Ransom, Roger L. *Conflict and Compromise: The Political Economy of Slavery, Emancipation, and the American Civil War.* Cambridge: Cambridge University Press, 1989.

Ray, Frederic E. *"Our Special Artist": Alfred R. Waud's Civil War.* Mechanicsburg, Pa.: Stackpole Books, 1994.

Reid, William. *Arms through the Ages.* New York: Harper & Row, 1976.

Richardson, Albert D. *A Personal History of Ulysses S. Grant.* Hartford: American Publishing Co., 1868.

Roberts, Marcia. *Looking Back and Seeing the Future: The United States Secret Service, 1865–1990.* Edited by Winston Fitzpatrick. Alexandria, Va.: Association of Former Agents of the United States Secret Service, Inc., 1991.

Robertson, James I., Jr.:
Common Soldier (National Parks Civil War series). Conshohocken, Pa.: Eastern National Park and Monument Association, 1994.
Soldiers Blue and Gray. Columbia: University of South Carolina Press, 1988.

Robertson, James I., Jr., and the Editors of Time-Life Books. *Tenting Tonight* (The Civil War series). Alexandria, Va.: Time-Life Books, 1984.

Rollins, Richard (ed.). *Pickett's Charge: Eyewitness Accounts.* Redondo Beach, Calif.: Rank and File Publications, 1994.

Ross, Ishbel. *The General's Wife: The Life of Mrs. Ulysses S. Grant.* New York: Dodd, Mead, 1959.

Sandburg, Carl. *Abraham Lincoln: The War Years* (Vol. 4). New York: Harcourt, Brace, 1939.

Sanger, Donald Bridgman, and Thomas Robson Hay. *James Longstreet: Soldier, Politician, Officeholder, and Writer.* Gloucester, Mass.: Peter Smith, 1968.

Schlesinger, Arthur M., Jr. *The Almanac of American History.* New York: G. P. Putnam's Sons, 1983.

Scott, Robert Garth. *Into the Wilderness with the Army of the Potomac.* Bloomington: Indiana University Press, 1985.

Sears, Stephen W. *George B. McClellan: The Young Napoleon.* New York: Ticknor & Fields, 1988.

Second Manassas (Voices of the Civil War series). Alexandria, Va.: Time-Life Books, 1995.

Simpson, Jeffrey. *Officers and Gentlemen: Historic West Point in Photographs.* Tarrytown, N.Y.: Sleepy Hollow Press, 1982.

Smith, Gene. *Lee and Grant: A Dual Biography.* New York: McGraw-Hill, 1984.

Smith, James Power. *With Stonewall Jackson in the Army of Northern Virginia.* Gaithersburg, Md.: Zullo and Van Sickle Books, 1982.

Sperber, Hans, and Travis Trittschuh. *American Political Terms: An Historical Dictionary.* Detroit: Wayne State University Press, 1962.

Spies, Scouts and Raiders (The Civil War series). Alexandria, Va.: Time-Life Books, 1985.

Steele, Janet E. *The Sun Shines for All: Journalism and Ideology in the Life of Charles A. Dana.* Syracuse, N.Y.: Syracuse University Press, 1993.

Steiner, Paul E. *Disease in the Civil War: Natural Biological Warfare in 1861–1865.* Springfield, Ill.: Charles C. Thomas, 1968.

Stewart, George R. *Pickett's Charge: A Microhistory of the Final Attack at Gettysburg, July 3, 1863.* Dayton: Press of Morningside Bookshop, 1980 (reprint of 1959 edition).

Sutherland, Daniel E. *The Expansion of Everyday Life, 1860–1876.* New York: Harper & Row, 1989.

Sword, Wiley. *Shiloh: Bloody April.* New York: William Morrow, 1974.

Symonds, Craig L. *Joseph E. Johnston: A Civil War Biography.* New York: W. W. Norton, 1992.

Thomas, Emory M.:
Bold Dragoon: The Life of J. E. B. Stuart. New York: Harper & Row, 1986.
The Confederate Nation, 1861–1865. New York: Harper & Row, 1979.

Trager, James (ed.). *The People's Chronology.* New York: Holt, Rinehart and Winston, 1979.

Trudeau, Noah Andre:
Bloody Roads South: The Wilderness to Cold Harbor, May–June 1864. Boston: Little, Brown, 1989.
The Campaign to Appomattox (National Parks Civil War series). Conshohocken, Pa.: Eastern National Park and Monument Association, 1995.

Trulock, Alice Rains. *In the Hands of Providence.* Chapel Hill: University of North Carolina Press, 1992.

Tucker, Glenn. *Hancock the Superb.* Dayton: Press of Morningside Bookshop, 1980.

Urdang, Laurence (ed.). *The Timetables of American History.* New York: Simon & Schuster, 1981.

Utley, Robert M. *Cavalier in Buckskin: George Armstrong Custer and the Western Military Frontier.* Norman: University of Oklahoma Press, 1988.

Vandiver, Frank E. *Blood Brothers: A Short History of the Civil War.* College Station: Texas A&M University Press, 1992.

Vinovskis, Maris A. (ed.). *Toward a Social History of the American Civil War.* Cambridge: Cambridge University Press, 1990.

Walker, Peter F. *Vicksburg: A People at War, 1860–1865.* Chapel Hill: University of North Carolina Press, 1960.

Ward, Geoffrey C. *The Civil War: An Illustrated History.* New York: Alfred A. Knopf, 1990.

Warner, Ezra J. *In Blue: Lives of the Union Commanders.* Baton Rouge: Louisiana State University Press, 1964.

Webb, Willard (ed.). *Crucial Moments of the Civil War.* New York: Fountainhead Publishers, 1961.

Wert, Jeffry D. *General James Longstreet.* New York: Simon & Schuster, 1993.

Wheeler, Richard:
On Fields of Fury. New York: HarperCollins, 1991.
The Siege of Vicksburg. New York: Thomas Y. Crowell, 1978.
Voices of the Civil War. New York: Thomas Y. Crowell, 1976.

Witness to Appomattox. New York: Harper & Row, 1989.
Witness to Gettysburg. New York: Harper & Row, 1987.

Wiley, Bell Irvin:
The Life of Billy Yank: The Common Soldier of the Union. Baton Rouge: Louisiana State University Press, 1981.
The Life of Johnny Reb: The Common Soldier of the Confederacy. Baton Rouge: Louisiana State University Press, 1980.

Wilkeson, Frank. *Recollections of a Private Soldier in the Army of the Potomac.* New York: G. P. Putnam's Sons, 1887.

Williams, T. Harry.:
Lincoln and His Generals. New York: Alfred A. Knopf, 1952.
P. G. T. Beauregard: Napoleon in Gray. Baton Rouge: Louisiana State University Press, 1955.

Wills, Brian Steel. *A Battle from the Start: The Life of Nathan Bedford Forrest.* New York: HarperPerennial, 1993.

Wilson, James Harrison. *The Life of John A. Rawlins.* New York: Neale Publishing, 1916.

Winks, Robin W. *Canada and the United States: The Civil War Years.* Lanham, Md.: University Press of America, 1988.

Winters, John D. *The Civil War in Louisiana.* Baton Rouge: Louisiana State University Press, 1963.

Worsham, John H. *One of Jackson's Foot Cavalry: His Experience and What He Saw During the War 1861–1865.* New York: Neale Publishing, 1912.

Who Was Who in the Civil War. New York: Crescent Books, 1994.

PERIODICALS

Castel, Albert (ed.). "The War Album of Henry Dwight, Part III." *Civil War Times Illustrated,* May 1980.

Meyer, Eugene L. "The Odyssey of Pvt. Rosetta Wakeman, Union Army." *Smithsonian,* January 1994.

Schultz, Jane E. "Race, Gender, and Bureaucracy: Civil War Army Nurses and the Pension Bureau." *Journal of Women's History,* Summer 1994.

Sears, Stephen W. "God's Chosen Instrument." *American Heritage,* July/August 1988.

Sword, Wiley. "The Battle of Shiloh." Conshohocken, Pa.: Acorn Press (Eastern National Park and Monument Association), 1982.

OTHER SOURCES

"Shiloh: National Military Park, Tennessee." Washington, D.C.: National Park Service, 1961.

INDEX

TIME-LIFE® BOOKS Time-Life Books is a
division of Time Life Inc.

TIME LIFE INC.

PRESIDENT and CEO: George Artandi

TIME-LIFE BOOKS

PRESIDENT: John D. Hall
PUBLISHER/MANAGING EDITOR: Neil Kagan

THE AMERICAN STORY

War Between Brothers

EDITOR: Sarah Brash
DIRECTOR, NEW PRODUCT DEVELOPMENT:
Curtis Kopf
MARKETING DIRECTOR: Pamela R. Farrell

Design Director: Dale Pollekoff
Deputy Editor: Mary Grace Mayberry
Picture Editor: Sally Collins
Text Editors: Robin Currie (principal), James Lynch,
Glen B. Ruh
Art Director: Ellen L. Pattisall
Associate Editors/Research and Writing: Mary H. McCarthy,
Jacqueline L. Shaffer, Katya Sharpe, Jarelle S. Stein
Copyeditor: Judith Klein
Picture Coordinator: Catherine Parrott
Editorial Assistant: Patricia D. Whiteford

Special Contributors: Ronald H. Bailey, Timothy Cooke,
Thomas A. Lewis, George Russell (text); Philip Brandt
George (administration); Barbara Fleming, Ruth Goldberg,
Stacy W. Hoffhaus, Daniel Kulpinski, Barbara Levitt,
Maureen McHugh, Mary Davis Suro, Marilyn Murphy
Terrell, Elizabeth Thompson, Robert H. Wooldridge Jr.
(research and writing); Ellen Gross Gerth, Catherine
Chase Tyson (pictures); Gerald P. Tyson (editing); Barbara
L. Klein (index).

Correspondents: Christine Hinze (London), Christina
Lieberman (New York), Maria Vincenza Aloisi (Paris).

Vice President, Director of Finance: Christopher Hearing
Vice President, Book Production: Marjann Caldwell
Director of Operations: Eileen Bradley
Director of Photography and Research: John Conrad Weiser
Director of Editorial Administration: Judith W. Shanks
Production Manager: Marlene Zack
Quality Assurance Manager: James King
Library: Louise D. Forstall

The Consultant
Colonel John R. Elting, USA (Ret.), a former associate
professor at West Point, is the author or editor of some
20 books on military history, including *Amateurs, to Arms!:
A Military History of the War of* 1812–1815, *American Army
Life, The Battle of Bunker's Hill, Military Uniforms in
America, The Superstrategists,* and *Swords around a Throne.*
Colonel Elting also wrote *Battles for Scandinavia* in Time
Life's World War II series and served as a consultant to
The Civil War and The Third Reich series.

Library of Congress Cataloging-in-Publication Data
War between brothers / by the editors of Time-Life Books.
   p. cm.—(American story)
   Includes bibliographical references and index.
   ISBN 0-7835-6251-9
   1. United States—History—Civil War, 1861–1865—
Campaigns. 2. United States—History—Civil War,
1861–1865—Pictorial works.
I. Time-Life Books. II. Series.
E470.W33 1996
973.7'3—dc20   96-20773
                            CIP

Other Publications

HISTORY
Voices of the Civil War
The American Indians
Lost Civilizations
Mysteries of the Unknown
Time Frame
The Civil War
Cultural Atlas

SCIENCE/NATURE
Voyage Through the Universe

COOKING
Weight Watchers® Smart Choice Recipe Collection
Great Taste–Low Fat
Williams-Sonoma Kitchen Library

DO IT YOURSELF
The Time-Life Complete Gardener
Home Repair and Improvement
The Art of Woodworking
Fix It Yourself

TIME-LIFE KIDS
Family Time Bible Stories
Library of First Questions and Answers
A Child's First Library of Learning
I Love Math
Nature Company Discoveries
Understanding Science & Nature

For information on and a full description of any
of the Time-Life Books series listed above, please
call 1-800-621-7026 or write:

Reader Information
Time-Life Customer Service
P.O. Box C-32068
Richmond, Virginia 23261-2068

On the cover: Shortly before his return home in
1865, a weary Union veteran of the 8th Pennsylvania Volunteers displays his unit's tattered flag, stark
symbol of a country ravaged by four grueling years
of civil war. Soldiers who survived the ordeal laid
down their weapons but continued to carry the
memories of death, self-sacrifice, and heroism.